THE MINDS OF MARGINALIZED BLACK MEN

PRINCETON STUDIES IN CULTURAL SOCIOLOGY

*Paul J. DiMaggio, Michèle Lamont, Robert J. Wuthnow,
Viviana A. Zelizer*

A list of titles in the series appears at the back of the book.

THE MINDS OF MARGINALIZED BLACK MEN

MAKING SENSE OF MOBILITY, OPPORTUNITY, AND FUTURE LIFE CHANCES

Alford A. Young, Jr.

PRINCETON UNIVERSITY PRESS   PRINCETON AND OXFORD

Copyright © 2004 by Princeton University Press
Published by Princeton University Press, 41 William Street,
Princeton, New Jersey 08540
In the United Kingdom: Princeton University Press,
3 Market Place, Woodstock, Oxfordshire OX20 1SY
All Rights Reserved

Library of Congress Cataloging-in-Publication Data

Young, Alford A., Jr.
The minds of marginalized Black men : making sense of mobility,
opportunity, and future life chances / Alford A. Young, Jr.
  p. cm.—(Princeton studies in cultural sociology)
Includes bibliographical references and index.
ISBN 0-691-09242-7 (cloth : alk. paper)
1. Poor men—Illinois—Chicago—Attitudes—Case studies. 2. African
American men—Illinois—Chicago—Attitudes—Case studies.
3. Social mobility—United States—Public opinion. 4. Equality—
United States—Public opinion. 5. Social stratification—United
States—Public opinion. 6. United Staes—Race relations—Public
opinion. 7. Social perception—Illinois—Chicago—Case studies.
I. Title. II. Series.
HV4046.C36.Y68 2003
305.38′896073′077311—dc21   2003041862

British Cataloging-in-Publication Data is available

This book has been composed in Sabon

Printed on acid-free paper.∞

www.pupress.princeton.edu

Printed in the United States of America

10 9 8 7 6 5 4 3 2 1

Contents

Acknowledgments

FIRST, I thank the men who shared their stories, opinions, and points of views with me so that I could write this book. They willingly and courageously let me step into their lives and let me listen to them express their hopes and dreams, their tragedies and failures. I fully believe that they deserve a better day, and hope that this work, in some small way, might lead to making that possible.

My first serious consideration of African American men as a population in crisis began after I was accepted into the membership of the Archbishop's Leadership Project, a program of the Roman Catholic archdiocese of New York that aimed to cultivate and enhance the leadership skills of African American male youth (it has since become a coeducational program). I thank the founder and initial director of the project, Father John T. Meehan, for providing me with the arena for beginning to think about this issue. I also thank the alumni of the project, who inspired, educated, and supported me as I gradually entered into academia in a sincere quest to address and (in whatever ways possible) redress the plight of African Americans.

My decision to become a scholar, and my eternal rethinking about what it means to function responsibly as one, is due in more ways than I can count to Jerry Watts. If the people involved in the Leadership Project are central to what I think about in terms of social uplift, then Jerry is central to how I think about it. In the past twenty years, when I was not in conversation with these people about the plight of African Americans or the means for their social uplift, then I often was with Fred Wallace. Rest in peace, Mr. Wallace, and know that at least one other person out there is trying to follow your example.

In the course of constructing the research that went into this book, I benefited from, and thus thank immensely, William Julius Wilson. He gave me support, resources, guidance, enthusiasm, and many of the concepts that became core emphases in this project. Others who nurtured me as a young researcher trying to make some sense about social inequality include Edgar G. Epps, Moishe Postone, George Steinmetz, Richard Taub, Thomas Holt, and Michael Dawson. I am fortunate to have benefited from this collection of brilliant minds.

Early in the course of turning this project into a book I was approached by Michèle Lamont, who determined to offer me the kind of guidance and support that scholars usually reserve for their students. She read every word of multiple drafts of this work. That is more than an author should ask of anyone and, it turned out, really the least that she has given to me throughout the time that it took for me to pull this off. Charles Lemert served as a masterful mixture of constructive critic and supreme cheerleader for this work. In his own unique way, he encouraged me to realize the promise of this work, and this carried me through each chapter.

Howard Winant, Ann Arnett Ferguson, Roseanne Anderly, Howard Kimeldorf, Mark Chesler, Andy Modigliani, Rick Lempert, Karin Martin, Barbara Laslett, Amanda Lewis, Geoff Ward, Mario Small, and Nasha Vida read parts of this work and said many things, big and small, to help it turn out as it has. The faculty of the School of Social Science at Hampshire College, the Great Barrington Theory Circle, and the members of the Race and Racial Ideologies Workshop and the School and Schooling Workshop at the University of Chicago provided helpful criticisms and assessments over the years. The same holds for audiences at Northwestern University, the University of Richmond, and Columbia University.

Ian Malcolm, acquisitions editor, and Mark Bellis, production editor, at Princeton University Press, guided me—and more importantly, kept me at ease—through the publication process. The editing done by Kristin Gager and Jodi Beder has made this material much more comprehensible. Their efforts allowed me to understand better the need to write not for oneself, but for other people.

Reuben May, Mary Pattillo, Ray Regans, Nick Young, Jolyon Wurr, Sandra Smith, Mignon Moore, Jim Quane, and the people associated with the Center for the Study of Urban Inequality at the University of Chicago challenged me, laughed with me, and kept me aware of the sheer joys and pleasures of doing scholarship. Dan Cook and Sudhir Venkatesh are two people who are brimming with provocative ideas and good spirit. Thanks for sharing both with me.

My colleagues in the Department of Sociology and at the Center for Afroamerican and African Studies at the University of Michigan welcomed me into their communities and helped me to make them my own. They stimulated my thinking from the first day of my arrival in Ann Arbor. James S. Jackson, director of the Center, provided crucial support for the editing and final preparation of the manuscript, and I am grateful for his doing so.

My mother, Anne Young, and my sister, Elizabeth, had little idea of what I was up to with this work, but like excellent family members, they were completely supportive nonetheless. The same holds for my son, Alford III, who somehow was able to practice patience (a rare feat for him) whenever "daddy really had to get some work done." Finally, one family member—my wife, Carla O'Connor—knew all along exactly what I was up to, and because she did, she determined to step into this work with me (editing and evaluating it) while knowing how to keep the rest of the world out of it when I needed that to happen. She has sacrificed her time and energy to help me get it done. If there ever was an example of how much one individual could help another to get through a challenge, then she is it. Love you, sweetie.

Preface

THIS BOOK aims to deliver a new message about young, low-income African American men, a population that is well known to be in a state of crisis. I wrote it because I aspired to say something that is not widely known, or at least not very much talked about, concerning poor black men. I came to the project that resulted in this book because I wanted to get a sense of whether poor black men looked beyond their immediate surroundings and circumstances when thinking about the future. Hence, the story told here is about how these men think about themselves as members of a larger social world—not just their communities and neighborhoods, but American society.

A major concern for me was whether these men thought about what other people do to get ahead in American society, and, if so, how that might serve as a basis for what they might do in order to advance themselves. Having quickly discovered that they do think about all of these issues, the more central questions became, (1) In what specific ways do they think about how other people get ahead? and (2) How might their past experiences and contemporary situations relate to differences between them in their thinking? Popular commentary gives a great deal of attention to the behavior and public demeanor of poor black men, but little to their thoughts about the world and their place in it. These thoughts, however, provide the foundation for their functioning.

I went to the Near West Side community of Chicago to explore these questions. African Americans have a long and rich history in Chicago, especially poor black men. Yet the west side of town has never received the kind of scholarly and media attention focused upon the South Side, where the massive public housing project—the Robert Taylor Homes—and other residential developments stood in what was known throughout the twentieth century as Bronzeville, the Chicago black belt. Thus, I went to a less familiar part of Chicago to explore a less examined set of issues concerning poor black men.

While there I found that some of these men had much to say about racism, deprivation, and other factors that matter for getting ahead in American society, while others said little. Some had detailed explanations of how social relations unfold across race and class lines in American life, and others did not say much about the topic at all. Accordingly, this book delivers an argument about why men who may appear to be of the same ilk and disposition when seen on the streets of Chicago have a wide range of views and visions of how mobility operates in American life, and how it might operate for them in the future.

My desire to undertake research on these questions is rooted in my own past growing up in the East Harlem section of New York City. My experiences there as a child and adolescent have ingrained in me a lifelong preoccupation with the social situation of poor black men. For the past three decades, East Harlem has been a community that rivals the Near West Side of Chicago in the severity of the poverty, social ills, and large-scale socioeconomic immobility that afflict its inhabitants. There are two crucial differences, however, between my experiences in East Harlem and the experiences of the men of the Near West Side. First, although a sizable African American presence can be found there, East Harlem is predominantly Latino (hence, it is best known by its other identifiers, Spanish Harlem and El Barrio).[1] The predominance of Latinos did not prevent me from establishing close ties with a large number of African American males while growing up in the midst of the immediate post–civil rights era.[2]

The second major difference is that, unlike many of my neighbors, I came from a solidly middle-class family. My father, who lived with the family until my mid-adolescence, was a college graduate and a certified public accountant. While this placed our family below the elite strata of mainstream America, I was from one of the most financially secure families of all of the youth in East Harlem with whom I associated. As a young child I had a general sense of the difference in socioeconomic status between myself and most of the youth that I knew. This social difference was, perhaps, best made clear by my being the first child that I knew of to leave the neighborhood public elementary school in the early 1970s in order to integrate a Catholic school near the vastly more elite midtown part of Manhattan. By the time that I went to college I was a few years into knowing full well that I was positioned to do much better than my neighborhood peers, and by any objective measure I certainly did.

A few of my neighborhood friends completed college, but many others received no more than a high school diploma, and some not even that. This situation taught me how much family-based capital could do for you (even though I never thought to use that term when I first had such realizations two decades ago). More importantly, it also led me to realize that black men who came from the same community, while often holding the same views, could hold very diverse opinions about various aspects of society. Over the years, I talked a lot with neighborhood friends and associates about the struggles affecting African Americans. Our views on these matters were informed by the fact that we lived less than a mile away from one of the wealthiest urban communities in the country, the Yorkville section of New York. We often ventured into that community to go to the movies, and the precious few of us that were able to escape public school went to parochial and nonsectarian private schools there as well.

Yorkville is not separated from East Harlem in the way that Chicago neighborhoods are separated by viaducts, railroad tracks, vacant land, and other robust physical barriers. The only barrier is East 96th Street, four lanes of busy traffic entering and exiting the Franklin Delano Roosevelt Drive (a thoroughfare running up and down the east side of Manhattan). East 96th Street can be crossed in about ten seconds by taking a leisurely stroll at the green light. Living in the absence of formidable physical barriers meant that East Harlem residents saw a lot of wealthy people everyday in addition to the poor people that inhabited our community.

As I moved on to Fordham Preparatory High School, one of the most expensive Catholic high schools in New York City, I began to notice how different my life trajectory was turning out to be in comparison to the paths taken by many of my neighborhood friends. Those who fell behind (or simply remained behind given that they started out with too few resources to ever stay on course), continued to think critically about the situation of African Americans in society. These friends and I talked about racism, poverty, and power differentials, quite often in conjunction with some kind of police action in our community.[3] Throughout these discussions I grew more intrigued by the fact that people who were beginning to live extremely different lives than my own continued to share my views on some issues, yet did not think about others in the same way. My favorite example is the debate about why anyone would want to go to a school like Wesleyan University, as I eventually did, to study something called liberal arts, when they could learn about business or trade skills, which most of my friends believed would lead more directly to making large sums of money. We worked through our similarities and differences on playground benches, in the public schoolyard across the street from my apartment building, in the barbershop, or just on the corner. What stayed with me over the years, especially as I went to the University of Chicago for graduate studies, was that a great deal could be learned about other people from extended conversations about mundane, everyday matters.

My experiences in New York City were forefront in my mind when I began my research in the Near West Side of Chicago with a plan to have extended conversations with young black men. Before I began my work, however, I took a long look at some of the questions that psychologist Albert Bandura had asked in the course of his studies on locus of control and control orientations (for discussions of his approach see Bandura 1977, 1978, 1982, 1986). Bandura was interested in the extent to which people feel efficacious in or constricted by the social world. He wanted to know how much control they believe themselves to have over certain social outcomes and processes. To this end, he asked his subjects a series of questions based on dichotomous responses (e.g., yes-no, agree-disagree). The questions were framed in terms of statements about whether or not people felt in control of various spheres of their personal lives or in response to social processes.

I decided to ask some of my friends in East Harlem about these issues. Rather than asking them to agree or disagree, or to say yes or no, I simply asked them to talk out their reactions to statements such as "Everyone has the ability to get ahead in the world because it's simply up to each person to do so" or "Nobody gets ahead by himself because factors beyond one's control matter most of all in determining who gets ahead in society." Hearing what they had to say, and did not say, both intrigued me and committed me to conducting the kind of open-ended interviews that I did with the men of Chicago's Near West Side. I was convinced that this approach would shed some new and important light on their current and future behavior. This book is the culmination of my work using that new approach.

This book is divided into three parts. Part 1, "Logics," establishes the analytical foundations for the book. The introduction presents the call for a renewed cultural analytical approach to the study of low-income African American men. Chapter 1 explores the modern legacy of urban ethnographic research and policy-centered discussion on the culture of the urban poor. In doing so it explores why and how certain frameworks of cultural interpretation have emerged for poor black men, and ends with a discussion of the concepts and ideas necessary for a renewed approach toward analytical frameworks for cultural analysis that have been applied to low-income African American men.

Part 2, "Lifeworlds," explores the men's own accounts of their past and contemporary circumstances. It is here that the experiences and situations that have positioned them as poor, urban-based black men are explored. Chapter 2 provides a vision of the social contexts that circumscribe these men's lives and shape the comments and opinions that they shared with me. It also reveals the narrow range of social contacts that these men have experienced in their everyday lives and what this means for their capacity to apprehend the complexities involved in living in American society. Chapter 3 moves back in time to explore the men's recollections of schooling, family life, peer associations, and other past experiences, connecting this background to their present-day thoughts about getting ahead in life.

Part 3, "Worldviews," explores how the men *frame* their understandings of mobility processes in American life.[4] In speaking to the men about these issues, I aimed to gain an understanding of how they positioned their own life chances within the broader framework of their vision of American social and economic mobility: why they believe some people get ahead in American society and others do not. My discussions with them touched on how they believed society to be organized in terms of who possesses the most power and influence, who the least, and what, if anything, can be done to alter these core arrangements.[5] Each of the chapters in part 3 uncovers the degree to which subgroups of the men differ in their interpretations of social processes and the social world. Each also connects these differences back to particular patterns of individual life history or social experience that either provided or denied access to people across race, class, and experiential boundaries.

As we shall see, the men's framing of the issues of stratification, inequality, and prospects for mobility was shaped by the level of contact they had with people of other races or higher class standing. During the course of the interviews it became increasingly clear to me that the closer the men got to experiences with overt or perceptible social difference, the better able they were to talk about how these issues factor into the social order of American life. The men who, for a variety of reasons, had contact with people outside the immediate surroundings of the Near West Side showed a greater capacity to talk about the centrality of race and class in the American stratification scheme and to specify who gained or benefited from social inequality. On the other end of the spectrum, those men who rarely or never left the neighborhood, and therefore encountered few non-blacks or college-educated people, were unable to frame their own life circumstances in terms of these broader structures of race and class. Accordingly, this latter group of men was more likely to identify with the individualistic virtues associated with the "American Dream." Not surprisingly, different experiences with the world outside of the neighborhood inspired the men to make use of varied structural elements while constructing their frames of understanding.[6]

Chapter 4 covers the men's vision of how stratification and inequality are structured and how they function. This includes how these men frame understandings of social relations and social hierarchies in American society. Chapter 5 does the same for their vision of social mobility and attainment, or how people are understood to move through these social structures. Chapter 6 explores the men's beliefs about their prospects for personal mobility. It concentrates on what they see as possible, probable, and desired outcomes for their futures, and how their past experiences factor into the emergence of such differences. Chapter 7 addresses how the men imagine activating personal mobility in order to move toward desired ends. Finally, chapter 8 revisits the merits, for scholars, policymakers, service providers, and other interested parties, of employing this

new cultural perspective that situates poor black men as culturally en-
dowed actors.

I have strived to steer this book away from being too much of a chroni-
cle of my experiences in the field. Instead, my hope is that the book brings
to light some underacknowledged issues that concerned people should
take into account when thinking about low-income black men. Although
it is unavoidable that this book will be about me in many ways, I hope
that it does not simply introduce these men as interesting case studies, but
rather motivates readers to think about whether they have considered the
situation of low-income African American men with appropriate depth,
and, if not, how they might go about doing so in the future.

THE MINDS OF MARGINALIZED BLACK MEN

Part One

LOGICS

Introduction

Making New Sense of Poor Black Men in Crisis

LARRY[1]: I'd like to get away from around the projects. I'd have my own apartment man, you know, my own place jack. I'd come home and just relax man. I'd like to have something like that, a little car. . . . Man, if I could just move out them projects, man, and get my own spot, get a nice paying job man. . . . I mean what more can I ask for man? I mean I'd be satisfied with that right there, you know. . . . I could talk about it but I know it ain't going to come true, man. . . . Seems like every time I try to get away I end up back there. And that just kills me jack. It seems like something just keeps pulling me back.

DEVIN: The main thing I want to be is a good father to my kids and to my wife. . . . I'm leaving out of Chicago and start over in Mississippi. . . . It's better down there for me. I don't have to hear that confusion that's going on now and I ain't got to gangbang. It's a country part where I could build like I want to live and do what I want to do.

CASEY: Regardless of my situation I know exactly who I am. . . . So if you have a lot more material things that you manufactured—that you made sure that *you* can only have—doesn't make me no difference. I got life. I got a family now that I love. I'm a real person. I feel like I have emotions and I'm not scared to say it. I'm a black man in a white man's world. I don't have that fear, you know. And it's *their* world, believe me.

These are the words of young black men who were born into urban poverty. The men were living in the Near West Side of Chicago, one of the most destitute urban regions in the United States. They were born and reared in the Henry Horner Homes, one of the Near West Side's most infamous public housing developments. They continued to reside in or nearby the development.[2] These men shared a common ground of a life without much material comfort and in the midst of despair and violence. Yet, in significant ways their personal histories are strikingly different. Larry, age 24 in 1994, had never held a full-time job for more than a month or two at a time. He and his siblings (three brothers and one sister) grew up with both parents at home (a rare occurrence for the men discussed in the following pages). He still resided with his parents because he had not yet been able to create a secure and independent life for himself. Although he had little luck at finding work, he had never seen the inside of a jail cell, nor associated much with men who often did. Unfortunately, staying out of trouble did not mean that Larry ever came close to staying employed.

Devin, age 21, was an active gang member, on parole after serving time for possession of narcotics. He spoke his words in 1994, less than two months after surviving a hit-and-run attempt by rival gang members. This was by far the most severe of several life-threatening encounters that he experienced in nearly ten years of gangbanging. Devin's involvement with gangs began early in his adolescence. Since then, he had been shot at, had fired upon other people, sold drugs, fenced stolen goods, and had spent nearly the same amount of time in jail or on parole as he had attending high school. Although he claimed to have a more notorious reputation in the neighborhood than any of his close peers, he said that their lifestyles were similar to his own. Devin had never had any formal employment in his life.

Casey, a twenty-five-year-old ex-convict, stands somewhere between Larry and Devin in terms of participating in the illicit activities associated with the Near West Side. When he first spoke to me in 1993, he had recently completed a drug rehabilitation program that helped him to curb his addiction for the first time since he began using drugs as a teenager. His work history consisted of packing bags in supermarkets. The rest of his income came from hustling and drug dealing. Casey had an older brother who was a neighborhood gang leader until he was killed in the early 1990s during a gang-related conflict. Although his brother was heavily involved in gang activity, Casey managed to avoid that life. Casey's ability to avoid the gang life was largely due to his brother's reputation in the community, which created a protective shield for the rest of the family. Being a sibling of a high-profile gang member meant that Casey did not have to gangbang in order to reap its most esteemed social benefits: status and deference in the neighborhood. Casey still got into some trouble of his own, combining a small-scale career in drug dealing with a great deal of personal drug use. After serving a few years in jail and a few months in rehabilitation, he was back on the streets of the Near West Side and, as he said, eager to begin pulling himself together.

To the outside world these men represent the underclass.[3] Their accounts reflect an all-too-familiar depiction of poor black men as some of the most disenfranchised and despair-ridden people on the urban landscape. It may not surprise anyone that such men are upset about many aspects of their lives, and would prefer to be free of their present situations if possible. Without a more nuanced exploration into their lives and worldviews, these men would seem to reflect little more than the views and attitudes of the ultra-marginal, socially disconnected people that urban poverty scholars have been studying for the past two decades. There is no doubt that the lives of these men have been deeply affected by facets of urban life such as chronic unemployment, violence, and crime. Yet, these same men do more than merely stand either as passive reactors to such potentially debilitating outside social and economic forces, or as violent-prone individuals who mindlessly lash out at the world with hostility and aggression. Men such as Larry, Devin, and Casey are also men who critically react to the conditions in which they live, and who create a range of worldviews that help them to assign meaning to the social world around them. Unfortunately, their beliefs and thoughts—the material that comprises worldviews—have been given too little analytical attention by scholars of urban poverty.[4]

This oversight in the field of urban poverty stems in large part from a lack of dialogue between two arenas of sociological inquiry. One, the sociology of urban poverty, offers a long-standing and rich tradition of cultural analysis concerning poor black men. Yet that tradition has focused upon the presumed values and norms adopted by these men while reducing investigations of beliefs to the notion that the men think that their path to a better life is obstructed by their entrenchment in the turbulent and pernicious social world of the inner city. Values and norms have been emphasized in this tradition because they are viewed as the causal factors for behavior, and because beliefs were taken to be relatively easy to grasp and consistent over time. As we will explore a bit later, the concepts of values and norms continue to function as core terms in urban poverty research, even as debate has unfolded over the ramifications of using these terms. Unfortunately, that debate has not involved critical assessments of the historical use of other cultural attibutes, such as belief systems or worldviews.

The second arena of sociological inquiry is the more recently established field of cultural sociology. Here cultural analysis has extended far beyond a mid-twentieth-century preoccupation with norms and values in order to explore the social and political implications concerning the construction of meaning systems in everyday life. A large part of the research agenda here is to explore how it is that patterns of thought become "common sense" for certain kinds of people, yet unfamiliar or odd ways of thinking for others. In the sociology of culture, questions and issues about meaning have exploded across research agendas, yet far too little of this agenda has seriously incorporated the case of poor black men. Drawing on the tools of cultural sociology, the central goal of this book is to combine these two perspectives in order to develop a richer and more textured portrait of how poor black men make sense of their lives—how they think creatively about their lives and their future prospects—given the structural conditions that they face.

The stories told here reveal aspects of the lives of poor black men that have been neglected in the scholarship. In order to counter the traditional, often troublingly simplistic pictures of these men as either extremely passive or overly aggressive respondents to the external forces of urban poverty, *The Minds of Marginalized Black Men* employs the men's own words. These words reveal the extent to which the men function as more complex creative actors in response to those forces, weighing various possibilities for their futures and making conscious choices. The remarks by Larry, Devin, and Casey quoted above provide a unique entry into the worldviews of poor black men that lie hidden beneath the standard images of them as angry, hostile, and alienated. That entry necessitates constructing a new cultural lens on these men. I interviewed twenty-six men between the ages of twenty and twenty-five in two of Chicago's best known housing projects in the Near West Side, the Henry Horner Homes and the ABLA housing development. After introducing the setting for this initiative, we will return to a more complete presentation of the objectives for this investigation.

The Setting

The Near West Side of Chicago is the kind of place where one easily finds young black men such as Larry, Devin, and Casey, who seem to be completely left out of the flow of American social and economic mobility. The region is geographically and socially isolated from downtown Chicago and the opulent western suburbs, and resembles a holding pen for the economically immobile. It is surely one of the most difficult urban communities in which to grow up. While empty lots are quite visible, so are many large-scale public housing units. In the early 1990s public housing comprised approximately 20 percent of the total housing as well as a large portion of the residential space for the African American population of Chicago's Near West Side. Except for the Congress Expressway—a major thoroughfare that runs through the west side of Chicago—about a mile of small houses and abandoned lots separates the Henry Horner Homes from the ABLA Homes. Not surprisingly, low-income and working-class African Americans reside in the units that divide the two housing developments. Little of this neighborhood is noticeable to the suburban commuters who come into downtown Chicago on the expressway in the morning and head back to the suburbs in the evening.

The Governor Henry Horner Homes were built in the 1950s and are just about a mile west of downtown Chicago. The development is comprised of 19 buildings with 1,774 units, almost all of which are occupied by African Americans. According to early 1990s statistics, over 85 percent of the households receive public assistance, and only 8 percent of the households are supported solely by the employment of a member of the household (Chicago Housing Authority 1992). The United Center, the home of the Chicago Bulls of the National Basketball Association and the Blackhawks of the National Hockey League, stands across the street from the eastern edge of Henry Horner. This arena replaced Chicago Stadium in 1994 and is the only part of the community regularly ventured into by people other than poor black Americans. Nearby parking facilities and a large coterie of police officers keep the Center crowd from having much to do with Horner residents. In *There Ain't No Children Here* (1991), journalist Alex Kotlowitz tells of the intermittent interaction between two brothers from Henry Horner, the central characters in his book, and fans in need of parking for Bulls' games. The men I interviewed spoke very little of this interaction. Except for a few cases in which some got lucky and found short-term jobs, the stadium area remained a foreign country to these men. The same can be said of interaction with West Town, a community located about a half mile north of Henry Horner that is home to a vibrant Latino community, but is also a place of gentrification. Increasingly, white-collar professionals can be seen driving and walking around the area they have made their home.

I conducted interviews with the young black men from the Henry Horner Homes at the 28th Ward alderman's field office, which sits on the western edge of Henry Horner on Western Avenue. Running from one end of Chicago to the other, Western Avenue is a major north-south thoroughfare that forms the western boundary of the Near West Side (and the divider between Horner and Rockwell Gardens, another large public housing project that has a similar statistical profile and quality of life for its residents). The alderman's office has a storefront structure with a near-floor-to-ceiling window in the front. A row of hard plastic and metal chairs sit with their backs against the window. Two desks make up the only other furniture in the front room. Denise, who was the only staff member present every day that I conducted my interviews, occupied one of the two desks.[5] It was her job to greet anyone who entered the office, answer questions, and try to solve basic problems. Whatever Denise could not handle resulted in a scheduled appointment with Diane, the office coordinator who sat in a small office on the other side of the wall behind the front area.[6] Diane was my contact for fieldwork around Henry Horner. A large, affable, woman—I would guess in her mid-forties—she acted like a mother figure to many of the men who came to see me. Diane spread the word around the housing development that I was interested in speaking to young men, and it was thanks to her that the first wave of men came to the office to see me. I later found out from some of the men that she had also asked them to look out for me while I was doing my project, thus giving me some measure of protection for my time at the site.

I conducted interviews in a corner of the large room behind the wall separating the front area from the rest of the office. That room was also the space for the monthly community meeting and other large gatherings. Diane's office at the south end of the large room was actually a space carved out of the larger room and enclosed with drywall and a door. Although she closed her door whenever she came in and saw that I was already at work, her voice, full of the boisterousness that one might find in dialogue among friends at the beauty parlor or barbershop, would always seep through the wall and spill over onto my tape recordings. I'll never forget her "Hey baby! How you feel?!" that came through her opened office door whenever I entered the office after she had already got to her desk. It could be heard out on the street corner. Her overall cheeriness was a stark contrast to the bleak moods and words expressed by the men in the course of the interviews.

The ABLA Homes are located one and a half miles south of Henry Horner. ABLA contains 160 buildings and 3,505 units. At mid-century ABLA operated as four different residential developments—the Jane Addams Houses (built in 1938), Robert Brooks Houses (built in 1942), Loomis Courts, and Grace Abbott Homes (both built in the 1950s). The amalgamation of low-rise and high-rise buildings in such proximity led to the cohesive development named by the acronym. Like Henry Horner, ABLA is almost entirely populated by African Americans. Over 75 percent of the households in ABLA receive public assistance, and slightly more than 8 percent of the households are supported solely by the employment of one of their members (Chicago Housing Authority 1992).[9] The University of Illinois at Chicago is located just east of ABLA, and St. Ignatius Loyola, a Catholic high school largely attended by middle-income white youth, stands just across the street from ABLA's eastern end. Despite the geographic proximity of these predominantly white institutions to the African-American housing developments, a gaping social distance separates these two worlds. The white students coming from downtown got off the city bus in front of the high school, a few blocks from my own stop at ABLA. I never saw any of the high school youths or college students around on the ABLA grounds. West of ABLA is private housing, occupied by low-income residents much like those that live in the public development. The area about a mile to the south is the beginning of a European American ethnic enclave that forms part of the community of the Lower West Side.

At ABLA I worked out of an office located at the northern end of a facility on Loomis Street, right in the middle of ABLA Homes. The building housed the Local Advisory Council (the official ABLA tenants' association) and other community groups. The facility is much larger than the alderman's field office at Henry Horner. It is a one-story structure with rows of offices on both sides of a corridor that forms the perimeter of an open-air playground that seemed to remain unused. Around the corner to the right of my office, across the hall and about five doors south was the main office, where Ms. Beverly, my contact for that site, occupied the largest and most decorated office in the building. She was the president of the tenants' association, and, like Diane at Henry Horner, introduced me to the local men and created a public identity for me in the neighborhood. I saw much less of her than I did of Diane, but she was equally accommodating and warmhearted. Every now and then she would stop by to make sure that things were going well and that the men were "acting right."

As a series of programs were housed in the same space, I often would observe children's, teenager, and adult groups come and go throughout the day. Sometimes program directors would invite me to have lunch with a group if I was not busy (this would occur most often with the programs that included men). At both sites, I spent moments of free time on the street corners with some of the guys. Sometimes we sat on benches at bus stops; other times we watched games of pickup basketball played on cracked cement courts with bent rims and rickety backboards. These more casual conversations supplemented what I learned from the formal interviews that constitute the heart of this work.

The Mandate

When poor black men from urban communities are asked to reflect upon their life situations and future goals, one might expect their comments to be riddled either with anger, conflict, and animosity, or with hopelessness and despair. Both kinds of responses would seem to validate the standard portrait of young black men from the inner city as depicted in the print media, on television and in movies, and in certain genres of rap music. Surely, young men such as Larry, Devin, and Casey appear frustrated and angry about aspects of their lives such as pervasive racism, the lack of employment prospects, and the violence that often accompanies life in urban poverty. That part of their story, however, is not the core concern of this book. Rather, this work aims to show that research that focuses on these men's anger and hostility hinders a more complex exploration of how they take stock of themselves and the world in which they live.

As much as poor black men from urban America can appear to be despondent or angry about their future, they also show a capacity to critically assess the world around them with a profundity and complexity that is often left out of the public debate. Moreover, as my interviews with these men show, they also articulate a variety of hopes, dreams, and interpretations that matter to them greatly, but that usually get buried in the traditional stereotypical portrayals of young black men from urban communities as alienated, angry, and violent. As different as these men's lives appear when compared to more affluent Americans, it is essential to recognize that they function quite similarly to the rest of us in how they assess their social world, how they make sense out of what they see around them on a daily basis, and how they ground their visions of their futures.

The Minds of Marginalized Black Men explores the capacity of young black men to think critically and creatively about the ways in which mobility and opportunity operate in American society, showing how they situate their own lives within the broader social and economic forces that surround them. As the title suggests, rather than privileging the actions and behaviors of these men, this book seeks to place their minds at center stage. By doing so, it is my aim to break from the standard way of assessing how people see themselves in regard to the world around them. In both public policy and most scholarship on urban life, that standard approach has been to formulate a picture of what individuals think based solely on their actions. Indeed, urban ethnography, the branch of sociology that is primarily committed to observing and documenting behavior in public and private settings, has played a crucial role in sustaining the notion that what people think can be derived from what they do. Ethnography has sustained the notion that what people do with their family members, friends, and associates conveys how they make meaning of themselves, other people, and varied aspects of the social world. The flaw in this approach is that one's behavior is not a transparent reflection of one's underlying thoughts. For example, the fact that an individual is chronically unemployed and does not go to work on a regular basis (his behavior) tells us nothing about the complexity of his thoughts on the intricacies of the modern labor markets (his thoughts). Similarly, if someone has opted not to continue high school, this does not mean that she does not have a keen sense of how and why a college education might help one to get ahead in life. Thus, it is important to pay attention to what people articulate as their own understanding of how social processes work and how they as individuals might negotiate the complex social terrain, rather than simply looking at their actions. Accordingly, the main goal of this book is to uncover these men's worldviews on issues such as mobility, opportunity, and future life chances. These particular kinds of worldviews, consisting of depictions of how social processes and outcomes are constructed, must be given sufficient analytical space if the lives of low-income black men are to be more fully understood.

In order to advance this type of understanding, this study seeks to elucidate these men's worldviews about a particular range of issues and concerns related to socioeconomic mobility. The critical issue of socioeconomic mobility is the main terrain upon which these men form ideas and meanings central to how they understand their lives and approach their futures. The part of their worldviews that concerns mobility functions as a central part of their everyday lives inasmuch as it is directly implicated in their status as disenfranchised and immobile citizens on the American social landscape.

By focusing on beliefs and worldviews touching on mobility, opportunity, and future life chances, *The Minds of Marginalized Black Men* seeks to uncover some hidden domains of thought in the minds of poor black men. In working toward this objective, this work explores thoughts about aspects of the social world that are most familiar to these men, such as the Near West Side of Chicago, and those aspects that, given their socioeconomic situation, are seemingly far beyond their purview. The following pages seek to explore how the men's capacity to make sense of these issues relates to their larger visions of how other groups of people approach the future. By attending to this often-overlooked dimension of meaning-making in the lives of poor black men, this work aims to uncover the underrecognized complexity of their lives. In short, the following pages dare to consider low-income black men as something other than public menaces who are inclined toward violence, or as a downtrodden and dispirited constituency that lashes out at the world with brutality and insensitivity. Instead, the men are portrayed here as social thinkers—as people who have the capacity to interpret the world around them and who actively compare their situations to those of others.

In addition to bringing these men's thoughts to the forefront, the book also establishes important grounds for understanding how and why their future behavior takes on a particular form. As anthropologist Clifford Geertz (1973) pointed out some time ago, one's worldview, or system of meaning, constitutes a basis for future behavior. This formula is a reversal of the flawed logic of the researchers discussed earlier, that behavior is the source of insight about certain cultural attributes. Beliefs, then, are not deducible from behavior, but rather help to create the cultural fabric that informs and encourages such action. In other words, the way people think about the processes of social and personal mobility inform us about how they choose to act with respect to future prospects and possibilities. With this analytical framework in mind, the importance of bringing to light the actual worldviews and beliefs of low-income black men becomes evident.

Indeed, the remarks of Larry, Devin, and Casey cited at the outset provide but a brief glimpse into the complex arena of images and understandings that shaped their worldviews and how they came to terms with constraints and obstacles that factored into their schemas. Clearly these men were faced daily with a set of daunting obstacles. Yet, each of the men I encountered developed very different sensibilities about the nature of those obstacles and how to manage them. For instance, Larry focused on his inability to figure out how to get away from the Henry Horner Homes. Most of what he had to say about his aims and goals for the future related to what he wanted to get away from rather than what he hoped to move toward. As we will see, Larry's life revolved around trying to distance himself from problematic people and circumstances rather than on crafting a detailed plan for a better future. Devin, however, articulated a clear sense of where he needed to go in order to have a chance at a better life. His immersion in the world of gangbanging, vice, and violence led to his coming to terms with how these activities increasingly closed options for his personal mobility—options that were already prematurely narrowed simply by his being a young poor black man. Devin fully believed that he could not overcome the obstacles placed before him in Chicago. Hence, he imagined that Mississippi, the state where he was born and which he left at the age of three (too early for him to remember anything about it), would be his best bet for turning his life around. Mississippi remained an option for him because his mother had grown up there and told him about her experiences. Finally, Casey, who had grown up across the street from the Horner Homes, might not have been sure of exactly where he was going in terms of future employment or quality-of-life prospects, but he claimed to know full well where he currently stood and what he was up against as a black man with precious few material or symbolic resources at his disposal. He had seen small pieces of the world beyond the Near West Side because he went to a high school considerably more integrated than those attended by most Near West Side youth. His hustling and dealing also brought him into contact with people from beyond the boundaries of his home base. Consequently, he had enough access to other people and places to aid him in defining precisely where he stood in "their world," as he put it, and what he believed he had to do to succeed in it.

For those who know little about men like Larry, Devin, and Casey, it is easy to create and maintain monolithic images of them as dangerous, consistently destitute black men who are poorly equipped to help themselves. In such a view, these men often seem as though they do not want to improve their prospects in the first place, at least not in terms of mainstream societal standards for personal mobility. Yet the words of Larry, Devin, and Casey reveal that when such men are asked about their thoughts—rather than being evaluated solely on the basis of their actions and appearances in the public—the picture that emerges highlights the deeper dimensions of their social character and comportment. Hence, the fact that black men such as these share the same general social position in the American social hierarchy, yet think very differently about where they stand and what they must do to improve their lot, gives rise to a host of questions about how life experiences relate to the formulation of ideas on mobility and opportunity.

A more enriched understanding of how these men's worldviews are formed begins by taking seriously the fact that they often create provocative and intriguing patterns of meaning about their social worlds. Even those patterns that appear provincial on the surface emerge out of a profound set of experiential circumstances and conditions. Such patterns are not adequately captured by analytical frameworks that highlight the capacity of poor people to focus only on their immediate situations, thus rendering them incapable of apprehending or planning for their lives in the long term. In challenging such flawed approaches, this work complements recent analyses that have called for more complex and provocative investigations of the culture of the African American urban poor, and poor black men in particular. It also represents a new approach for overturning a long legacy of urban ethnographic and related modes of research that has served to construct the standard and overly simplistic image of the underclass in general and of low-income African American men in particular. By offering a new perspective, *The Minds of Marginalized Black Men* strives to reconstitute that image. Accordingly, the book revisits the standing claims about the contemporary "crisis of the black male" in order to reshape the sociological analysis of poor black men—and, by implication, all low-income African Americans—by putting forth a new cultural perspective for assessing their lives. At the center of this new perspective lies the assumption that the behavior of these men emerges not simply from the adaptation of stretched values or alternative norms, but more fundamentally from the stocks of knowledge that they accumulate about how the world works, and how they might work within it. A careful and critical assessment of what these men have to say attunes the observer to the rationality inherent to their assessments of personal life experiences. It is this very rationality that is suppressed or denied when behaviors are assessed only at a surface level, thereby leading to assumptions about poor black men's capacity to function in ways that middle-class America regards as proper and appropriate. By challenging this suppression and denial, then, this work seeks to de-pathologize the image of poor black men.

The following chapters, therefore, seek not to accentuate what these men did when they had a firearm or packets of cocaine in their possession, nor any other exotic exploits or endeavors usually associated with life in the bowels of urban squalor. Rather, this book brings to light what these men have to say when asked to define the social hierarchy of American society and their place in it. Their answers to these and related questions provide insight into their capacity for future action, and how they understand past behaviors when they talk about their future prospects. The book explores what men like Larry, Casey, and Devin understand the "good life" to be, and whether they believe that such a life is within their reach. A large part of the study focuses on the men's orientation toward the world of work because this is key to their prospects for getting good jobs in the future. My analysis takes into account what is and what is not included in their thoughts on these issues by exploring how their personal histories and present-day realities have made it possible for them to come to certain realizations about mobility and opportunity in American life. [7]

The degree of exposure that the men have had to the world beyond the Near West Side emerges as key to understanding the differences in the breadth and depth of their worldviews. Such exposure might have come about for some through a few months of work in a downtown fast food restaurant, for others, through incarceration in a penal institution. Whatever the circumstances, such exposure provided opportunities for these men to interact across racial and class lines. Overall, interaction with other worlds led to the acquisition of a more profound understanding of the inequities in social power and influence, and how these forces can affect individual lives. Quite often it led to intimate encounters with racism. The men who never experienced this kind of contact found it much harder, if not impossible, to express how these and other external factors mattered for mobility and future prospects. Without a greater knowledge of the social world beyond the Near West Side, these men's accounts of mobility rested almost solely on individual skills and abilities.

We will see that the men's varied ideas about the social world are strongly rooted in what they learned from parents, guardians, and other family members. In most cases, the people surrounding them saw little of the world beyond the Near West Side and thus could offer limited information about the broader social world. In other cases, the men associated with elders who were born and reared in the deep and rural South, the place of recent family origin for many Chicago-based African Americans. For most of these migrants, the Near West Side, as bad as it was, represented a far better place, with better opportunities, than the South. Nevertheless, coming from the rural South often meant having no firm grip on the social dynamics of urban Chicago. Although this book introduces the reader to men who have had the kinds of experiences—including drug abuse, joblessness, and gangbanging—that are well documented in urban ethnography, a very different kind of story is told here. This study does not dwell on how the men handled these and other turbulent aspects of their lives. Instead, it explores how they think about the nature of the world in which they live. This focus sheds new light not only on why these men have acted as they have throughout their lives, but also on what the potential for future action might be. That potential is found in taking careful note of how access to people across race, class, and social experiential boundaries provided these men with the capacity to build different mental maps of how the social world works and how they could or could not work within it. The ideas that they present open up entirely new arguments about how such men should be thought about and approached by the public sector, or other parties that interface with their lives. While the contemporary mandate may be one of increased social control via incarceration or police-based surveillance, this study illustrates that the men's future capacity to act is built upon how they evaluate and articulate their past and present circumstances together with their sense of how the social world operates. That package of ideas, more so than any amalgamation of values and norms, speaks to what they are prepared to do in the future. Consequently, beliefs or worldviews deserve a central place in the configuration of cultural impulses for action.

Chapter One _____

The Past and Future of the Cultural
Analysis of Black Men

THE PHRASE "the crisis of the black male" has come to have great salience in the public imagination over the past two decades. This crisis, in all actuality, pertains to low-income black men. A range of measures and indicators make the notion of a crisis legitimate. Sociologist William Julius Wilson (1993, pp. 25–34) reported that by the late 1980s less than half of the prime-aged black men (those between 22 and 58 years) with less than a college education worked full-time. In early 1970, 70 percent of such men worked in full-time employment. John Kasarda (1990a, 1990b, 1990c, 1995) argues that this drop was due to the decline in urban sector manufacturing jobs: between 1967 and 1987, Philadelphia lost 64 percent of its manufacturing jobs, New York 58 percent, Detroit 51 percent, and Chicago 60 percent, a total loss of over a million such jobs.

Another key dimension of the crisis concerns crime and incarceration. Delbert Elliott (1992) reports that for men, the adolescent years are the time of peak involvement in criminal activity. After the age of twenty, men decrease their involvement in such activity. The decline for black men, however, has been substantially less than that for whites. When in their late twenties, black and white men show a differential of involvement in violent crime of 4:1. Elliott attributes the difference to the much higher rate of unemployment for black men. In another take on crime and incarceration, Marc Mauer (1999) argues that 7 percent of black men are incarcerated in prison or jail on any given day of the year. Further, 13 percent of all black men, about 1.4 million of them, are currently or permanently disenfranchised because of a felony conviction (Fellner and Mauer 1998).

Tables 1.1 to 1.5 further elucidate the current distress in the condition of young black men and how exacerbated it becomes over time. These data show the greater severity of these statistics for black males between the ages of 15 and 29 in comparison to white males of the same age category. As revealing as these data may be, they provide but a snapshot of the modern-day crisis of the black male. Studies abound that tell a more complete tale.[1] While there is not much debate about whether a problem exists for black men, the dialogue about its causes is substantial. The crisis

TABLE 1.1
Death Rates in the United States, Men, Aged 15–24 (per 100,000)

	Black	White
1970	321	171
1980	209	167
1990	252	131
1991	278	128
1992	271	124
1995	249	122
1997	216	109
1998	194	106
2000	180	104

Source: U.S. National Center for Health Statistics, 1994, 2000, 2002.
Note: Hispanics included in both black and white categories in year 2000 measures.

of the black male has been attributed to two kinds of factors: structural and cultural. Structural factors include the transformations occurring in urban economic and employment sectors, and the effects of persistent race-based residential segregation on mobility prospects.[2] Poor black men have limited control over such external or structural factors. Cultural factors refer to behaviors and attitudes that prevent successful immersion in the world of work and the pursuit of upward mobility. These cultural factors are understood to be alterable by black men themselves, which, in turn, is often taken as evidence that these men cause their own plight.

Debates about the relative significance of cultural and structural factors in poverty persisted throughout the twentieth century (Katz 1989a, 1989b). Essentially, conservative thinkers assert that cultural factors cause black men to fall toward the bottom of the structural arrangements in American society in terms of employment, socioeconomic standing, and so on. In their view, changes in the behavior of black men matter more than anything else for improving their prospects for advancement (e.g., Mead 1986, 1992). Liberal thinkers reverse the order of cause and effect and maintain that the calamitous cultural traits that draw the greatest public attention are due to structural factors (e.g., Wilson, 1991). They claim that cultural factors, even if relevant in explaining social outcomes, are secondary in importance to the structural domain.

Many researchers argue that structural and cultural perspectives deserve equal attention. In this view, whatever the principal causal force, certain behaviors and attitudes serve to reinforce the already problematic social predicament of black men.[3] While this approach seems the most fruitful, most studies that address the crisis of the black male still focus too narrowly on behavioral traits and the presumably "abnormal" normative and value systems associated with them. A proper cultural analysis of low-income black men must not rest solely on an exploration of values and norms, but must thoroughly interrogate how these men formulate worldviews, ideologies, and belief systems regarding their life circumstances and possible futures. While these elements of culture have been incorporated in some recent discussions of poor black men, they have not been given the same degree of attention as have norms and values. Consequently, the cultural dimension of the crisis of low-income black men must be rethought to include proper attention to the social processes and implications of these additional aspects of meaning-making. The first step toward doing so involves a more precise consideration of the normative and value-laden logic for the cultural analysis of African American men and the research community's preoccupation with their behavior.

Cultural Inquiry and the (Incomplete) Representation of Black Men

Scholarly and popular attention to the situation of urban-based, low-income black men ultimately converges on one theme: why these men seem to function so differently from mainstream Americans. Throughout the twentieth century a plethora of research on these men strove to gain some understanding of their social character and behavior. Studies documenting broad-scale social outcomes for low-income black men usually examine large-scale survey, census, or other aggregate data. Although they reveal crucial information about the social status and well-being of poor black men, these findings ultimately provide only a thin description of the public image of black men.

In contrast, the tradition of urban ethnography has succeeded in presenting the most vivid images and accounts of the behavior of low-income black men. Urban ethnography has provided a window on the everyday life effects and implications of the crisis of the black male. Peer groups, street corners, and formal institutions are the usal focal points for these studies (Anderson 1978, 1990, 1999; Billson 1996; Hannerz 1969, 1972; Hunter and Davis 1994; Kornblum and Williams 1985; Laseter 1997; Leibow 1967; MacLeod 1995; Majors and Billson 1992; Rainwater 1970; Sullivan 1989; Tolleson 1997, and Venkatesh 2000). These studies have revealed how poor black men come to grips with living in poverty by assessing why they engage violent behaviors, how they manage turbulence and insecurity in family life, and what they do about goals and dreams that seem far from their current station in life. The basic vocabulary of cultural inquiry—norms, values, attitudes, behaviors, and beliefs—serve as the core analytical tools for these investigations. Urban ethnographers employ this vocabulary in order to construct cultural interpretations of behavior. The central challenge faced by researchers in this tradition has been to associate what often appears as unique, adverse, and even exotic behavior with the normative, attitudinal, and value systems that sustain it.

Cultural analysis in urban ethnography is the site of lively debate. In short, one side of the debate asks whether black men adopt or promote distinct cultural patterns that contribute to, if not cause altogether, their demise. The other side asks whether these men, who are taken to be cultural actors in the ways that other groups of Americans are, might simply experience unique life circumstances and conditions that overdetermine the social outcomes comprising their everyday lives. It is not surprising that what black men do in the course of their lives is sometimes harmful to themselves and others. This can be the case irrespective of whether the blame is placed on them for adopting profligate behavior or on external factors such as the declining employment opportunities or the lack of social support mechanisms in their communities. Wherever urban ethnographers fall along this continuum of perspectives, the tradition of cultural analysis, despite its crucial role in framing a robust image of poor black men, has nonetheless helped advance an incomplete cultural framework for interpreting their life situation. In this framework, the notions of beliefs and worldviews have been overshadowed by other analytical terms; norms, values attitudes, and behavior. In fact, two terms, *norms* and *values*, became the bedrock of cultural analyses of poor black men (and, for that matter, of poor black Americans in general). This is because norms and values are viewed in this tradition as significantly more relevant to behavior than are beliefs.[4] Norms are rules that guide behavior, and violating them makes the transgressor susceptible to sanctions. Depending on the formality of the rules, sanctions can range from the loss of personal freedom (e.g., incarceration), to experiencing disdain or loss of respect from peers and associates. Values are the goals or ideals associated with behavior. Values constitute the ultimate aim or objective of individual and collective action.

The formation of belief systems, worldviews, and other related meaning-making processes concerns an entirely different, yet equally important, set of cultural properties which do not always lend themselves to moral evaluations in the same way that norms, values, and behavior do. Because the cultural interpretation of African American men has been largely steeped in moral evaluation, the terminology that facilitates this orientation has become standard. In essence, the cultural attributes of black Americans—especially its poorest constituents—that appear flawed, underdeveloped, or most threatening to the mainstream cultural fabric in American society have been those that have received the most attention.

When beliefs and worldviews are acknowledged in this research tradition, such acknowledgment often has occurred in either of two highly problematic ways. In one case, beliefs and worldviews are inferred from an analysis of behavior. For instance, general claims about how black men conceptualize the social world are formed not from focused inquiries into their beliefs and worldviews, but from observations of their behavior. In the other case, beliefs and worldviews are given a distinct place in the analytical framework, but are then largely reduced to assertions that poor black men believe their situation to be traumatic (e.g., they believe themselves faced with inadequate work opportunities, a turbulent and threatening community, etc.). Attention then turns to how these men respond, behaviorally or emotionally, to this realization rather than to more critical and penetrating interrogation of the subtleties and complexities associated with thos beliefs. Hence, even when beliefs and worldviews are given explicit analytical attention, norms, values, and public behavior become the focal concerns, rather than a more elaborate cultural inquiry that included greater attention to the processes and outcomes of meaning-making.

The narrowed application of this cultural vocabulary, taken together with a preoccupation with capriciousness and volatility as core features of the public behavior of poor black men, has resulted in an exceptionally myopic view of their humanity. The quest for a new cultural framework concerning the crisis of poor black men is ultimately a plea for a more complex understanding of their plight. In order to achieve this, we must first take a closer look at how public behavior became the preeminent concern in studies of this population, and how a narrowed cultural vocabulary was employed such that it led to a view of these men as culturally underdeveloped.

Validating Public Behavior and Cultural Incontinence: The Origins of the Cultural Paradigm

The centrality of the public behavior of African American men in urban ethnography is lodged in a deep tradition of social scientific investigation into African American urban life. In the 1960s white American and European scholars first made their wholesale independent ventures into the African American urban community to conduct ethnographic research. The 1960s initiatives followed a long history of ethnographic and quasi-

TABLE 1.2
Homicide Rates, Men, Aged 20–24 (per 100,000)

	Black	White
1990	162.2	18.1
1995	155.5	18.2
2000	116.3	12.2

Source: U.S. National Center for Health Statistics, 2000.
Note: Hispanics included in both black and white categories in year 2000 measures.

ethnographic exploration of the African American urban experience stretching back to the late nineteenth century and flowering in the 1930s and 1940s. These earlier studies differed from the 1960s studies in two crucial ways. First, the early studies were usually conducted either by African American scholars working with white scholars in the field (Davis and Dollard 1940; Davis, Gardner, and Gardner 1941; Dollard 1937), or by African American scholars who adopted the theoretical and methodological tools of their advisors, all of whom were white (Davis 1946, Doyle 1937, Frazier 1932, 1934; Johnson 1934a, 1934b, 1934c, 1934d, 1941).[5] Second, most of the researchers who conducted these early urban-based studies also investigated the lives of African Americans in rural South, and drew from that work to formalize the initial cultural frameworks and arguments about urban lower-income African Americans.

This early work was produced between the publication of W.E.B. DuBois's seminal work, *The Philadelphia Negro* (1899), and the end of World War II, when St. Claire Drake and Horace Cayton published *Black Metropolis* (1945). Beginning with DuBois's work, arguments in the early tradition have ranged from pejorative accounts of the behavior of lower-income people to more compassionate social reform–minded commentaries. More importantly, by asserting that the culture of low-income African Americans was a source of their problems in attaining social advancement, that era of research laid the foundation for the studies produced in the 1960s.

Throughout the early phase of research, comparisons with more well-to-do black Americans and with Americans more generally drove home the vision of poor black Americans as culturally deficient.[6] The claims made about norms and values boiled down to the view that lower-income black Americans were not equipped for modernity. More specifically, they were not used to functioning in highly organized, hourly wage-earning economic sectors—the sectors that began to typify the American work sphere as the twentieth century progressed. Poor blacks were seen as ill-prepared to follow the rules and mandates of that system, or to effectively partake more generally in a social world profoundly shaped by urban industrialization. Much of the early research argued that low-income black Americans needed encouragement and material support in order to improve their lot so that they might achieve socioeconomic and emotional stability.[7]

The cultural domains of belief systems and the social processes of meaning-making were given scant attention in these discussions. This oversight was due in part to the shared belief by black Americans that the city represented the land of opportunity. Accordingly, discussions of black Americans' belief systems focused on illustrating how deeply they subscribed to this notion, and how much the idea served as an impetus for northern, urban migration away from southern-based Jim Crow oppression. This focus left little room for a deeper exploration of their belief systems (such as precisely whether and how they imagined navigating the industrial arena in order to get ahead, or precisely what kind of obstacles or barriers they imagined to stand in their way). Thus researchers did not undertake rigorous interrogations of beliefs and worldviews because they assumed that poor blacks wholeheartedly shared these dimensions of culture not only with other African Americans, but with the American populace more generally. The researchers believed that norms, values, and behavior formed the terrain upon which cultural differences were to be found between black and white Americans. It followed that these areas drew the most scholarly attention.[8]

Formalizing the Paradigm

The post–World War II era brought forth a slew of research that extended and solidified the contemporary depiction of the norms, values, and behaviors associated with low-income African Americans, especially men. As sociologist Lee Rainwater put his classic work, *Behind Ghetto Walls: Black Family Life in a Federal Slum* (1970: 362–73), by the 1960s social science had adopted a concrete notion of lower-class subculture. Although anticipated by the research of earlier years, the idea of a lower-class subculture was created and sustained in large part by ethnographic studies of European-American ethnic enclaves in urban areas (Gans 1962, Suttles 1968, Whyte 1943) and studies and commentaries about lower-income Americans of various racial and ethnic backgrounds (Berger 1960, Bordua 1961, Cloward and Ohlin 1960, Cohen and Hodges 1963, Coser 1965, Gans 1969, W. Miller 1958, Rodman 1963). A wave of ethnographic studies of low-income black Americans, primarily done by white Americans in the 1960s, gave even more intellectual ammunition to a conception of lower-class subculture (Abrahams 1964, Hannerz 1969, Liebow 1967, Rainwater 1970, F. Riessman 1962, Schultz 1969).

This body of work advanced the general argument that subcultures were created by members of subordinate social groups contending with the difficulty of achieving the goals and desires that the larger social system considered legitimate. These goals and desires either were beyond the means of members of the lower echelon group to achieve, or not attainable in the ways that they were for those in more privileged positions. As anthropologist Hyman Rodman (1963) argued, functioning without the resources necessary for mobility, or means to achieve them, resulted in the need for members of the subordinate group to stretch their values. This was a process whereby individuals occupying subordinate status could justify or reconcile their alternative behaviors and attitudes in ways that kept them somewhat in line with behaviors and attitudes regarded as mainstream. Thus, for example, immediate gratification was taken by scholars to be a value of the poor because that behavior would allow them to feel a level of satisfaction or fulfillment similar to that felt by wealthier people. It is disturbing irony that many subcultural theorists asserted that poor people differed culturally from the more economically secure without truly interrogating the cultural attributes of the more privileged. As poor black Americans began to take center stage in urban ethnographic inquiry, they became central victims of this flawed thinking.

The 1960s also saw the development of the notion that black Americans maintained their own cultural repertoire, which was reflected in their manner of speaking, styles of bodily expression, and basic attitudes toward life (Keil 1966).[9] Indeed, by the 1960s, many people began to regard African American expressiveness as "cool." That expressiveness became all the more acceptable in an American social landscape that was beginning to be more tolerant of different forms of cultural expression and public demeanor. This era of tolerance began with the establishment of the "beat" generation and ended with a highly visible countercultural movement. Arguments that legitimized the notion of lower-class subculture emerged in the midst of these developments, which opened the door for public acceptance of alternative cultural styles. The notion of an African American lower-class subculture represented an amalgamation of alternative styles. Although some researchers questioned the legitimacy of this notion, it lingered as an importnt construct for serious cultural analyses of African Americans.

A major point of reference in the lower-class culture debate, and one that had strong ethnic overtones, was the culture of poverty thesis associated with the work of anthropologist Oscar Lewis (1959, 1961, 1966). Lewis coined the term "culture of poverty," and expounded upon it in his series of studies of Hispanic and Mexican families neighborhoods in the

United States and Mexico. Essentially, Lewis's culture of poverty thesis argued that the behavior and values of the poor led to an enclosed and self-perpetuating world of dependence. Lewis presented this mind-set as a way of life, passed down from generation to generation as long as successive generations lived in the same conditions of poverty. It is important to realize that Lewis is given less credit than he deserves for balancing the focus on culture with an affirmation of the relevance of structural conditions in affecting how poor people responded to their situation and how they viewed their chances for escaping poverty. Thus Lewis's framework left room for the notion that escaping the conditions of poverty could release one from the hold of the culture of poverty. Most importantly, Lewis also stated that one could live in poverty without sharing in the culture of poverty. Unfortunately, he said little about precisely how the structural context mattered and how it intersected with culture. This gap in his thinking meant culture reigned supreme in reactions to his work and elaborations on his ideas by other scholars.

Whether read accurately or not, Lewis's work sparked extensive discussion about the relationship between poverty and culture. More importantly, it solidified an enduring social-scientific conception of the power of cultural forces in determining the social outcomes of those living in poverty.[10] While research in the pre-1960s era asserted that black Americans generally believed in the possibilities for a better life, the 1960s research agenda assumed that the poorest African Americans increasingly saw little or no possibility at all for improvement. Accordingly the research agenda turned to detailed considerations of the norms, values, and behaviors exhibited by people who held fatalistic visions of their future. Both liberal and conservative thinkers in the 1960s incorporated aspects of this conception in their investigations of the black urban poor (Banfield 1970, Harrington 1962, Moynihan 1965, F. Riessman 1962).[11]

Modern Urban Ethnography's Contention with Culture

As we have seen, the culture of poverty thesis greatly influenced the public mind-set about the relationship of culture, poverty, and urban life during and since the 1960s. The thesis was not without its critics, however. Essentially, four basic points of criticism emerged; (1) its lack of emphasis on the community or other external factors as bases for the behavioral outcomes of the urban poor, (2) its lack of emphasis on the agency of the poor, (3) its faulty implication of the nuclear family as a necessary model for family organization in low-income communities, and (4) its uncritical assumption that mainstream culture was a cohesive, positive, or problem-free normative referent for comparative analysis (Valentine 1966).

TABLE 1.3
Civilian Labor Force—Employment, Men, Aged 16–19 and 20–24, Non-Institutionalized, High School Education or Less

		Black		White	
	Age	Employed	Unemployed	Employed	Unemployed
1993	16–19	59.8	40.2	82.4	17.6
	20–24	77.0	23.0	90.5	9.5
2001	16–19	69.5	30.5	86.2	13.8
	20–24	82.6	17.4	92.3	7.7

Source: U.S. Census Bureau and U.S. Bureau of Labor Statistics, 1994 and 2002.

Note: Hispanics included in both black and white categories in year 2000 measures. The population of the civilian labor force includes those who work or remain on government records as seeking employment.

The penetrating criticisms of the culture of poverty thesis did not prevent it from impacting the content and forms of the urban ethnography of the 1960s and later. Urban ethnographers have rejected certain aspects of the culture of poverty thesis, endorsed other aspects, and grappled to specify and refine that which could not easily be rejected or endorsed.[12] The thesis was modified to include greater attention to structural issues such as the absence of stable and substantive employment prospects for urban-based low-income African Americans. The leading ethnographies of the 1960s made specific claims about how good work prospects were essential for change in the cultural milieu of the black urban poor. In doing so, they made cultural factors secondary to the absence of adequate work for explaining the persistence of inequality (Hannerz 1969, Liebow 1967, Rainwater 1970).[13] This focus on employment issues continues in more recent urban ethnographies (Anderson 1990 and 1999, Bourgois 1995, Glasgow 1980, Newman 1999, Sullivan 1989, Venkatesh 2000). However, the lingering effects of the culture of poverty thesis still remain, primarily in the urban ethnography tradition's inability to broaden its terrain for cultural inquiry beyond the standard categories of values, norms, and behaviors.[14]

At least one 1960s-era work, *Soulside* (1969), by Swedish anthropologist Ulf Hannerz, addressed the importance of looking at beliefs and worldviews in a broad fashion. Hannerz discussed the ways in which public interaction helped individuals to cement beliefs and worldviews about various aspects of social reality. He noted that public interaction, among other things, acts as an information-gathering process. By dissecting what he called "street-corner mythmaking," Hannerz argued that public interaction is a principal site for black men to share ideas and create understandings about their world (1969, pp. 105–17). Rather than serving solely as a means for men to banter in order to feel good about themselves, Hannerz stressed, such activities are also a way for them to share ideas about people and occurrences in their communities. This communication is a critical means of providing the men with the tools for assessing who or what may be helpful and harmful in everyday life and why this is the case. The problem is that Hannerz did little more than note the analytical significance of this social process as a type of meaning-making activity. His focus was mainly on why myths are constructed by street-corner people rather than on the process of meaning-making itself.

Some recent studies in the urban ethnographic tradition have proved significantly more committed to unpacking the processes by which beliefs and meanings about mobility and opportunity are formulated. Those that address this concern do so by focusing on how low-income African Americans make sense of labor prospects in the fast food industry and other forms of inner-city low-wage employment (Newman 1999), how views about legitimate work opportunity relate to the choice to pursue illicit activity (Sullivan 1989), and how gang members rationalize their behavior despite their understanding that such participation throws barriers in the way of upward mobility (Venkatesh 2000). Overall, however, the focus on why and how low-income individuals come to hold their views remains a secondary focus on the literature. The preoccupation of the field continues to be the behavioral dimensions of low-income, urban-based African Americans, who by the 1980s were largely identified as or associated with the urban underclass.

Street Culture and the Public Persona of Black Men

The roots of the modern depiction of the social character of black men are in 1960s-era urban ethnographies (Hannerz 1969, Liebow 1967, Rainwater 1970). By introducing concepts such as "anomic street culture" (Rainwater 1970), these studies aimed to shed light on why low-income communities differed so much from more affluent ones in terms of the potential for violence and the absence of social and institutional buffers from physical, economic, and emotional threat. They also highlighted a finding that dates back to the turn-of—the-century work of W.E.B. DuBois, showing the importance of public space such as the street for recreational and social objectives for the African American urban poor who lacked access to private space for those ends.

A number of 1960s-era ethnographers argued that an anomic street culture in low-income communities caused the inhabitants to function in unique and sometimes aggressive ways in order to survive their social environment (Rainwater 1970, Schultz 1969). Subsequent research continued to employ this analytical framework focused on public behavior. These studies showed the extent to which despair, frustration, and tension form parts of the everyday lives of these men.[15] Researchers argued that African American men conveyed a public persona consisting of highly expressive styles of public engagement that reflected their effort to cope with these bleaker aspects of their lives. This persona included displays of bravado and overtly sensational forms of conduct, which were promoted in order to mask their weaknesses and vulnerabilities.[16] The emergence of this persona further encouraged the emphasis on public behavior in the literature on the African American poor.

Another development in the field that influenced the approach to studying poor black men was the sweeping public exposure to—and rapid acceptance of—the concept of the *underclass* in the 1980s.[17] The term implied that a criminally inclined, violence-prone, despair-ridden and culturally deficient group of individuals locked in an inescapable web of economic deprivation and pathology formed part of the African American urban poor. The underclass was made up of the most immobile and socially isolated of these urban dwellers. They had the fewest prospects for upward mobility, and they experienced little sustained interaction with those in more mobile positions (Wilson 1987). Most importantly, the concept of an underclass became an identifier of behavior and public demeanor (Auletta 1982). Violence, aggression, and idleness emerged as the personal characteristics and images most often associated with the term. Much of the urban ethnography of the past decade has centered on so-called underclass behavior (Anderson 1990 and 1999, Billson 1996, Bourgois 1995, Majors and Billson 1992).

The emergence of the notion of the underclass ultimately served to over shadow any remaining positive characteristics regarding the public behavior of poor black men found in urban ethnographies. Although some studies have offered images of poor black men managing the paucity of resources available to them, and maneuvering around the threats, dangers, and insecurities that constitute much of their everyday lives, the preeminent focus of the most recent work in urban ethnography has been the framing of poor black men as prone to violence and decadence, or at least to attitudinal dispositions that lead to such behavior (Anderson 1999, Glasgow 1980, Majors and Billson 1992).

Urban ethnography in the age of the underclass has been comprised of lucid arguments about black men's propensity for violence and aggression. A leading claim of such studies is that black men are psychologically wounded both by a labor market that does not provide them with what they need for sufficient living, and by a community rife with threats and uncertainty. The prototype that emerges from this ethnography is of a people responding to despair and futility by leveling their goals and desires. This portrayal is another of the enduring legacies of 1960s urban ethnography. While the best of that work offered more than psychological portrayals of the black urban poor, the image of despairing men continues to be one of the outstanding and enduring artifacts of this research. The danger is that this image comes to be accepted as representative of all low-income black men. It certainly is not. Black men offer a wide-ranging and diverse set of responses and reactions to the conditions that confront them. Yet, the emphasis on uncovering these kinds of cultural patterns in recent literature has overshadowed the search for other cultural manifestations such as the formation of worldviews and beliefs about daily life circumstances, especially those not directly connected to everyday life in poverty.[18]

Toward a More Complete Cultural Framework

Jay MacLeod's *Ain't No Making It: Aspirations and Attainment in a Low-Income Neighborhood* (1995) stands out as an exception in the literature. Unlike most other ethnographers of the urban poor, MacLeod pays attention to the cultural processes of meaning-making, including how these men frame images of the broader social world. The work explores how two groups of working-class and low-income young men, one predominantly white American and the other mostly black American, contemplate and work toward (and sometimes unknowingly against) their future goals. MacLeod deftly shows how meaning-making processes emerge as by-products of social interaction and socialization. He also argues that meaning-making processes provide a basis for how individuals determine which norms and values to adopt. For instance, one must have some understanding of a social context before determining what rules to follow within it, or what particular ideals and goals to maintain.[19] MacLeod formulates a unique argument about the importance of historical context on the formation of worldviews. He asserts that historical context shapes whether and how these men consider race and class as relevant factors in their orientation toward possible future mobility prospects.[20]

By exploring a range of outlooks across two groups of men, and by noting carefully how the same historical context matters for different readings of reality by the members of both groups, *Ain't No Making It* offers a much more complex exploration of meaning-making than is typically found in urban ethnography. In essence, MacLeod shows how these men employ race as a tool for ordering social reality. Not surprisingly, each group of men uses this tool in a different way. Race serves as an

TABLE 1.4
Employment Rates for African American Men Aged 16–24,
Non-Institutionalized, High School or Less Education

1979	0.62
1989	0.59
1999–2000	0.54

Source: Current Population Surveys (reported in Holzer 2002).
Note: Hispanics included in both black and white categories in year 2000 measures. Employment rates include those who are not listed on government records as seeking employment.

organizing principle for how they view their own life prospects, and for how they conceive of the prospects of the men in the other (racial) group.

MacLeod's work is particularly useful for an analysis of meaning-making because he explores race not solely as a descriptive trait for comparing black and white low-income and working-class men, but also as a lens for viewing social reality. Consequently, his work comes closest to the underlying logic behind the exploration of the minds of black men offered here. Most relevant to my own work is the fact that MacLeod's study is not preoccupied with furthering the psychological depictions that characterize 1960s-style urban ethnography. Rather than looking at interaction or overt public behavior, MacLeod moved closer to getting into the heads of the young men he studied. Still, as important as MacLeod's work is in terms of breaking with the paradigm of urban ethnography, his analysis is not completely free of the assumptions of that same tradition.

MacLeod's shortcomings are related to his efforts to be true to formal ethnography. He focused a great deal on behavior and interaction in order to ground his analysis of the men's understanding about the world and how they see themselves fitting into it. In doing so, he provided a highly provocative and theoretically sophisticated interpretation of how social experience and behavior connect with the formation of ideas about one's future. MacLeod's attention to the relationship between behavior and meaning-making, however, is underdeveloped because he did not sufficiently explore exactly what the men had to say about mobility and future possibilities. Instead, he restricted his analytical vocabulary to the terms aspirations and expectations, fitting what the men had to say about future goals and desires into one or the other. As important as these two terms are, they do not exhaust the wide range of potential conceptions concerning one's outlook on the future. In fact, aspirations and expectations cannot be appropriately understood in the absence of assessments of other kinds of future-oriented thoughts.

The meaning-making work done by low-income African American men about future goals and objectives includes much more than aspirations and expectations. Notions of the probable, the possible, and the desirable are also important to consider inasmuch as they contextualize and help determine those same expectations and aspirations. MacLeod addresses some of these points, but does not theorize carefully how these varied forms of meaning relate to one other. Instead, he focuses primarily on how social experience affects the formation of aspirations and expectations. In committing himself to these two terms, MacLeod's work is not inaccurate as much as incomplete.

The first step toward pursuing a broader inquiry on meaning-making is to expand the parameters of cultural analysis that have traditionally shaped urban ethnographic studies. An important addition to work that focuses primarily on behaviors or practice, or remains preoccupied with values and norms, is a careful examination of the meaning-making that shapes belief systems and worldviews. In fact, two related areas of meaning-making must be pursued more thoroughly. The first is the pattern of beliefs and worldviews about one's immediate life situation. This includes one's sense of the specific probable, possible, and desirable outcomes that may come one's way, as well as the barriers and obstacles that one may perceive to be associated with these outcomes. The second is one's pattern of beliefs and worldviews about how others in the social world manage their mobility prospects and options. This is important because ideas about the plight of others (especially those in similar life situations) may shape one's understanding about oneself (even if one eventually rejects the notion that the dilemmas befalling fellow members of a social category—racial, gendered, or class-based—will affect oneself).

Careful consideration of both areas leads to a more thorough understanding of this domain of culture. Moreover, what people think about themselves and others in the social world helps define their capacity for future action. An exploration of their thoughts on these issues also illuminates why they behave in the ways that they do, and what they think that behavior may mean for their future prospects.

The Analytical Objectives of a New Cultural Analysis

Belief systems and meaning-making processes remain the least developed of the conceptual terms that comprise the cultural vocabulary employed in modern urban ethnography. Ulf Hannerz may have provided a road map for undertaking more nuanced work with these terms, but he himself did not follow it. Jay MacLeod charted a path along that map, but did not go very far along it. Instead, two other branches of social science inquiry have led the way in exploring the belief systems of the African American urban poor. One consists of qualitative studies that address issues such as how people frame a sense of their own and others' moral worth (Lamont 2000). The other consists of quantitative assessments of how people gauge the shifts in mobility prospects over time for themselves and other Americans (Hochschild 1995). Thus, the fruits of a broader cultural inquiry on poor black men are found in having them talk at length about their sense of themselves, which the former approach favors, about the issues raised in the latter approach.

The immediate challenge is formidable. The central goal of this new cultural analysis will be to explore a wider range of poor black men's thoughts about the future, including how they think mobility unfolds for Americans in general. An important part of this task is to explain the extent to which these men consider and present themselves as similar to or different from other people regarding how they approach their future. Finally, this new cultural analysis must include an analysis of the social experiential bases of why the men say what they do about all of these matters. This broader focus on the sociological dimensions of meaning-making builds from and enriches the tradition of cultural analysis of low-income African American men. This new cultural analysis seeks to portray poor black men as more than hyper-stimulated reactants to a turbulent world, but rather as people like the rest of us—meaning-makers who have different degrees of insight and understanding about ourselves and the world we live in.

The Practical Objectives of a New Cultural Analysis

The practical goal at stake in constructing an improved cultural analysis is to provide a new insight into the effects of social isolation and poverty concentration. These concepts were introduced in 1987 by sociologist William Julius Wilson, just at the same time that the underclass concept reached its greatest popularity. While Wilson has since moved away from using the term *underclass* due to its highly and unnecessarily pejorative implications, social isolation and poverty concentration remain central concepts for his interpretation of the contemporary nature of urban poverty in America (Wilson 1996).

Social isolation refers to the lack of contact or sustained interaction with individuals or institutions that represent mainstream society (Wilson 1987, p. 60). Wilson explains that such isolation makes it harder for people to become tied to social networks that connect to jobs. It also generates behavior not conducive to good work histories, most especially the inability to organize one's daily life. *Poverty concentration* refers to the

TABLE 1.5
Percentage of Males under Penal Authority in the United States, Aged 20–29
(in prison, in jail, on probation, on parole)

	Black	White
1989	23.0%	6.2%
1994	30.2%	6.7%

Source: Mauer 1990, Mauer and Huling 1995.

social outcomes resulting from large numbers of impoverished people living in great proximity to each other. In introducing these terms, Wilson strove to counter the pervasive culture of poverty logic, which did not adequately account for structure. The introduction of the concepts of social isolation and poverty concentration created an analytical space for including and assessing the effects of an enduring lack of social and geographic connection between the urban poor and other, more affluent people. In doing so, these concepts drew attention to the structural dimensions of urban poverty. The major structural dimensions include the existence of social networks that are thoroughly saturated with chronically poor, especially ones who are far removed from the labor force, and of neighborhoods in which poor people live in extreme proximity of each other. With attention being drawn to the structural domain, researchers could no longer make the easy jump to assessments of the behavior of the urban poor as the principal source of their problems.

This inquiry accepts, but moves beyond, the basic assertion of earlier research that living in social isolation leads to the inability to participate in mainstream life and culture (Harrell and Peterson 1992, Jencks and Peterson 1991, Massey and Denton 1993). Social isolation is a multifaceted phenomenon that involves more than geographic and social distance from institutions and formal organizations. It can be relevant in assessing whether and how people interpret the social processes and structures that shape their lives, especially those processes that may be less familiar to low-income people (e.g., how large firms and businesses seek potential employees). By looking at what black men say about mobility, opportunity, and life chances, this book provides a detailed exploration of individual differences in the experience of social isolation, degrees of exposure to certain concentration effects, and the bearing that these differences have on the formation of contrasting worldviews about mobility and structural constraint.

To make the best possible sense of what these men present as their views of mobility and opportunity, we must first take a detailed look at how they describe the social world in which they live; that is, how they interpret their lifeworlds. Part 2 explores the social worlds of these men from their own perspectives. This exploration provides the necessary background for understanding the formation of their worldviews, which are explored in part 3. To be sure, actual lived experience, social worlds, and worldviews are connected dialectically. One's life experiences can lead to modifications or refutations of one's current worldviews, and one's worldviews can help shape future decisions. Therefore, the separation of the book into these parts should not be taken to mean that these domains exist independently of one another. Yet, we must first explore the social worlds of these men in order to provide an anchor for their worldviews. The analytical separation, then, allows us to highlight the heretofore missing element of worldviews without overlooking the key social foundations that help shape them.

Part Two ─────────────────────

LIFEWORLDS

Chapter Two _____

Time, Space, and Everyday Living

THE MINDS OF THE MEN in this book, as with all people, have been shaped in reaction to past and present experiences. Before looking at their interpretations of the social world, it is important to know something about the social world of the Near West Side of Chicago. In doing so we must take note of the meanings that these men give to the institutions, experiences, and individuals that they encounter in everyday life. This involves focusing not only on what is different about their lives in comparison to more privileged people, but also on what aspects appear to be the same, and how the two interconnect in their life histories. These men may face different options and possibilities than other people, yet they function quite similarly to the rest of us in how they read their social worlds, how they make sense of what they see, and how they think this affects their lives.

The bedrock for these men's visions of mobility and opportunity in the social world is the set of meanings that they give to past and present personal experiences. In order to effectively ground their future outlooks, it is imperative to understand their sense of the order and processes of everyday life, the types of people involved in it, and how they connect their pasts to the present. These initial understandings help illustrate how their experiences lead to what more privileged people may consider to be blind spots and biases in their testimonies about future possibilities. They also help to explain why these men talk about people and institutions that are relevant to mobility in ways that are odd or unfamiliar to the more well-to-do in American society.

Time and Space on the Near West Side

Listening to the men talk about everyday experiences provides a special view into the part of the world that they inhabit. Paying attention to this talk opens up this world in a way that observational analysis cannot. Watching them stand on corners, in front of abandoned lots, or near park benches does little to convey the specific ways in which they make meaning out of their everyday experiences. Contrary to what casual observation of such behavior might indicate, these men take life quite seriously,

especially because life on the Near West Side involves a great deal of uncertainty. There is no certainty that a job will come one's way on a given
day. Without work there remains no basis for daily planning, so time
comes to mean something different for these men. Being without work
means that schedules and routines are not the norm. Instead, the everyday
means continuous efforts at "trying to stay busy" or "not be idle," as
Conrad stated in trying to explain to me what his daily life was like in
the absence of work.

Conrad is a twenty-two-year-old resident of ABLA, where he lives with
his grandmother and her two foster children. He is a high school dropout
without a job and with a criminal record. He acquired that record when
he was stopped by the police a few years before while in possession of a
gun. Conrad told me that it all began when he won a fistfight with a man
from the neighborhood. Feeling that his pride was wounded, the other
man pulled a gun on Conrad a few days later. As Conrad explained, the
man walked up to him in front of a group of people and said, "I bet you
I could make your knee shake."

Conrad went on to say:

> I said, "I bet you can't." So he grabbed his gun from his boy, right, and he put
> it up to my leg. He said, "Man, if you was one of them niggers I wanted to kill,
> I'd kill you right now." So I felt like he let me live, you know. You know how
> people, see, coming up in the 'jects if you grant a man life, if you give him a
> chance to live, you know what I'm saying, you done just, you jeopardized your
> life right there. So on my way to get my revenge, you know, I thought this is
> the way of being tough, you know. But I just seen it was the way of being stupid.
> I got caught in the process.

Shortly after the encounter, Conrad acquired a gun and went looking
for his aggressor. In the midst of doing so, he was stopped by the police
during one of their routine street corner searches. He was arrested and
charged with illegal possession of a firearm. This was one of a few stories
that he told me about violent and near-violent encounters in his past. Prior
to this incident Conrad had been shot in the leg as a result of a conflict
with another man. This altercation was over a woman that Conrad was
dating at the time. The other man was interested in her as well, made that
known to him, and the matter eventually was handled like many are on
the Near West Side.

While Conrad could talk at length about neighborhood events like
this, he could not elaborate with concrete examples regarding "staying
busy" when I asked him about idleness. Conrad's inability to comment
further shows his difficulty in explaining how he occupies himself on a
daily basis. Still, his remarks spoke loudly about the dread associated with
having nothing to do. For Conrad and most of the other men, daily life

consists of little more than being in the streets and interacting with others in public space. Those without work share in a world of this kind of activity, watching and talking to each other as the days go by. This style of interaction is captured by Georg Simmel's (1971) notion of sociability, whereby people mingle with each other not for the purpose of garnering explicit or tangible returns, nor to offer them to others, but for superficial, for-the-moment encounters that preserve a sense of being alive, active, and vibrant. The exuberance implied in Simmel's definition is a bit of an overstatement when applied to the men of the Near West Side. For them, sociability is more about simply being present in a social space and passing time because there is nothing else for them to do. These men could expect or desire little more from their peers on the corner, as nobody had much to offer.

The men's daily rituals included something on the order of rising at the start of the day and venturing out into the neighborhood as men have been doing since the influx of African Americans into the urban arena nearly one hundred years ago. Occasionally, some of them would check in at one of the two sites where I conducted my interviews, either at the alderman's community office on Western Avenue if they were from Henry Horner Homes, or the tenants' association office if they lived in or near ABLA Homes.

I regularly witnessed men coming to both locations to say hello to staff members and see if some short-order work needed to be done. My presence in either place was one of the few unusual aspects of this otherwise near-daily pattern. The busiest people that I came into contact with were the staff working in these offices. On the streets, most people moved about as if there were nothing particularly important going on in their lives. The only exceptions were the drug dealers who could be found at certain corners (but who protected their affairs from overt visibility), and people who looked as if they were social workers or civil servants conducting official business in the community. Most of the men in the twenty-to-thirty age range seemed to be completely consumed by hanging out on the street and not having much to do.

Such behavior requires little orientation to time. My desire to meet and talk to these men served as one of the few formal obligations that they had to arrange in their daily lives. Their lack of familiarity with formal obligations meant that scheduling interviews with some of them entailed great difficulty. The everyday situation of these men led to an increasing inability to organize; there was little in their lives that compelled them to function in any other way.

Early on, I assumed that some of the men's failure to meet me at established times and places simply meant that they did not care. Their enthusiasm about being involved in my research, and more importantly, getting paid for it, did not overcome whatever unexplained occurrences or inclinations kept them from being in the right place at the right time. To be sure, many men did show up on time. Hence, I came to the conclusion that those who could not follow schedules perhaps did not care to, and there was really nothing more to the matter. Mild frustration over the inability to get some of the men to adhere to my scheduling soon gave way to my expecting that the first or second arranged meeting would probably fall through. As I became more immersed in the project, I accepted that this was the way things were going to be.

A different reaction on my part, more of bewilderment than frustration, occurred after witnessing another type of response to time. Rather than showing up late, some of the men often would arrive hours early at one of the offices or, on special occasions, at another meeting place.[1] In a handful of cases, men who were very late for a meeting would be extremely early the next time around, and it did not seem that they did so as a way of making amends for their earlier lateness. Instead, the consistent explanation for the early arrival was that they had nothing else to do that day, so they sought me out in order to talk. While they were not generally surprised if I told them that I was busy, they also did not expect that their sudden appearances would pose any problems for me. In most cases, the men simply waited until I was available to talk to them, not understanding that they might be infringing on another man's time or on my own until one of us spoke up to clarify the situation.

After several weeks of fieldwork, the men's different conception of time became the most pressing issue in my mind during times when I was not in the midst of scheduled interviews. My journey to the Near West Side took the form of a ninety-minute bus ride from the Hyde Park section of Chicago.[2] The distance in privilege, prestige, and degree of serenity between the two communities was perhaps the most staggering dimension of the divide between them. It was in the course of traversing this terrain late one night that I began to understand more fully what was going on regarding the men's responses to time. My understanding was influenced by an interview with Devin in the Near West Side alderman's office.

Devin came into the alderman's office early one June afternoon in 1994 and took a seat in the front-room waiting area. I did not notice if he spoke to anybody when he first came in, and I stopped taking notice of him soon after his arrival. I did take enough notice to draw the conclusion that he was experiencing particularly rough times, even in comparison to many of the other men that I met. He had bruises on his face, and a dirty bandage around one leg. The bandage was visible just below his sweat pants leg, which was rolled up to his kneecap. It looked as if it had been submerged in muddy water before it was wrapped around his limb. Never one to stare too long and hard at strangers—especially on the Near West

Side—I went back to my business. A busy and productive day commenced as I introduced myself to and conducted interviews with other men (all of whom, if I recall correctly, were on time that day). I thought that my day would end around six o'clock when I had finished speaking with Ken, a determined and focused ex-gangbanger and ex-convict who had recently found some stable work, and who looked like he might be able to leave some of his past behind him, even if work did not stay with him.[3]

It was getting late and I planned to follow up with Ken at another time. As I prepared to leave, I noticed Devin in the waiting area and glanced in his direction (making that wide-eyed gesture immediately followed by the obligatory nod that black men often direct toward each other in order to express recognition without actually having to utter a word). Devin looked up and said something on the order of "Hey, I'm looking for you."

At this point I had been in the field for over a year and had completed about five months of intensive fieldwork. I immediately understood that Devin was looking for the guy that was doing interviews with young black men, and who would pay them in cash as soon as all phases of the interview were complete. I did not need any further reply from him to understand all that was insinuated by his terse remark. At that point in the day I was very tired. My thoughts were on going home. More importantly, though, I did not want to lose a possible respondent. My judgment motivated me to lead him to the back room of the alderman's office where I convened some of my interviews. We went past a small assembly of volunteers, in attendance at a meeting that was the basis for the office being open so late on that particular evening. I unpacked the tape recorder, cassettes, batteries, and a writing pad from my bag, and began taking notes from the small talk that ensued. Within a half hour, I was ready to begin taping, for it was clear that Devin had an important story to tell.

Devin began by telling me about his membership in a gang and about his being on parole at the time of our meeting. Although he never mentioned it directly in the course of our dialogues, it was clear that his physical appearance was due to a gang-related murder attempt. What Devin had to say on the topic of black men and time came at the end of that day's discussion, around nine o'clock. Altogether, Devin had waited for over six hours to talk to me. The quality of our discussion was such that I forgot about the length of his wait until we were finished for the day. As I was packing up my materials again, this time for good, I asked him why he waited so long to talk to me when he must have figured that I would be around on some other day. He said that he had nothing else to do. I tried to conceal my puzzlement while searching for another question to ask. I wondered how he could have nothing to do for a six-hour period. I immediately realized that trying to turn that into a direct question was not the best thing to do, especially since I knew so little about him and

nothing about his emotional state of being. Instead, I asked about when
we could talk again. We made plans for future contact and I went on my
way home. His remark about having nothing else to do stayed with me
throughout that evening's ninety-minute bus ride. By the time I reached
Hyde Park, I had connected my thoughts about Devin with those about
the other men who showed up very late or very early for interviews, and
I grew more puzzled and intrigued about what was going on.

It dawned on me that as a researcher I functioned with a strict schedule
because I had an agenda that I was eager to complete. The completion of
that agenda was *the* major focus of my days. In the absence of obstacles
or barriers interfering with my daily goals, I did not have to think about
staying on schedule. I simply went about doing so. If obstacles or barriers
surfaced, then I became concerned and anxious about my schedule. The
men of the Near West Side maintained nothing like that level of commitment to schedules in their lives, nor had they had much reason to do
so. They did not have to manage formal commitments on a daily basis.
Consequently, it become quite apparent that what was unusual for me—
lateness, extreme earliness, or appearances on the wrong day altogether,
and the casual demeanor associated with such behavior—was, in fact, the
typical response for men who had no formal daily obligations, nor a history of having to manage them. I arrived at home that night having made
at least some sense of what time means, and does not mean, to men who
face the everyday with nothing to do.[4]

As the French social scientist Pierre Bourdieu found nearly forty
years ago when he studied unemployed Algerians, an absence of work
means an absence of the need to carefully organize daily life.[5] Concepts
such as laziness or irresponsibility might seem applicable to Devin's
case. However, those terms better capture an outsider's reaction to these
men than provide an adequate interpretation of their behavior. Such concepts reflect judgments made about the men rather than an informed analytical approach regarding how they came to function in this way. Indeed,
for an outsider to grasp how difficult it is for these men to act with conscious regard for time would require some profound distance from the
scheduled everyday lives of the those with stable employment. The degree
to which the employed are constrained with respect to time is the degree
to which the chronically unemployed are not. Such men do not have to
think about time in the same way as do people who have the luxury of
going to work everyday.[6]

Bourdieu masterfully conveys that what becomes most meaningful
about the absence of daily scheduling is not more free time for the unemployed, but an entirely different way of thinking about time. The application of this framework to the black men of the Near West Side offers the
starting point for a new approach to the cultural analysis of poor black

men. Rather than employing terms such as *norms* and *values*, a better assessment of these men's management of time necessitates the use of new and different concepts. One of the most important of these concepts— and one that originates in Bourdieu's work on Algerians—is *habitus*.

Since his first substantive discussion of the concept of habitus in the 1960s, Pierre Bourdieu has modified and refined his definition of the term quite extensively (Bourdieu and Wacquant 1992, Swartz 1997). One of his more recent elucidations, which actually elaborates, rather than simplifying, an already hard concept to grasp, is as follows: "[Habitus is a] system of durable, transposable dispositions, structured structures predisposed to function as structuring structures, that is, as principles which generate and organize practices and representations that can be objectively adapted to their outcomes without presupposing a conscious aiming at ends or an express mastery of the operations necessary in order to attain them" (Bourdieu 1990, p. 53).

Essentially, habitus is a statement about how individual action relates to external constraints or social structures. The concept speaks not only to the way that people think about the world, but how their positions in the social world facilitate those thoughts in the first place. Bourdieu had a long-standing interest in how individual action shapes as well as is shaped by social structure.[7] By employing the concept of habitus, he addressed the fact that much human action is performed without conscious awareness. Instead, much of what people do is done because they learned such action as a result of their membership in social groups that regularly function in such ways.[8]

All of this is to say that habitus is a coherent set of cultural artifacts (beliefs, actions, attitudes) that pertain to members of a social group. That group can be as large as a socioeconomic class, gender, racial, or ethnic group, or as small as a sports team or neighborhood association.[9] Habitus is made up of informal and practical cultural traits that allow people to function in their everyday worlds. This cultural package supplies them with the tools to make distinctions and choices for action. However, by virtue of their prior experiences in specific social contexts, habitus also creates for them some fluid boundaries around what they perceive to be viable or legitimate options for action.[10]

For example, engaging in violence to defend oneself on the Near West Side is seen as a legitimate means of handling certain situations (Conrad's experiences being a case in point). The patterns of interaction and socialization that emerge within a specific community are what gives legitimacy to certain kinds of individual responses. Thus those kinds of responses can be talked about in the kind of matter-of-fact style exemplified by Conrad, as if the experiences that came his way could (and, in fact, regularly did) happen to almost anyone else on the Near West Side. Clearly, those living without the encumbrances that come with life in urban poverty might view another approach, such as calling the police to resolve disputes or problems, or reacting with greater concern or consternation to violence or conflict in the neighborhood, as the most legitimate.

What appears to an individual as legitimate action is shaped by how that person and those that he or she associates with experience the social world. By *legitimate action* I mean something more than a normative arrangement. Legitimate action can include that which is valued, but it also includes that which is deemed necessary, taken as commonsensical, or viewed as the only available option in a given situation. These choices and options appear as rational or logical because they are set within a social world of people, circumstances, and conditions—in this case, on the Near West Side—that continually reinforce that vision of them (Bourdieu and Wacquant 1992, p. 53). Hence, the choice of certain residents in poor communities to engage violence is made because it is a logical way to behave. These individuals do not believe that other actions will lead them to desired ends in the environment in which they live. As soon as it becomes regular activity, violence simultaneously functions as a response to and facilitator of other violent encounters.

Habitus is important, then, because it helps explain how the men handled life experiences in formal institutions, in their neighborhoods, and in other settings that together constituted their everyday lives. It helps show how and why they made certain choices in the past, and how doing so resulted in their capacity to think about both their pasts and the future in the ways that they did. By allowing appropriate analytical space for thought and action, the concept becomes indispensable for expanding the cultural terrain included in studies of poor black men. The men did not consider arriving very late or very early for an appointment to be problematic, and they didn't consider that such behavior might be problematic for others. As it turned out, I thought about their lateness much more than they did. After all, experiencing daily life as an arrangement of scheduled events and circumstances was a part of the habitus of my social world, not theirs.

Everyday People on the Near West Side

Another important aspect of everyday life on the Near West Side, shown again by Conrad's experiences, is uncertainty about safety. For young black men, living on the Near West Side means being unsure that one will get through the day unharmed, or without having to harm someone else. Violent acts do not happen every day, but the enduring sentiment is that they *can* happen on any given day. The possibility of violence looms large because it is random and unpredictable. It can occur in the form of organized gang activity, the wrong thing being said to somebody during a street corner discussion, the misreading of someone else's intentions, or simply being in the wrong place at the wrong time.

When these men are not at home there is no place other than the street corner for them to be. However, it is not always an extremely comfortable place. Public social interaction, therefore, takes on special importance in areas like the Near West Side. That importance is reflected in these men's need to think a little bit more than do others about who passes them on the street corner, and what reactions they may generate by passing by other people. Chronic unemployment may leave these men with little to plan for or to organize around. The ever-present possibility of violence, however, forces them to plan very carefully regarding with whom they talk, as well as when and where they do so. Thus, they have to be very disciplined actors in this dimension of their everyday lives.

In talking about the possible dangers of the street corner, Ken said:

Being in the wrong place at the wrong time, you know. A lot of places that I hang out at, you know, [could end up as] me getting hurt. I always, you know, hope and pray don't nothing happen to me so I have to, you know, go on disability or have to not be able to take care of myself, you know. . . . Man listen, within seconds it could happen, you know. You know, shit, everyday somebody get hurt over there, you know. I just hope I ain't going to be the next one.

Like so many others, when asked about the possibilities of hanging out someplace else, or not hanging out at all, Ken said, "Yeah but then, you know what I'm saying, shit can happen anyway."

In response to these and related concerns, many of the men stressed the importance of behaving in certain ways while in public. Minding one's own business becomes important for a number of reasons. It means keeping one's nose out of the affairs of others as much as it means looking out for oneself when in the streets:

FELTON: You know, I just try to mind my own business and, you know when I first moved around here [*he moved to ABLA public houses from another residence in the same west side neighborhood*] I carefully picked my friends, you know. Cause sometimes, you know, the way people is today you got to study them first because you, somebody can tell you, "Well I'm your friend," or "I want to get close to you," but they might just want something from you, or try to hurt you. So I carefully picked my friends. . . .

JOSEPH: Most of the time . . . I was active to my own self. And I ain't really started affiliating with people around until I seen my brother [*an influential gang member in the community*] affiliating with them and then he coming in to introduce them to me. I was a person that stayed to myself. I was just happier by myself. . . . I look at it like this, if ain't nobody bothering me I won't bother nobody. I mean, you know, I'm known by people, I speak to people, they speak to me. That's it. They don't bother me, I won't bother them.

A third of the men said that they had not had serious, in-depth conversations with anyone other than some close relatives. For some, this was because they did not feel comfortable about having intimate exchanges with their peers. Barry was a self-described loner who said that he had no close friends. In discussing friendship he said:

Really I'm a, really I'm a loner, to tell you the truth. . . . I'm just a loner. [If] we do talk about something we talk about, just talking like, you know, just talking. It don't be nothing, nothing really serious. Everybody be trying to keep they business to theyself. I'm a loner that's why I really can't answer that.

These feelings lingered in the minds of many of these men while they went about their daily lives. On the surface there was a great deal of frivolity and playfulness in their public behavior. Underlying this was a constant mental state of being that made them pay more than casual attention to the people moving around them, especially strangers.

For many of the young men, the presence of gangs was a salient factor for neighborhood peer associations. Butch, Earl, Devin, Anthony, and Tito were the only men who reported ever being gang members. About half of the remaining men explicitly stated that they had never held such membership. The others provided no specific information one way or the other.[11]

All of the men discussed the presence of gangs as significant components of community life and, more specifically, talked about their own levels of association with gang members. There often were detrimental consequences in choosing either to avoid or participate in gangs. Those who avoided such affiliations usually had a smaller social network of peers and associates. For some of them, lack of gang affiliation led to an increased sense of fatalism, made evident by their emphasis on the lack of security in public space. For others, the absence of such ties meant feeling less socially connected in the neighborhood. Lastly, some men indicated that maintaining distance from gangs was itself a difficulty. Larry and Jake each addressed these points:

Was it difficult growing up to pretty much keep out of that whole scene [gangs]?

LARRY: Oh yeah, you know, cause you start to get forced, you know. There was this one guy, he used to always come asking me "man you ought to join this thing, you ought to join this thing." I was like "I'm not with that man." My brothers, none of us never were into that right there. That's one thing my father really taught us, you know. Because if you get into trouble, if you get caught with the crowd and hang with the bunch you swing with the bunch, or however they said it, you know. So I never would, we never was into that, you know. I couldn't, I ain't let nobody force me to be in no gang, you know. It was all up to me, whether I wanted to be there or not, you know. So I never was about that. . . . The majority of [my friends] were. I used to try to talk to some of them, you know, try to talk them out of it, you know. Most likely, you know, I could talk them out of it but, you know, some of them I just couldn't.

JAKE: You got a bunch of people living together man, and things changed when you got people living on top of each other like that, you know what I'm saying. You got, you saw sides of people, you know, because you was right there with them at all times, you know. You know, through the project system I found out about gangs. I never been in a gang, [I] got approached by the gangs, you know what I'm saying, but you know, one thing I was always taught, you know a man fights on anything. And it's kind of hard sometimes when people think you, you know, you meet somebody, "He's from the projects," you know. They automatically think you're in a gang, you know what I'm saying. But I just say, you know, it was cool. It was just like if you mind your business and, you know, I guess just chill, you know, and go, certain people get along with certain people, you know what I'm saying. You might have some people just don't like you just cause, you know, you're being you, you know. They might not like you cause of the way you're dressed in the morning. But, you know, that's the way it is, so you just have to learn how to deal with things like that, you know. So like I say I dealt with the gangs. . . . When it came down to it I just handled it the best way I could. And, you know, I came through with it, you know what I'm saying, so.

The gradual incorporation of Larry's peer group into a faction of the Vice Lord Nation left him with a nearly depleted network of social contacts and associates in the neighborhood. He told me that he socialized with his friends occasionally, but that he did not have the intense bonding with them that he believes they share with each other. He has been left outside of their support network. On the other hand, Jake appeared much more at ease about this predicament. However, he was very much aware of the stigmatization that he was subjected to by virtue of living in a gang-saturated community.

Anthony provides a contrasting perspective to these accounts. A dark-skinned, well-built man of twenty-five, he used to be active in a gang during his late adolescence. The gang served as his primary social network outside of his family. Later in his life he came to feel that gang membership led to many of the barriers standing between him and a better future:

> I figured if I had a bunch of guys behind me then I would be a little stronger instead of bringing my family into it . . . it made me figure that I could go outside with protection and, you know, like it put like a shield around me. It made it seem like I couldn't be touched then, you know what I'm saying. I go out there and if anybody did do something to me they was going to get it back but even worser, you know. It was just a shield I walked around with for awhile anyway.

For him and some others, gang membership provided the security essential for daily interaction in the community. While it provided some necessary short-term capital for dealing with the community, it also factored into his diminished prospects for upward mobility.

Gang membership was not always a source of problems and difficulties. For some men it provided an avenue to better options in life. Some of the men explained how membership could be a ticket to significant mobility. Twenty-five-year-old Earl, a muscular man of well over six feet and about 230 pounds, offered one of the more lucid accounts of gang-related mobility. One summer afternoon he made his way to the alderman's office to introduce himself to me. In stark contrast to his physical appearance, he was very soft-spoken and patient in responding to my questions. Earl was fresh from a two-year stint in prison. He was currently on parole after serving time for possession of narcotics with the intent to distribute. In talking about his gang-banging partners he said, "I have a few friends that gots some money, whatever they was doing to get it, but they took the money and invested it. They now own real estate . . . investing their money, doing the right things. They work for themselves."

Earl's partners were able to do with their returns from gang activity what he could not. In large part, he could not do what they did because he was arrested and served time for narcotics possession with intent to sell. Going to jail took Earl out of the game, leaving him broke and stigmatized as an ex-convict. Some of his associates fared much better. They saved their money from petty crime and drug distribution and transferred the funds into legitimate businesses.[12] As Earl has shown, a network of friends who are deeply involved in illicit activity can still serve as models of upward mobility. Furthermore, his comments illustrate that role models and key individuals can operate as exemplars of success while also engaged in illegal activity. Gang membership expanded Earl's vision of opportunity as much as it led to some crucial problems for his chances of accessing that vision. This is but one of the many contradictions that come with a lived experience in socioeconomic hardship. Earl went on to say the following about his fellow gangbangers:

Some of them is a lot better off than I am, some are poorer than I am. [The more better off are] pretty much the same person, you know what I'm saying, that I knew when they didn't have nothing. They treat me just about the same. They'll help, you know. Some of my friends just let themselves go, you know what I'm saying. It's just like they don't care no more. But some of my friends, the ones who I say just played it smart, you know what I'm saying, took what they had at the time and what they could do with it, and took advantage of it.

Later on during this part of our discussion, he put his views on friendship in perspective:

I have friends that mess with drugs, but you know they grown, you know what I'm saying. They have their own life to live and they know what they want. That's what they want, you know what I'm saying. I don't like it, but, you know what I'm saying, I just can't abandon them because we grew up together, you know. They was friends then, you know. They just, some just go through a period of time. Well, they might catch themselves, they might not, you know. I have friends that have died from drugs, drug overdose, stuff like that. But my main objective is just, you know, be there, you know what I'm saying, be friends to them, just be there.

Earl's account shows how the gang infrastructure of the Near West Side led to more than wanton violence. For a select few men, it became an alternative mechanism for upward mobility. While the existence of gangs and the proliferation of violence are not necessarily the same thing in low-income communities, gangs were the common point of reference in the men's discussions of why violence and related concerns must be taken into account in public life.[13] The gang infrastructure in the Near West Side mirrors that of many other low-income African American community areas in Chicago. Gangs became a much greater public concern when they assumed control of street-level drug trade in the 1970s (Block and Block 1993, Venkatesh 1997, 2000). That growth and development also established their central role in the escalation of violence in the communities where they operated, even if public accounts of gang-related violence are sometimes overstated (Venkatesh 2000).

Gangs in Chicago are generally divided into two cohorts: the People (largely comprised of multiple factions of the Vice Lord Nation), who are located primarily in low-income West Side communities, and the Folks (largely comprised of factions of the Gangster Disciple Nation) who populate the low-income South Side of Chicago. The People display symbols on the left side of their bodies (e.g., earrings in the left ear, the left pants leg rolled up—as was the case with Devin when I first met him) or tilted toward the left (hats, belt buckles, etc.). The People also display a five-pointed star as one of their primary emblems. The Folks display symbols to the right and display a six-pointed star. Graffiti reflecting these symbols is used to mark territory, and a series of hand gestures also distinguishes People and Folks.

Damen Avenue divides the traditional terrain of two gang factions (although since the 1960s, factions of each have established some presence in the terrain of the other). Going north to south, it runs right through Henry Horner and lies to the west of ABLA. Throughout the early and mid-1960s, the Vice Lords ran the area to the east of Damen Avenue and the Disciples controlled that to the west. Hence, almost all of the men interviewed for the book resided in Vice Lord territory. The factions most often talked about include the Conservative Vice Lords, the Mafiosi Vice Lords, the Four Corner Hustlers, the Undertaker Vice Lords, and the Traveling Vice Lords. Coupled with drug distribution, the regimented organizational structure of gangs has facilitated consistent and well-planned periods of gang-related violence (Block and Block, 1993). However, it was clear to the men of the Near West Side that while violence and gang activity overlapped, they were not necessarily the same thing. Furthermore, it was random violence, and not gangs per se, that was at the forefront of their minds when they talked about uncertainties in everyday life.

Despite the connection of gang association with violence, the regularity with which violence was acknowledged in discussions of daily life was astounding. In most other communities violence is an unusual and distant occurrence. People in other places only think about it intermittently, such as when they are moving about late at night or in unfamiliar places. In contrast, the men of the Near West Side associated their most familiar settings with violence. It was a common point of reference for talking about the everyday. Therefore, it crept into discussions with the same consistency that business people talk about deals and other occurrences at work.

> BARRY: [on living in Henry Horner Homes] Violent, violent. . . . Always had to look out, you know, it was pretty much mind your business, but then again never knowing when something might happen and you might be in the wrong place at the wrong time. . . . I stayed nervous a lot. . . .

> ANTHONY: [on ABLA Homes] Every day there was a shooting or something happened so you get used to that because you stay there and you know it's bound to happen. They only thing you do is worry about it is you going to be next or hope you don't be the next one that be on a piece of obituary or something, you know. . . .

Some men explained that they were always apprehensive when in public, yet they accepted this emotional state as a natural reaction to the environment in which they lived. Others lacked such a heightened level of anxiety, fear, or concern, but still made reference to it when talking about what daily life was all about.

Closely aligned with the men's discussion of the lack of safety and security was their sense that as they got older the quality of life on the Near West Side had steadily declined. Almost every one of the men with whom I spoke made this point. They spoke of their own childhood experiences as filled with greater safety and friendliness. Some also drew distinctions between the past and the present on the basis of their parents' descriptions of a more tranquil earlier era.

> BARRY: I think it changed over time because my mother used to tell us it wasn't always like that when she was coming up. So I just go by what she said, you know. She said it wasn't worser. The only way it got worser is when, you know, Martin Luther King died, and that was the riot. . . . [After that] new people moved in. It got worser, you know, cause then, you know, everybody new that was young over there done get fouled up trying to get put into a gang. It was mostly like something like [becoming] a boy scout. If you could move in they give you about a week. When you walk outside somebody want to know you or "Do you want to join in since you living in this building." "You know you can't go over there 'cause they going to whoop you 'cause they know you live over here." That what it was, it's mostly a dividing line against this building, that building, or over there. And there's certain stores you could go to without getting robbed or stabbed or beat up for going across to the other end.

Whether the past was significantly better or not, these men grew up in situations of conflict, strife, and insecurity, all of which were set within a larger context of community decline. They understood that violence was a commonplace feature of life, and they dealt with it as best they could. The staples of everyday life on the Near West Side, then, were stagnation and turbulence. The first was ever-present and unavoidable for these men, precisely because they went without work in their lives. The second was more capricious but, if the right steps were taken, often avoidable. However, a man's susceptibility to the second was greatly enhanced by being on the streets because of the absence of work. The spectrum of stagnation and turbulence had to be managed individually by each man. The fact that these two factors came together in this community area had more to do with the structural dimensions of life there than it did with individual choice-making and behavior. Those structural facts are firmly rooted in the recent socioeconomic history of Chicago and the Near West Side.

The Social and Economic Organization of Life:
Chicago and the Near West Side

While the street corners that these men occupied were some of the most
notorious in the city of Chicago, transformations in the city itself constitute much of the underlying source of their problems. Over the past three
decades Chicago has been a site of urban decline for many of its low-
income black American residents (Wacquant and Wilson 1989; Wilson
1987, 1996). From 1970 to 1980, the population living in Chicago's poverty areas increased by 62 percent. During the same time span the population living in *extreme* poverty areas increased by 162 percent.[14] These
figures capture the municipal-level social transformation occurring during
the early childhood years of the men in this book. Consequently, their life
stories are not accounts of growing up in stable contexts of socioeconomic
disadvantage, but of having municipal and neighborhood conditions actually worsen for them as they matured into adulthood.

The increased populations in poverty areas resulted from both an out-
migration of wealthier residents from inner-city neighborhoods and a decline in the economic fortunes of residents who remained in those communities. As a result of these transformations, the proportion of African
American Chicagoans living in extreme poverty areas went from 24 percent in 1970 to 47 percent by 1980. Moreover, the black male employment rate in Chicago declined from 62 percent to 48 percent during that
decade. A contributing factor to the loss of employment was the closing
of 38 percent of Chicago's 8,455 factories between 1967 and 1982 (over
3,000 of those closings occurring after 1970) and the decline in manufacturing jobs from 390,000 to 172,000 from 1958 to 1982. Retail trade
lost 64,000 jobs during that time span, and wholesale trade lost 47,000
jobs (Wacquant 1989, Wilson 1987). It takes little imagination to consider how the socioeconomic downturns in Chicago affected the institutional structure of low-income communities as support for banks, stores,
community groups, and civic organizations diminished during this time.

The decade of the 1980s saw the further deterioration of the manufacturing employment sector in Chicago. Between 1970 and 1987, Chicago
lost nearly 250,000 manufacturing jobs, and the service sector surpassed
manufacturing to become the major employment arena in the city (Israilevich and Mahidhara 1990). Service-sector employment went from
620,000 jobs in 1970 to 1.12 million jobs by 1987, while manufacturing
jobs declined from 950,000 to 660,000 during that same time span (Israilevich and Mahidhara 1990). Not all of the newly created service-sector jobs were high paying (nor were they necessarily higher paying than
some traditional manufacturing positions). However, the greater crisis for

the men in this study was not the increase in lower-paying service-sector jobs, but the decrease in jobs in the very sector of the labor market—manufacturing and manual skill jobs—for which they felt most suited and in which they most desired to be employed (what they have to say about this will be explored in chapters 6 and 7).

These historical patterns and trends circumscribe the labor market prospects that the men have been exposed to since their adolescence. In prior decades, many residents of the Near West Side found stable work in one of the large factories in the North Lawndale area, located immediately southwest. Sears, Roebuck and Company, International Harvester, and Hawthorne Western Electric put many transplanted African American southerners to work after they arrived in Chicago throughout the middle of the century. Between 1960 and 1984 all of these plants ceased operations, at least those that were located on the western edge of Chicago. This eliminated over 60,000 jobs, as well as diminishing major portions of the local economy that were dependent on the influx of workers into the community. While perhaps the largest transformation in local employment prospects, this unfolding was only one of a series that constituted the changing nature of work opportunity in Chicago for low-income African Americans.

The steady disappearance of manufacturing jobs since the 1960s resulted in most Near West Siders witnessing successive cohorts of neighbors and associates having fewer job prospects. Moreover, the changes in the quality of life in the Near West Side has reshaped residents' capacity to consider what tenable labor prospects currently exist or might exist in the future. It was first with mild amazement, and then intrigue, and finally, growing sympathy that I spoke with men who talked about going to work as nothing but an abstract thought because they knew of few men in their age group who went to work everyday.

In talking about the relevance of work to how they went about their everyday lives, the majority of the men said that they were always looking for whatever might come up. A minority talked about specific employment options that they pursued, most of which they heard about through friends on the street. Indeed, approximately one-third of the men asked if they could work for me while I conducted this research.[15] They generally did not believe that potential employment existed. Thus, the common logic was "There's no point in seeking that which is not there in the first place." Some of them said that they sometimes acted on impulse in determining to pursue an employment opportunity. At other times, employment opportunities emerged by serendipity. These circumstances made it virtually impossible to codify any pattern of response toward employment prospects. Peter, a young man of 22 years of age who said that he sought work, stated:

I've been eagerly pursuing a job. It's almost like they've eluded me. I worked one job that short time with a contractor driving cause I have my CD air license. And so I do want a job and I have searched for a job. I would go back to school but the financial [cost of school] is too much. And then I have a lot of other friends who gone to school and it's not an encouraging thing to see your friends that have gone to school and they're unemployed or they're making $6.00 and they're not even working in the field that they were trained in. It's very discouraging.

The myriad ways and manners in which these men approached work prospects must be understood as part of their repertoire of responses to the challenges of being in poverty, which is another aspect of their habitus. Included in this repertoire was the general sentiment that jobs were not available (as evidenced by so many of their peers being out of work) so that there were none to seek. As shown in the appendix to this chapter, much of their interaction was with individuals who were not attached to networks that could either produce or inform them about employment options. Thus, while they understood work to be essential for achieving better lives, they knew very little about what it meant to go to work, or exactly how work becomes central to one's daily existence.

Today there is no strong employment sector in the predominantly African American part of the Near West Side (which is all but a narrow slice of the eastern edge of the area). Together with some small manufacturing and light industry businesses, a large complex of medical centers is near the eastern end of the community, closer to downtown. Cook County Hospital, the public facility used by the uninsured low-income residents, is there along with the private Presbyterian-St. Luke's Hospital, the West Side Veteran's Administration Hospital, the Chicago State Tuberculosis Hospital, and the Research Hospital and Medical School of the University of Illinois. The only other large-scale facilities near Henry Horner and ABLA are the Department of Public Aid, located on Western Avenue across the street going west from Henry Horner; the Juvenile Temporary Detention Center, near ABLA; and the University of Illinois at Chicago, which is a few blocks northeast of ABLA but socially a whole world apart from the housing development.

Although poverty was very much a part of the picture in the 1960s, the Near West Side and the neighboring community areas that house Chicago's west side African American community were nonetheless ripe with activism and enthusiasm. The Chicago chapter of the Black Panther Party kept its headquarters there. Some of the older residents that I came across expressed pride and reverence when talking about Mark Clark and Fred Hampton, two leaders of the chapter that were killed by Chicago police during a raid in 1969. Hampton in particular was talked about as having a zest for organizing. People listened to and respected him. Furthermore, it was the west side that Martin Luther King chose to visit and reside in when he came to Chicago in the late 1960s. The effects of riots there following his assassination in 1968 are still felt in the community, embodied by vacant lots and abandoned buildings that have been untouched since the fires were put out. Since the riots ended, the most concentrated residential areas have been those occupied by public housing.

As two of the three major public housing projects on the Near West Side (Rockwell Gardens is the third), Henry Horner and ABLA are prototypical public housing developments in Chicago, resembling containment centers more than residential communities. Buildings lack secure front doors, and hallway and lobby lighting is a luxury. Other than a few basketball rims, the grounds around each building contain no facilities, swings or monkeybars, just patches of grass and dirt in open space. With clear and easy entry to buildings and lobbies, these open spaces make periods of gang conflict or other random violence especially dangerous. At such times, bystanders can become sitting ducks because there are so few places to hide from gunshots. It is around these housing developments, and the small houses, stores, and vacant lots that public life is re-created every day by and for these men and the other inhabitants of the Near West Side. While the situation made some men angry or despondent when they talked about it, most sounded like Jake:

> Well the projects is the projects man. You know I guess you got to see it, I mean it's for each person to see how it is, you know. But for me I was, ah, it was okay. I mean, you know, I mean you have gripes about the building sometimes. The elevator is not working sometimes, and sometimes how nasty the building is . . . [but] that's something that me myself couldn't change. So, you know, I like wouldn't be worried about it.

Social Contacts, Social Networks, and Social Capital

Thus far, the discussion has centered on framing the physical environment of the Near West Side and the way the men approached their daily lives in terms of "keeping busy" in the absence of good employment prospects. A more complete account of what life on the Near West Side means to these men must include an exploration of the range of their social contacts. Who is included in these networks and who is not tells much about the kind of social reality that shapes the men's lives. (See the appendix to this chapter for the tabular range of people present in the men's lives.)

In the course of our discussions, each man was asked to what extent his relatives, friends, and acquaintances possessed a range of social characteristics (the column headings of each table).[16] Each type of social tie plays an important role in shaping one's social exposure. Family and close friends, who constitute the most intimate social ties, provide some of the most crucial human resources for helping the men to gain exposure to ideas, possibilities, and prospects for mobility. Acquaintances, who constitute more distant social ties, may also serve as such resources; at bare minimum, they can exemplify different lifestyles and social possibilities, thus broadening one's conceptions of what the social world has to offer (or, alternatively, reinforcing one's narrowed vision of what is extant in the world if such acquaintances do not greatly differ from what one person has already encountered in social life).

Table 2.3, then, represents the depth and breadth of one's weak ties and affiliations.[17] The evidence in these tables reveals that over half of these men did not know or regularly interact with a single person who they knew for certain was a college graduate. Over sixty percent had exposure to no more than two people with white-collar professional status. The same held for exposure to people in blue-collar employment. Less than a third of the men experienced social contact of any regular kind with non–African Americans. By far, their greatest degree of social exposure was to African Americans who were unemployed and who did not complete high school. They knew and interacted regularly with dozens of people who were out of work. Accordingly, a consistent theme in their comments about their friends was the minimal utility that they provided for each other in matters that related to upward mobility. As Conrad stated, "Most of my friends that are, you know, they either been in jail or, you know, or they 'The Man' out here. They selling, you know, doing that, so I guess if they going to get ahead they going to get ahead in a game and not as far as [legitimate] jobs or anything like that."

Conrad could not recall any serious discussions with his friends about getting ahead in life or planning for the future. When asked about the type of discussions he does have with his friends, he said, "There ain't nothing we talk about like everyday. We just, we just be hanging out, just kicking it. We talk about females, or if a tournament going on we'll talk about the tournament or something like that, basketball, that's all."

Whether the men talked about being social or keeping more to themselves, the consistent statement was that issues of getting ahead do not punctuate their discussions with friends. When twenty-three-year-old Joseph, a slender guy who was missing a tooth on the upper left side of his jaw, was asked about the attitudes of his friends toward getting ahead, he said, "I can't answer that because I don't know what they are."

Devin held a similar point of view. In talking about what his friends may hope for their future, he said, "To be honest I don't know. . . . I don't talk with them, I don't talk to them about that." He said that what he did talk about was "Girls, money, and who we can get next [through gang actions]."

Men like twenty-four-year-old Dennis felt that there was a lack of initiative within their friendship network to improve their lives:

> They ain't got no desire for getting ahead in life. . . . They out here running around drinking every day, thinking about what they can take from somebody, so I don't think they want to get ahead. . . . See my attitude is trying to get out of here and finding a job, doing something positive. They attitude is getting high or something like that. I don't like that. That's not my attitude, trying to get high. I ain't really trying to jaw now. I can get high, but I better find a job then being in the streets just thinking about where I'm a get my next money from, drinking, or doing drugs. Naw, I rather find a job.

Given that he was no further ahead in life than his friends, one could easily regard Dennis's comment as posturing. Still, his words express strongly the depth of the deficiencies in resources offered by the peer networks of the Near West Side.

Despite what has been said so far, one must be very cautious about highlighting only the negative aspects of friendships and peer networks in the Near West Side. Problematic as they were, it was these very friendships that also helped the men to survive. Some of the men talked about how their fellow gang members risked their lives to protect them during periods of gang conflict. They also discussed how street corner dialogue with their friends often provided them with the chance to make sense of the events and circumstances in their lives.[18] Finally, a select few had friends who were exemplars of achievement and opportunity. Altogether, friendship was a profound and intricate part of the lives of these men. In some instances it brought them enrichment, yet at other times it brought them harm and misfortune. As in so many other aspects of their lives, friendships involved a profound blend of complexity and contradiction.

Contextualizing Everyday Life: Taking Stock of Capital

Peer associations and family ties on the Near West Side involve much more complexity than can be conveyed by a mapping of connections. The social environment for the men of the Near West Side was comprised of their social relationships and the amalgamation of social conditions and forces that affected their everyday lives. As we have seen, those connections were embedded in a social environment that inhibited mainstream mobility while simultaneously encouraging outlooks and behaviors that facilitated community-specific security and stability. The kind of comfort and security found in more privileged communities was absent for them.

The same held for the kinds of social ties and relationships that could possibly help them to achieve better lives. Both tables 2.1–2.3 and the testimony provided by the men reveal an absence of the kinds of resources and support mechanisms that could benefit their prospects for upward mobility. In short, what these men lacked was the kind of capital that matters for achieving upward mobility in modern American life.

Like habitus, *capital* is a crucial concept for understanding the link between life experience and thoughts about future mobility, opportunity, and life chances. Also like habitus, *capital* is a term that was brought into contemporary social-scientific analysis by Pierre Bourdieu (although he was not alone in doing so, as a number of other scholars employed the term as well; see Portes 1998 for an overview). Generally speaking, capital is anything that is a resource for engaging strategic action toward a desired end (Bourdieu 1986). It is the fuel not just for mobility, but for the capacity to think about mobility in the first place. For the men in this study, capital is that which they accumulated (or did not accumulate) through their past and present experiences such that they found themselves in positions near the bottom of the American socioeconomic hierarchy. Capital is also a resource for being able to interpret and plan action in the social world. It takes both material and ethereal forms. Money is a prime example of a material form of capital. An ethereal form is knowledge of how to negotiate interactions with social elites in order to get whatever one desires from them.

The range of entities and ideas included in the definition of capital led Pierre Bourdieu to continuously modify his definitions of its forms and content (1977a, 1977b, 1986, 1990; Bourdieu and Wacquant 1992). However, he has always regarded capital as a symbolic entity that represents anything that is a valued resource in social relations (1990). It serves as a signifier or a representation of power, status, or influence. No form of capital in and of itself constitutes power or influence. Instead, people attribute power and influence to various kinds of matter (like the paper and ink that, when put together, become currency) or different mentalities (like knowing how to engage elites or dignitaries such that one can accrue resources or deference from them that can help in furthering one's personal goals).[19]

There are gains and losses in making use of a broad term like capital. The fact that it can be applied simultaneously to so many objects and ideas makes it a useful construct for creating a leveled analytical field. For instance, capital allows a researcher to think about how money, social relations, and individual-level skill at social interaction come together to create or limit one's sense of how social hierarchies are maintained and how to move up in the world. Consequently, the concept helps explain how some people without much money are located higher in social hierarchies than some of those with a great deal of money, as well as how someone moves up in the world without much money, but with the benefit of other resources.

On the other hand, the breadth of the term *capital* renders it problematic as an analytical construct. One runs the risk of lacking coherence and focus when employing it to explain the relevant factors for a social phenomena or occurrence. To avoid such problems, capital will be defined here in four distinct ways.[20] Perhaps the most straightforward is *human capital*: the skills or abilities needed to perform specific tasks.[21] Another fairly straightforward form is *financial capital*, which can be thought of as the material resources that allow one to acquire other forms of capital.

The other two forms of capital are significantly more complex and less precise. *Cultural capital* is the knowledge of how to function or operate in specific social settings in order to mobilize, generate responses from, or affect others such as social elites. Finally, *social capital* has a twofold definition. On one hand, social capital depends on the degree to which an individual is embedded in social networks that can bring about the rewards and benefits that enhance his or her life. In this way, social capital is seen as a precursor to the acquisition of other forms of capital (money, information, social standing, etc.). On the other hand, social capital has been identified as the package of norms and sanctions maintained by groups so that positive or desired outcomes occur for all members, especially those that no single member could achieve on his or her own. The functioning of a neighborhood "watch group" is a prime example of this form of social capital. By each neighbor being attentive to strangers or unusual circumstances in the neighborhood, each benefits from an extended security measure in the community.[22]

Of course, desired outcomes in one instance may be associated with problematic developments in another. For example, joining a gang may be done in order to receive protection from community-based threats. That action may be read by outside observers—or even at later points in time by the central actors involved—as detrimental because it increases one's potential involvement in violence, incarceration, or other circumstances. This example is indicative of the way in which the accumulation of certain forms of social capital on the Near West Side can simultaneously help and hinder one's life situation.

The types and depths of capital that one accumulates are an indication of where one stands in the social world, and more importantly for this project, how profoundly one is able to interpret that world. Consequently, what these men framed as social reality, and indeed whether some things were framed at all, was contingent upon how much capital they had acquired. Moreover, their thoughts about and reactions to events and circumstances in their past (constitutive elements of their habitus) were affected by how much capital they possessed.

The tables in this chapter reveal the depth of social capital accumulated by these men through an exploration of their friendships and associations. These ties sometimes led to the accumulation of the kind of capital that is most relevant for everyday living in the Near West Side (e.g., immersion into social networks for protection and defense against threats from others in the community). Those men with the fewest ties to others in their neighborhood often were the least comfortable negotiating everyday life within the neighborhood. However, those who maintained strong ties with people who could deliver the kind of capital that helped in surviving the threats found on the New West Side also found that such capital was quite often detrimental for mobility in mainstream America. For instance, friendship ties with gang members (for someone not already a member) could help a man to accrue capital that was advantageous for living on the Near West Side. Such ties could also result in a man having to involve himself in criminal activities or risk exposure to violence—neither occurrence being an asset for getting ahead in mainstream American life. Hence, capital accumulation on the Near West Side was not a process with simple outcomes. Instead, it was riddled with contradictions and complexities.

The relationship between friendship ties and capital extended far beyond issues of gang affiliation. Whether gang members or not, friends mostly were unable to function as sources of information about anything that concerned upward mobility, especially goals and strategies for its pursuit. Friends were generally incapable of encouraging personal mobility quests. The tables provide the clearest evidence that the social networks of these men were not laden with people who possessed or could provide access to other forms of capital.

One might wonder in the end how much things could have been different had the men been in association with other types of people. Getting with the "right" kind of people, however, was not a realistic possibility. As we have seen, there are a variety of reasons why associations with other types was not an option for these men. The changes in the economic arenas in Chicago, and the Near West Side in particular, left many people out of work and separated from resources that could benefit their lives. Thus, it was not simply that the men were associating with the wrong type of people. It was that their associations took place with the only kind of people available in their immediate social world—those who were unemployed and unattached to labor market prospects. This lack of broader social contacts, as well as the kind of capital that is accrued from them, inevitably had a profound effect on the formation of these men's worldviews, especially those concerning their prospects for a better future.

Appendix to Chapter Two _____

Range of Social Contact

In the following three tables, a few of the column heads require clarification. *College+* includes relatives (table 2.1), friends (table 2.2), and acquaintances (table 2.3) currently in college, college graduates, graduate school attendees, or graduate school graduates. *No HS* includes relatives (table 2.1), friends (table 2.2), and acquaintances (table 2.3) who did not *complete* high school. *Professional* includes attorneys, physicians, businesspeople, and buiness owners. *Criminal activity* refers to relatives (table 2.1), friends (2.2), and acquaintances (table 2.3) regularly involved in such activity. The statistics refer to the number of men (and the percentage of men) that reported the number of ties indicated in each row. The columns are not mutually exclusive; the men were asked to account for the number of people that they knew in each category, irrespective of whether they fit into other categories as well.

TABLE 2.1
Distribution of Relatives into Social Categories

	College+	No HS	Professional	Fire/Police	Blue-collar	Unemployed	In gangs	Criminal activity
None	15 (58%)	3 (12%)	11 (42%)	17 (65%)	7 (27%)	3 (12%)	8 (31%)	14 (54%)
1–2	4 (15%)	4 (15%)	9 (35%)	4 (15%)	5 (19%)	1 (4%)	8 (31%)	6 (23%)
3–5	4 (15%)	9 (35%)	1 (4%)	4 (15%)	6 (23%)	11 (42%)	2 (8%)	2 (8%)
6–10	2 (8%)	2 (8%)	2 (8%)	0 (0%)	3 (12%)	4 (15%)	2 (8%)	3 (12%)
10+	0 (0%)	7 (27%)	2 (8%)	0 (0%)	4 (15%)	6 (23%)	5 (19%)	0 (0%)
Don't Know	1 (4%)	1 (4%)	1 (4%)	1 (4%)	1 (4%)	1 (4%)	1 (2%)	1 (2%)

TABLE 2.2
Distribution of Friendships into Social Categories

	College+	No HS	Pro-fessional	Fire/Police	Blue-collar	Unem-ployed	In gangs	Criminal activity	White	Hispanic	Asian-American
None	14 (54%)	4 (15%)	13 (50%)	7 (27%)	6 (23%)	3 (12%)	10 (38%)	17 (65%)	9 (35%)	13 (50%)	21 (81%)
1–2	4 (15%)	3 (12%)	3 (12%)	11 (38%)	4 (15%)	2 (8%)	1 (2%)	0 (0%)	5 (19%)	5 (19%)	2 (8%)
3–5	2 (8%)	2 (8%)	7 (27%)	4 (15%)	5 (19%)	2 (8%)	2 (8%)	0 (0%)	4 (15%)	2 (8%)	1 (4%)
6–10	3 (12%)	0 (0%)	2 (8%)	3 (12%)	3 (12%)	1 (4%)	0 (0%)	0 (0%)	2 (8%)	1 (4%)	0 (0%)
10+	2 (8%)	16 (62%)	0 (0%)	0 (0%)	7 (27%)	17 (65%)	12 (46%)	8 (31%)	5 (19%)	4 (15%)	1 (4%)
Don't Know	1 (4%)	1 (4%)	1 (4%)	1 (4%)	1 (4%)	1 (4%)	1 (4%)	1 (4%)	1 (4%)	1 (4%)	1 (4%)

TABLE 2.3
Distribution of Acquaintances into Social Categories

	College+	No HS	Pro-fessional	Fire/Police	Blue-collar	Unem-ployed	In gangs	Criminal activity	White	Hispanic	Asian-American
None	13 (50%)	4 (15%)	17 (65%)	17 (65%)	9 (35%)	3 (12%)	4 (38%)	10 (38%)	10 (38%)	17 (65%)	21 (81%)
1–2	4 (15%)	1 (4%)	2 (8%)	1 (4%)	4 (15%)	2 (8%)	3 (12%)	3 (12%)	3 (12%)	1 (4%)	3 (12%)
3–5	5 (19%)	2 (8%)	5 (19%)	3 (12%)	6 (23%)	5 (19%)	2 (8%)	3 (12%)	3 (12%)	0 (0%)	1 (4%)
6–10	1 (4%)	0 (0%)	0 (0%)	4 (15%)	0 (0%)	0 (0%)	0 (0%)	1 (4%)	1 (4%)	7 (27%)	0 (0%)
10+	2 (8%)	17 (65%)	1 (4%)	0 (0%)	6 (23%)	15 (58%)	16 (62%)	8 (31%)	8 (31%)	0 (0%)	0 (0%)
Dont' Know	1 (4%)	2 (8%)	1 (4%)	1 (4%)	1 (4%)	1 (4%)	1 (4%)	1 (4%)	1 (4%)	1 (4%)	1 (4%)

Chapter Three ———————————

Coming Up Poor

> Oh, coming up at the time that I was living with her, yeah, [my mother and stepfather] was very strict and very hard. . . . Okay, my mother was very strict and she very, very religious. We couldn't come outside. We could only come outside for an hour and then go back in the house. . . . [S]he was overprotective at times.

These are Devin's recollections of his early childhood years. They do not easily fit with the person that he became as a young adult. Although he entered adulthood in possession of a criminal record and a public image as a menace to the community, Devin said that his life began over twenty-one years earlier in a household steeped in discipline and good intentions. He recalled his mother as being not only encouraging, but also intensely afraid of letting him get too close to the world beyond the doors of the family's apartment in Henry Horner Homes. His mother's overprotective impulse came from her deep desire that he not succumb to the temptations of the streets.

Having no other recourse to keep him off of the streets, she quite literally locked him in the house. Devin recalled that she put gates on her second-story apartment building windows and installed a padlock on the front door to keep him from going outside whenever she was not at home. While it might be hard to imagine someone getting away with such behavior, the general negligence of Chicago Public Housing officials translated into tenants having to do all sorts of things to their apartments without official sanction.[1] Devin said the following about his mother's and stepfather's views on his education:

> Yes, they had attitudes, they had opinions about our education because they wanted us to get the education that they didn't never get. . . . Most of the things they said was stay in school, don't join gangs and try to do something with my life besides what I'm doing [gangbanging].

This was encouraging advice, but it was not very elaborate or informative, especially for helping a young man handle the kind of life experiences encountered in an urban, low-income community. Devin's mother was ill-equipped to contribute much else to her son and his five siblings as preparation for their achieving better lives. She stopped her own schooling shortly after the eighth grade. Three years after she gave birth to Devin in

Mississippi, the family moved to Chicago. During most of Devin's childhood she received public assistance. There were brief periods when she would find work as a store clerk or cashier. Given her life experiences, her main goal was for her children to attain a level of education that she was unable to acquire for herself. The problem was that she was unable to provide them with the proper guidance and guidelines for avoiding some of the social calamities associated with life on the Near West Side. His mother's only measure of control, at least when Devin was very young, revolved around attempting to control his access to the neighborhood.

Devin's stepfather was a part of his life for only a few of his teen years. Except for having left a negative impression, the time was too brief for Devin to regard him as a critical factor in his life. Devin could not recall any meaningful conversations with him. When asked further about the specific information that either parent shared with him about getting ahead in life, he said, "No they didn't never have anything to say. They never did set my life. They just told me to stay in school and make something out of myself, as they say."

Devin's mother chose to lock him inside the home because she knew no better strategy to protect him from the world that he soon enough would have to confront on his own terms. Unfortunately, this strategy served only to heighten Devin's curiosity about that forbidden world on the other side of the window. This yearning was further compounded by his desire to erase the "mama's boy" image that he acquired because of the limits that his mother placed on his social engagements. As Devin explained:

> Going to [elementary] school then was a good experience because I got out the house a lot and I got to meet a lot of kids and play with them. . . . If only I could stay there and learn instead of playing and goofing off. . . . I guess cause I wasn't getting enough of a childhood time to myself to be with kids my age, you know what I'm saying. I was called a mama's boy, got to go in, got to do this, can't do that.

In late elementary school and junior high, Devin was determined to find better ways to establish himself in the eyes of his peers. Eventually, he went down the path leading to gang membership and an enduring pattern of self-destructive behavior, all occurring despite his mother's initial hard work toward achieving the opposite outcome. As a result of his gradual but ultimately successful immersion in the streets, as Devin approached early adolescence the mama's boy image quickly began to dissipate:

> I wanted to start moving and get acquainted with the crowds and stuff. So I started sneaking outside and stuff, and once I get caught I took the whooping, and that's it. After I start coming outside to a lot of stuff, trying to get used to

the atmosphere and the crowd that I was just hanging around, it was rough trying to come up.

What made it so rough, Devin quickly learned, was that the streets were controlled by gangs. Depending on where he was going and with whom, his movement from block to block meant having to confront gang members:

> I didn't never want to gangbang until an incident that went on in school when a group of boys tried to push on me for crossing Damen [Avenue] at that time, and we couldn't cross Damen [because we were] living down on the other end. So therefore they tried to push on me because I was going to see my cousin and his relatives down there. And they just always thought I was Vice Lord, until I got tired of them trying to push on me all the time, so I became a Vice Lord and started fighting back, and fighting back with the weapons that they wanted to fight with.

Devin was thought to be a Vice Lord because he lived on the east side of Damen Avenue—the part of Henry Horner that was located in Vice Lord territory. It was a fact of life on the Near West Side that young men would be associated with whatever gang factions controlled the territory around their apartment building or block. The police and community residents also made these associations, usually with different consequences. Any kind of personal business conducted on the street, especially if it was with other young men, could easily appear to observers as gang activity. Being identified as a gang member by community residents could give the individual feelings of greater security, or, alternately, could place him in a more insecure position, depending on where he went and with whom he interacted. A visit to a part of the community where one did not live often was read as an act of encroachment upon another group's territory. As for how one's actions were interpreted by the police department, being identified as a gang member meant greater likelihood of being harassed, arrested, or even assaulted.

In a move that cemented his career in gang activity, Devin eventually joined the Four Corner Hustlers, a young and increasingly aggressive faction of the Vice Lords. As an adolescent, his days were filled with petty thievery, distribution of narcotics, and regular participation in violent activity. Devin talked about being thrown out of Dett Elementary School and becoming labeled "behaviorally disordered" due to his increasing involvement in violent activity:

> [I was first thrown out of school because] I pushed a teacher down the stairs. . . . I pushed a teacher down the stairs for hitting me in my arm for accusing me of stealing something that I didn't steal, and she put a green mark on my arm. I'm very insulted as it is. As we were going up the stairs I stuck my foot out and tripped her. And then she had me locked up, kicked out the school. I didn't

care. . . . I went to [a school with a program for the behavioral disordered]. . . .
It was a fun school. I graduated from there. I got a chance to do what I want
to do.

By that point in his life gangbanging had become the only regular activity in his life:

> You get a reputation in BD [behaviorally disordered classroom assignment],
> that's a slow and behavior problem classroom, so a lot of people like to try you,
> and you have more fights and you won't get expelled for it because you already
> got a label on you. So at that time it was fun. . . . I used to go around school
> kicking off fights cause I thought I was the tough one around there. I tried to
> get everyone scared of me.

Devin found much success in his efforts. Asked about how people responded to him, he said, "Somewhat, I got my props [respect from school-
mates]. That's what I can say."

Upon finishing junior high, Devin proceeded to high school. Once there
he began a path that led to his expulsion or self-initiated departure from
almost every public high school that served the residents of public housing
on the Near West Side. He explained that his mother and stepfather tried
to punish him in order to keep him on track. He said that he "used to
catch hell" after being thrown out of school. Whatever early results his
parents' efforts to keep him out of trouble had, they diminished altogether
as he got older. When talking about his early teen years while living with
his stepfather, Devin said, "I just slowly stopped listening to him because
I had grew up. It got to a point, 'You ain't my father. You can't tell me
what to do. I'll do what I want to do.' "

By his mid-teens Devin gave almost no thought to academic achievement:

> To be honest, I wasn't into learning. I was threatening teachers at that time,
> telling teachers what to do. . . . I went to Crane [High School] for my first
> year because everybody was going, all my buddies and everything. . . . I had
> started gangbanging. I became a Four Corner Hustler. And then we get into it
> at school, they had Disciples in there. And I got into it with some boys and I
> shot a shotgun in the school, and they kicked me out. . . . I had got a transfer
> to Marshall. . . . I had a reputation. They wasn't nothing they could do. Mar-
> shall, it was so-so. . . . It was just too far from home. They wasn't the type of
> gang that I wanted to be around. They used to try to jump on me all the time.
> Some of [the members of my gang] were there, but it didn't matter . . . I just
> stopped going to there and just got a transfer. Got to Creiger. . . . I was going to
> school, gangbanging. I was still in my first year [of academic standing] because I
> had got demoted. I picked the grades up, got to be a junior. My junior year I
> just got carried away.

The experience at his third high school initially was more positive because Devin's mother and stepfather tried a new motivational technique: they bought him a car. The vehicle did not come from a dealership or standard used car transaction, but rather through a neighborhood fence, a route by which many poor people get access to goods normally beyond their means. Devin said, "I was a car freak, man . . . so it wasn't nothing I could do but try [to do well in school]. So I tried it, and I just got into it [gangbanging] again."

Despite his newly found and initially successful commitment to schooling, Devin could not leave his past behind so easily. He continued to draw the attention of rival gang members inside and outside of school. He said, "Students, gangbanging. That's the main problem . . . there was plenty shoot-outs. I could remember a lot of shoot-outs."

Without finding any refuge from his immediate past, Devin soon got caught up in gang matters again, immersing himself into violence and crime. In evaluating his experiences in his third high school, he said:

> Creiger, that was a good school because everyday I went to school at Creiger I knew it was going to be somebody that I'm going to break going to school. And see [it] was all a Disciple school. I was the only Vice Lord in there. They looked up to me 'cause I told them I kill one of you, and then they gave me my props. . . . I was the only Vice Lord with the first and second years, after that brothers [other Vice Lords] would start coming in.

Rather than being expelled, Devin departed from his third high school on his own terms:

> I didn't get [thrown out], I just left. I just didn't go back because it was getting, it was really getting a little too deep. I was getting really carried away with it. . . . I was getting shot at, then my brothers and sisters, they still stayed on the other end [in schools closer to the family's apartment], and I had to chill out before one of them end up hurt.

That left him with one final option. "I went to Austin [High School] for a week, then I stopped going. I just got tired of school."

With school having more to do with bullets than with books, it is understandable that Devin grew weary of the institution. With the exception of a couple of months in high school, by adolescence Devin lacked any commitment whatsoever to formal education. School had instead become a site for negotiating the other, more pernicious, interests in his life. He said that it was not until sometime near our first meeting that he began reflecting on his life's seemingly dead-end path. Since leaving high school his life had revolved around gangbanging, drug dealing, and incarceration. When I first encountered him in the spring of 1994 he was living with his girlfriend in a Henry Horner apartment not far from the one in which he grew up. He was caring for their four-year-old son along with her three children from other involvements (a seven-year-old boy, a one-year-old boy, and a four-year-old girl). Although he had blood ties to only one child in the household, he called this assembly of people his family. He also was quite certain that his past history prevented him from being able to do much for his family, at least if they remained in Chicago.

Given his past and present circumstances, one might have figured that Devin was a product of a non-nurturing household. He said, however, that this was far from the case. In fact, the very ways in which discipline and control were administered in his household factored greatly in his moving toward the seedier side of life. Devin's story reflects the full spectrum of tensions and constraints that characterized the lives of these men. However, his story reveals that a life history on the Near West Side (or any other poor community) is not always, exclusively, or even primarily, one that tells of a dangerous person and his violent acts. The importance of looking at Devin's own account of his past is that it illustrates how the context of living in an urban, low-income community, densely concentrated with poor people and their problems, combined with his own conscious decisions of how to live his life, could lead him down the path of gangbanging and crime. Devin's story is an account of the failure to accumulate the right kinds of capital for combating, deflecting, or resolving the factors that stand in the way of escaping urban poverty. The capital that he did acquire—the agency provided for him by having a gang affiliation, deference from other gang members, the ability to intimidate other people—certainly was relevant for successful navigation of the streets. It was the very kind of capital, however, that limited his prospects in other domains of life. The inability to accumulate certain kinds of capital not only affects where one ends up in the social hierarchy of American life, but also how one conceptualizes mobility and opportunity both as aspects of the social world and as factors in one's own life. Exploring the processes of capital accumulation in the life histories of the other men will help to explain why they spoke as they did about mobility, opportunity, and their future life chances.

The Promise of the Focused Life Historical Inquiry

JAKE: Well you know how we fellas get together, you know, we run, you know, play, you know, play "it" through the building, catch one catch all, stuff like that, you know what I'm saying. I mean it was pretty fun.

LARRY: Hang out with my partners, you know, ride bikes, you know. We go on bike rides, you know. We used to go skating a lot, or go to the show, go swimming, go to the boys club. I stayed at the boys club a lot.

TITO: Well, when we was young it was like just me [and] seemed it was like twelve other guys out, all my buddies, you know.

These men were responding to my question about their early elementary school years. Unlike their current situations, many of these early life experiences were replete with the activities and joys of young children elsewhere. The men talked about playing in the neighborhood without an acute regard for the dangers and dilemmas that were seen as regular features of life by their adolescent years. For almost all of the men, the early childhood years were recalled as a less stressful time.[2] It seemed to them that more people had jobs back then, and by objective measures, as we have seen, it was a better time. We saw in chapter 2 that labor market transformations occurring between the 1960s and the 1980s eroded the employment prospects of the population of the Near West Side. In providing accounts of their life histories, this chapter explores how the men articulated the personal side of this transformation.[3] Our ultimate aim is to provide some background that makes clearer how and why these men spoke about mobility and opportunity as they did.

Before proceeding, it should be noted that when exploring the situation of people whose social and economic mobility is limited, it can be tempting to look for causes for why things turned out as they did. However, after completing the interviews with these men, I found it impossible to think in terms of direct cause-and-effect arguments about their lives.[4] Instead, I discovered that the heart of the story of how they came up and remained in poverty lay in the interrelation of various aspects of their life experiences, the structural context of urban poverty, the degree to which they realized and made sense of the impact of that context, and their subsequent behavior. All four dimensions contributed to the ultimate place of all the men near the bottom of the American social hierarchy. Consequently, the following analysis does not aim to show how the absence or presence of specific factors or conditions (a father figure in the household, the possession of a high school diploma or a criminal record, etc.) leads to specific social outcomes (seeing a way to get ahead in personal life, or understanding exactly how certain categories of people function in society). Rather, this chapter will illustrate how an amalgamation of factors in the men's past framed their capacity for certain kinds of agency.

Prior engagement with the social world is a precursor for developing the capacity to interpret it. Therefore, a look at these men's past experiences helps to make better sense of how they thought about the present and the future, and how they saw their places within each. For most of them, the small part of geography that is the Near West Side formed their entire social world. The choices that they made within narrow parameters eventually left them submerged in a world of disadvantage. This situation positioned them to think in certain ways about how different groups of people approach their futures, and how those examples related to their own sense of personal prospects for the future. A few of the men did have some limited experience outside of the world of the Near West Side. Yet, even those men regarded the Near West Side as the space with which they were most familiar. Hence, for the majority of the men, life outside of the Near West Side was unfamiliar, if not altogether exotic.

The Structure of Family Life

Jason, Lester, Ted, Roy, and Larry were the only men who grew up with their fathers in the home.[5] The absence of fathers in the household is a topic of grave concern in American society.[6] On the Near West Side, however, the absence of fathers in the household is a normal state of affairs. Adult males would come in and out of the men's lives. Whether their mothers had boyfriends who stayed with the family for a while, or got married and brought stepfathers into the home, the male presence was short-lived (in no case longer than three years), and almost always insignificant in the men's recollections of important family experiences. Single-female-headed households were the norm for most of the men, and all but seven of the mothers worked regularly in low-wage jobs throughout their son's youth. Employment was generally of the blue-collar type, including school security, store cashier, short-order cook, and home attendant. The mothers or guardians without the benefit of such work in the nooks and crannies of a diminishing urban industrial sphere received public aid.

It was often difficult to reconstruct who stood as the main authority figure in the household, due to the difficulty the men had in trying to make sense of the authority relations in their households. One might assume that people would have little trouble recalling the composition of their childhood households and the authority relations within them. Not so for these men. In the course of our discussions, each of them sat with me trying to reconstruct the composition of the household year by year. What I assumed would be an easy task turned out to be the hardest part of the interview for some of them. Crises and uncertainties were common features of family life. Relatives came and went regularly over the years as a response to the loss of a job, the inability to pay rent, or the need to avoid a threatening or problematic resident in their own domicile. Still, recollections of the arrival and departure of relatives took a back seat to memories of unplanned and unpredictable events. Consequently, the men could recall problems and crises much better than they could how these events effected the changing composition of the household.

Another characteristic of the transitory quality of household membership concerned siblings. Only one man, Barry, had none. The others had between two and eight. The birth and departure of siblings throughout their childhood, coupled with the temporary (but sometimes extremely lengthy) household hosting of aunts, uncles, and cousins, made family life an unstable, if not altogether turbulent, experience.

The same events that caused the ever-shifting nature of the households also often worked against the men's capacity to achieve upward mobility. Additional relatives at home could mean less food or material resources to go around, as well as the discomfort of less private space and time at home. Furthermore, relatives coming into and out of the household often meant changes in authority relations. Sometimes a grandmother would come into the household to take charge of things. In other families, a grandmother would move in to be taken care of by relatives. These varying circumstances led to the uncertainty mentioned above regarding whether a grandmother was the head of the household.

In perhaps four cases, a grandmother was the head of the household for the duration of the men's youth. Whether they resided with their grandmother or not, over two-thirds of the men discussed the centrality of their grandmothers in their childhoods. Twelve of them recalled having regular conversations with their grandmothers about preparing for the future. Usually, these talks were motivational. Additionally, grandmothers were often the best source of information for the men about the trials and tribulations in the history of black American life. Finally, some of the grandmothers were extraordinarily dominant figures in the household, creating a blend of adoration, fear, and awe in the men. Twenty-five-year-old Travis said the following about his grandmother:

When I had left Chicago and went to Mississippi for a little while my grandmother, she really pushed me man. . . . She put me on punishment, you know what I'm saying, to let me know that education comes before anything, see . . . she was the one that had pushed me to go, you know, because at first I was in a lot of trouble as far as in school, like going to high school. I was going to really flunk out until my grandmother, you know, stepped in. My grandmother, you know, took the place of my mother. . . . I thought mothers couldn't be that aggressive, but my grandmother was that aggressive to be an old lady.

Like some others, Travis's explained that his grandmother was that way because she survived the harsh realities of being a black woman in an earlier age.

I'll say the depression years, like that, you know [made her so resilient]. I figure something like that cause she told me a lot about the depression and stuff, I mean like wow, picking cotton, something I never had nothing to do with, you know what I'm saying, so I'm like man. And they had to do this, they had to work hard, you know. . . . She was always telling me stuff like, "Be someone. Don't get into nothing like ganging, all of that stuff," you know, "Do something with your life," you know what I'm saying.

The men heard stories of hard times and struggle from their grandmothers and other elders. Having survived some extremely difficult years, these women were apt to respond with the kind of tough love that made their grandsons respectful of them. Yet, this negative reinforcement alone was not enough to help the men deal with their present-day situations. While grandmothers and other adult figures often talked to the men about the virtues of a good education, the nature and quality of their own educational experiences did not equip them to provide concrete information to help the young men as they were about to encounter the first formal organizational setting of their lives: the Chicago public schools. In almost all cases the grandmothers were reared in the South, where their educational opportunities were severely curtailed. What education they did receive came in Jim Crow–era southern institutions that lacked the resources and bureaucratic complexity of Chicago public schools.

The educational background of the next generation was slightly better. Fourteen of the men's mothers received high school diplomas and another two received associate degrees sometime after their sons completed childhood. Ten of the women received diplomas from high schools in the South (in most cases from Mississippi). Altogether, sixteen mothers were born and reared in the South. For the most part, whatever education the women received was southern-based, which meant that they were exposed to educational environments that were much smaller in scale than was the Chicago public school system. Paradoxically, even given the poor reputation of the Near West Side schools, compared to the racially segregated, rural southern schools of their youth, they were considered by most of the men's parents and guardians to be tickets to opportunity.[7]

Family discussions about education were pretty much limited to these comparisons and contrasts between the Chicago and southern schools. The sons reported that their parents rarely discussed other aspects of schooling with them. Even more rare were discussions of the growing national criticism of public schools in low-income, urban communities such as their own. Instead, the parents just told their sons to take advantage of whatever the school provided. Larry captured the essence of these discussions when he said of his parents, "Yeah, they say, you know, go as far. You're going to go all the way, you know. You know, like, they tell us to go all the way." Essentially, these parents and guardians were woefully underprepared to offer the kind of guidance and advice that would benefit their children as the latter attempted to navigate the intricacies of the

Chicago school system. The parents' and guardians' limited encounters with schooling reveal the extent to which cultural capital, the knowledge of how to maneuver and manage in institutional settings, was lacking for these men. This cultural capital simply did not form a part of their habitus.

The Process of Family Life

A resident of ABLA, Lester was twenty-three years of age when we first met in 1994. A shade under six feet, but weighing over 200 pounds, he spilled out of the chair across from me in the ABLA community center when he sat down to begin telling me about himself. Lester had not been employed for more than a few months out of any single year of his adulthood. He was one of the few men who had both a mother and father at home for a substantial period of his childhood. Any tribulations he eventually encountered did not result from an absence of encouragement and careful planning on the part of his parents. In fact, he had a lot to say about how his parents tried to prepare him for a constructive future. In talking about the strict rules and guidelines that his parents established for him and his younger brother and sister, Lester shared with me an example of what his parents did to help him attain the better things in life:

> They'd give us certain days to study, and certain day we can go outside. On like Tuesdays and Thursdays, that was always study days. . . . They wanted all of us to be someone man, graduate and do something. . . . My whole plan for junior high through high school was to play football, try to get a scholarship, and then from that point I wanted to go into the military.

Unlike some of the men, Lester had developed a concrete plan that he hoped would carry him through to adulthood. As indicated by his parents' approach, schooling was a crucial part of the agenda. However, as was the case for many young black men, athletics had a place in the plan as well. Unfortunately, shortly after Lester started high school his family began experiencing grave problems that disrupted his plans. At that time the family moved to Texas for what Lester was told was a better work opportunity for his parents. He later found his parents had moved in an attempt to evade legal authorities. While in Chicago, his father had been transporting contraband across state lines. His father eventually went to jail for doing so. As Lester explained, "It didn't go out like that. . . . My father went to jail. . . . You know, we didn't know that [my parents] was doing something illegal, you know."

As the eldest child, Lester ended up having to do a lot of the daily care of his brother and sister while his parents were engaged in the complicated court case that preceded his father's incarceration. This new set of duties and obligations caused Lester to radically adjust his plans for the future. Lester withdrew from high school and was never able to make use of his athletic skills in order to get into college. Lester's strategizing for his future might have been more complex than many of the other men I interviewed. Yet, the problems in his family situation that ultimately led him to alter his plans look disturbingly familiar. Like others in his cohort from the Near West Side, Lester came from a family that tried to provide for him and his siblings through counterproductive and even illegal activities that eventually undermined that goal.

Lester was unusual in that his father was a full-time participant in illicit activity. Others, like Devin and Ted, had parents who got involved in such affairs on an ad hoc basis to help meet pressing needs. Devin's stepfather occasionally fenced stolen goods, mostly car parts. Ted's father periodically participated in hustling in a neighborhood bar. Whether parents were full-time hustlers or just in and out of the game as needed, the sons understood that their parents ultimately wanted to gather the resources needed to make things better for their children's futures. Such contradictions abounded in these men's family experiences. Far from being unusual or abnormal, these patterns of behavior are often found in families that function without the kinds of capital that could better sustain them. The uncritical observer might begin with the assumption that family behavior in the Near West Side and other disadvantaged communities takes one of two forms: the heroic or the tragic. The heroic model is exemplified by the resilient effort to shield the children from the perilous dimensions of social life and promote their academic and social development. It includes fostering the hard work ethic at home, especially as the surrounding community seems to have so many people who look like they are wasting time because they are without work. It also includes laying down firm moral guidelines, which appear to contrast starkly with the cultural orientations of members of communities rife with crime and deviance. Alternatively, the tragic model is reflected by images of irresponsible parents carelessly surrendering themselves and their children to the vices of the street.

Lester's situation demonstrates the convergence of both models. His parents sought the best for him, helped him to see how he could acquire it, and tried to marshal resources through illicit activities to make it happen (doing so without ever telling Lester exactly how they went about acquiring those financial resources). In the end, good intentions were paired with bad practices. This duality meant that Lester's parents, the very people who were trying to provide for him, became the pivotal factors in preventing him from ever reaching his intended goals.

Lester's complicated family situation points to the need for new critical analysis of the social dynamics of low-income African American families. An enduring issue in research on black families is the extent to which they value education and encourage the children to pursue schooling as a route to secure employment in their future.[8] What these men have to say about their family experiences in regard to preparing them to engage mobility provides crucial insight into the kinds of messages and ideas they recalled about getting ahead. The next step involves assessing how the men connected events and circumstances in family life with those messages. This new approach incorporates family-centered behavior into the picture in a very specific way. For the men in this study, family-centered behavior unfolded in a state of minimal capital accumulation. Ideas and ideologies for attaining mobility were transmitted between generations, but without much depth. In paying attention to these messages, it is as important to consider what was not said as what was. Both perspectives are essential for understanding how this dimension of family culture helped or hindered these men to make appropriate sense of the world in order to secure better futures.

Lester's family consistently asserted the importance of education. Unfortunately, the assertion alone was not enough to produce the desired outcome. In Lester's case as in others, the message was overshadowed by the illicit actions that often were taken in an effort to negotiate life in the Near West Side. Sometimes the messages themselves reflected a lack of awareness of the necessary educational prerequisites for significant upward mobility. For example, Earl said:

> Well my father stressed it [education] but he wasn't really strict, you know. He was, like I said, he busy trying to make sure we had a place to stay and had clothes. . . . Yeah my mother used to talk to me about education. She used to tell me that it will take you a long way, that's what you're going to need to get by in the world today.
> *Did they tell you how much education they thought you should get in your life?*
> They was basically saying like a high school diploma.

When asked if they ever encouraged him to do more than finish high school, Earl added that high school was all that his folks really knew about. College, for example, never entered the picture.[9] Unlike Earl, Jake did receive a high school diploma. Yet, when talking about his mother's attitudes toward education, it became clear why Jake also had no idea that college could become a part of his life, despite having received a lot of support and encouragement from her about schooling in general:

> She didn't talk about it [her own education] much, but I think back in her times [*the 1930s and '40s in Delano, Mississippi*] I think eighth grade was like maybe

as far as most people went because they had to get out and work, you know what I'm saying. I mean she talked about her school sometimes, about her life stories, you know. She wanted us to know about that. . . . And when I was coming up the priority was my sister, my younger sister and my brother. And it was like, you know, trying to just hold on to what we had because we didn't have much. . . . I mean everybody was pushed to graduate, you know what I'm saying . . . she figured that, you know, right now at least graduate out of high school, and if college came it came, you know, but she didn't have the money to pay for it so it was like, you know. But the point was just to get that high school diploma . . . she gave you a kind of outlook . . . it's not what type of job, the point is to try to have a job, you know what I'm saying. Whatever you do, she would just tell you to be the best at it, you know what I'm saying. So she never did try to tell us, lead us into any direction. She left it up to us to do that.

When family members did have something to say about their sons' schooling, it most often promoted a false sense of what education was necessary for leading a successful and independent adult life. Had the quality of parental information been any better, the question still remains as to whether adequate opportunities for information sharing could have existed. Time and materials had to be carefully shared and managed in households with minimal resources. With insufficient time and energy available to make ends meet, there was little opportunity for parents to involve themselves in their children's schooling more fully.[10] It is not so puzzling that their parents, amidst the concerns of raising other children and trying to meet family needs, would have little time for such interaction, no profound sense of how to pursue it, nor even the capacity to think of the importance of doing so.[11] Rather than there being a vacancy in the right kind of values in the family, there was a vacancy in delivering the right kind of information.

In a few cases, as we have seen, explicit and detailed guidelines about schooling were communicated to the sons. In these cases, the parents' plan usually consisted of an expectation that the son would complete high school and attend college via an athletic scholarship. The military was promoted as an alternative option for those who could not go to college through sports.[12] Again, we return to the situation of Lester. In addition to his parents' encouragement, Lester also explained how extended family members contributed much to his strategic plan for personal advancement:

My grandfather, he's from way back, about early 1900s when he was born, and he's real kind of, he's strictly, he's real strict on education too because you know he only completed the fifth grade, but he went to World War II and throughout and then he retired, and now he working for housing and all that. The only thing he got is a fifth grade education. . . . He told me pursue my career in college, play football, but the main thing about him, he an old veteran so he wanted me to go, you know, participate in the air force.

We already know what ensued for Lester in his pursuit of this plan. What this additional information helps us to understand is the degree to which a detailed plan, in the face of other circumstances, could not provide the necessary leverage for upward mobility. Lester's case shows the complex and complementary roles played by extended family members. Older extended family members had rich histories to refer back to and draw upon in their communication with the men.[13] They helped the men to see some way of coming to terms with their own life situations. Yet, the portraits they painted were far from sufficient to make upward mobility a reality for the young men.

Church attendance was another mechanism that parents and guardians employed in the effort to inculcate certain moral codes in their sons. Most of the men went to church fairly regularly throughout their childhoods. They recalled their mothers taking them there in the hope that this experience would expose them to the type of moral codes that could help them along in life. However, there was no compulsion to continue going to church after reaching adolescence. As the men began to deal with the rigors of community life, they came to find that church was no longer pertinent to them. These responses capture the sentiment of most of the men:

BARRY: I enjoyed church, yeah, but it wasn't my decision. That's probably why I didn't stay there. You know how when you're growing up because your mother said "You going to church. You going to Sunday school." And you don't want to disrespect mom. I'm going, you know. I would just stay there an hour, we'd be all right, I'd be back out in the street, basically that's what happened.

GUS: I was in the choir. I was an usher. I kept going to Sunday school and stuff like that. [But I stopped going] like right before I went to high school. . . . I started getting fast, you know what I'm saying. I started liking girls a lot more, and I started spending my weekends doing stuff like that instead of going to choir rehearsal and stuff like that.

Even the few that said that they had attended church in the past year or so did not go regularly. Damon, a young man who suffered from repeated bouts of alcoholism and substance abuse, said that the main reason that he no longer went to church regularly was that he did not have the right kind of clothes to wear to services.

Every one of the men attested to believing in a Higher Being. Their rationale was that a Higher Being must exist because they had little else to rely upon as explanation for how they made it to adulthood when so many of their peers did not. In reflecting on his life, Donald said, "I figured He done had His arms wrapped around me because I haven't been in no type of trouble, and I've been all around it. I've been all around trouble so I figured I've been blessed right there."

Additionally, the former churchgoer Damon said, "I wake up in the morning, I've got to say 'thank you Jesus,' because that's the only way I'm waking up I guess. Well that's what I was told, and that's the way I feel. I don't know about nothing else."

Finally, Conrad said:

> My mother kind of like said that when I was young, you know, like being into truth or whatever, you know how that go, that things will be better for you. And I guess it will be because man, it's just messed up out here. You need something, you know. Some type of guidance I guess, man. Being religious, going with God, will help I guess.

However, when asked about whether religion mattered at all in his life, he paused for a while and then said, "I don't know. I don't know the difference from being in church or being out here."

Even after this cursory glance at the childhoods of these men, it may still seem reasonable to wonder why things still went so wrong for them. To be sure, not all parents were perfect, and many engaged in criminal activities. We have seen that most of the fathers were not around. Additionally, some mothers battled substance abuse and other problems that made them less capable, if not altogether incapable, of contributing to their children's well being. Such circumstances led other relatives to step in to play parental roles. Despite the hardships, parents and guardians seemed to have been caring enough, if not adequately informed, to help their sons do better with their lives. Most parents encouraged their sons to take schooling seriously. They went so far as to offer accounts of their own lives to their sons as examples of the troubled consequences of a lack of schooling. Some of them also strove to protect their sons from the perceived and actual dangers of the community in order to diminish, if not prevent, access to the social forces and conditions that worked against upward mobility. The ideas and understandings about upward mobility that were cultivated within these families can be viewed as a rudimentary form of cultural capital. However, they were too rudimentary to make much of a difference for the men. The messages either were too embryonic or simply not relevant enough for helping the men to negotiate the kinds of everyday life experiences that they encountered. As we shall see, the same themes appear in the men's discussion of their schooling and adolescent years. Once again, the internal dynamics of family life ran up against the brutal realities of social life on the Near West Side.

Schooling

Many of these men first approached their school years with their minds fixed on something other than obtaining a quality education. When asked to reflect upon their early schooling years, rather than talking about the quality of their learning experiences the men discussed whether their teachers were nurturing and supportive. Coming from homes filled with stress and anxiety over a lack of money, their emphasis on security should come as no surprise. As Anthony said:

> I had a lot of good teachers in there [elementary school]. And one of my teachers, . . . if you come to school with your hair nappy she'll make sure she'll comb it . . . and at the end she'll take pictures of you and put them up on the classroom door for every month. . . . And she'll give it back to you like at the end of the month so you could carry it home to your mother. . . . If you do good and you have, your paper be corrected good, she always kept a whole bucket of candy in the closet that she give to us every time we leave. If you been bad you don't get none. And she made, she made, she made learning fun, you know what I'm saying.

Meeting the grooming needs of students is not a traditional duty of elementary school teachers. Yet attending to these issues can make all the difference in the world to poor kids. By the time these boys had started school, they had begun to see that life was not altogether good to them. Thus, they recalled early schooling experiences as positive to the extent that their teachers helped them cope with the pressures and concerns that came with living in low-income conditions. Remarkably absent in the men's recollections of their school days were details about the learning experience. In those early years, the men valued schooling when it provided them with a sharp sense of emotional, and sometimes physical, security. For some, the inability to find this kind of comfort kept them out of school on a regular basis. Dennis explained how:

> I believed in school, but you know, sometimes, you know, when you don't have exactly things to wear or, you know, you feel embarrassed . . . so sometimes I would dis school cause I didn't have nothing to wear, you know what I'm saying. And it was hard, you have to go to school and you look like a bum.

This was not an uncommon response for many of the men as they spoke about their excessive absences from school during periods of severe financial crisis. Absences occurred for a lot of reasons, but more than a few of them had to do with being uncomfortable with how they looked. The contrast between better-off students and these men is quite striking. A part of the culture of schooling in elite communities is that the school grounds become a place where new styles of dress, appearance, or the latest material acquisitions can be displayed. For the men of the Near West Side, going to school became a source of extreme anxiety if they were not clean, did not look healthy, or did not have clothes that fit correctly.

For many reasons—the risky trip to and from school, the quality of the school environment—schooling and education played a very different role in these men's lives than in the lives of other American youth from better-off communities. The normative view of education is that it is a process that offers tools for handling life experiences. Schooling helps by enhancing skills or abilities (defined earlier as human capital), by expanding understandings of the social world and ways to maneuver in it (cultural capital), or by developing relationships and ties with people who are connected or can create connections to desired resources or goals (social capital). These processes do not easily occur in public schools on the Near West Side. The surrounding environment penetrates the classroom and impedes students from growing more efficacious in developing the coping tools they need (especially those needed for the mainstream world). That dilemma is compounded by the school's shortcomings regarding teaching skills and learning opportunities.

At the time that the men were in elementary and junior high school, Chicago public schools were capturing the nation's attention as particularly troubled. In the late 1980s, then–secretary of education William Bennett considered the Chicago public school system to be the worst in the country. This view was sustained by an in-depth expose on the system done in 1988 by the *Chicago Tribune*, one of the city's major daily newspapers. The men in this book made no mention of these investigations, nor did they say anything about public perceptions of Chicago's schools. As all but two of the men experienced public schooling as their sole educational experience, they were well positioned to be victims of the system due to their lack of knowledge of the history and culture of Chicago public schools.[14]

The public elementary schools near Henry Horner included Henry Suder, located right across the street from the development, Dodge, Dett, and Victor Herbert. Almost all of those living in and around ABLA went to Medill Elementary. The major public high schools of the Near West Side were Crane, Collins, Creiger, and Marshall. All but a few of the men attended these institutions. At both the primary and secondary level, these institutions were generally considered to be at the bottom of the already indicted urban school system. According to statistics from the late 1980s, student enrollment at each of these schools never dipped below 97 percent

African American.[15] No less than 95 percent of the students in each of them were from low-income households (meaning that such students qualified for free or reduced-cost lunch); a few of the schools almost always stood at the 100 percent mark throughout the 1980s.

In the elementary schools, throughout the 1980s, between 75 and 90 percent of the student body performed below the national grade level on the Iowa Tests of Basic Skills, a standardized sixth-grade math and reading test. The standout school was Victor Herbert, where scores dropped to no lower than the fiftieth percentile; the outstanding elementary school on the Near West Side, then, was no better than average in the nation. As for within-city comparisons of sixth-grade math and reading scores, aside from Victor Herbert, each school regularly ranked in the bottom 25 percent out of over four hundred public schools in Chicago. Victor Herbert consistently placed between the bottom third and the middle.

All of the four area high schools graduated somewhere between 15 and 30 percent of their students throughout the late 1980s. During this time the percentage of the student body taking the American College Test (ACT)—a crude gauge of how many students are thinking about any form of post-secondary education—ranged from less than 10 to no higher than 40 percent. In terms of test scores, none of the four high schools consistently ranked above the first percentile nationally; in other words, the ACT scores in 99 percent of public schools in the country were better than those of Near West Side schools. Test scores certainly do not convey everything about the status of a certain public school. The statistics cited above, however, do highlight the extent to which achievement was an uncommon feature of Near West Side public schooling.

The Near West Side schools, like the other community-based institutions, function in a public space that is replete with the negative and even criminal elements of low-income communities. The students' experiences in the schools is shaped by what is happening on the surrounding streets. The events on the streets help determine what emotional and attitudinal baggage the students bring into the classroom. Those events and conditions also play a role in determining what objects (e.g., guns, knives) the students bring into the school.[16] It is not too hard to imagine that, despite the best intentions of the faculty and administrators who care the most, schools cannot easily operate as safety zones in these communities. A routine part of the school day for the young men of this study was the interruption of instruction as they and their classmates ducked under their desks when gunfire rang out in the streets surrounding the school building. Without having the assurance of safety, it was that much harder for these schools to function as sites for learning and intellectual development.

These chaotic conditions plagued the men throughout all of their school years. At times, some of them were agents in producing such violence. Yet, they also reported that, as exemplified by the conduct of certain instructors and administrators, school was not always fair to them. As black men, some of them knew that they were often being read as symbols of trouble, irrespective of whether they were causing it or not. For some of the men schooling was the first formal institutional setting where they bore and began suffering the stigma of being black and male in American society.

Nine of the men neither completed high school nor received a General Equivalency Diploma (GED). Of the seventeen that did complete high school, a few went on to additional programs of study. Casey and Kurt went to trade school after receiving their high school diplomas (Casey got a certificate in bricklaying, and Kurt in commerce), but neither went further in the liberal arts. Donald and Damon each spent a single term in community college, while Peter attended a public four-year institution for only one term. All three withdrew from their respective institutions due to financial constraints.

None of the men was older than twenty-five by 1995. Given their relative youth, one might expect that, aside from family matters, schooling experiences would constitute the major portion of their life histories. In some sense this was the case, but not in ways that have much to do with formal academic learning. Their stories do not include much about formal educational experiences. Rather, their histories are replete with other experiences in school, including elaborate tales of conflict, confusion, and turbulence. The men's underachievement can be attributed to an amalgamation of factors, some in and some beyond their control. For most of them, the barriers to real learning were in place almost from their first days in school. By junior high school, external events began to interfere seriously with the men's ability to focus on school. Earl, who started junior high school in Chicago after his family moved from Mississippi, said:

> It was a whole different experience because when we first started going it was like, it was a different peer pressure, you know what I'm saying . . . and it was more like kids teasing us about where we was from, things like that. Things was like hard at first, and then like, you know, I had got so I just said I'm going to have to do what I have to do and go on to school.

At first glance, Earl's account seems to parallel the woes of any child in a new school. Yet, a closer look reveals that the situation of coming into a school in a low-income community involved particular stressful circumstances. Earl and his family had moved into a community riddled with the violence and social turbulence that pervades everyday life wherever large-scale drug activity and other illicit activities exist. The gang recruitment that was common in the schools became a major obstacle for very early in his junior high school experience. Recall that Earl was well over six feet and about 230 pounds. While somewhat smaller as an adolescent, he said that back then he still looked like a prime recruit for a gang. He recalled the daily pressure he experienced in school to join one of various gang factions. Gang pressure was not the only distraction he experienced in school. He explained that he was a slow learner who had long been intimidated by school starting back in Mississippi:

> There's one particular experience that I had when I told this Catholic teacher that I would like to learn how to read. By me being in fourth grade I couldn't read so I asked her to learn how to read and I was like ignored, you know what I'm saying. She told me sit down, you know. . . . All she wanted to do was be there and for us to be there, but she didn't care if you learned or not.

Thus Earl had fallen way behind academically before leaving Mississippi. He said that upon arriving to Chicago, he wanted to give school another chance. As it turned out, the Chicago public schools did not do much to help him out. Unfortunately, Earl continued to slip through the cracks (which, given the deteriorating situation of the schools, might best be conceived of as gaping holes). Soon the problem with gangs and recruitment took a tragic turn.

> And then there was a different peer pressure [in high school] because it was like gangs, something I never experienced before, and I remember a time when I used to break for lunch. I used to go to the store and guys used to stand on the corner and put pressure about "can I have a quarter, give me a quarter," and all this. So I had been going to school for like almost about three months, and I just got fed up with it and I got into a conflict with one of the guys and stabbed him. And so what happened is he went to the school too, so I was ejected . . . they kicked me out of school.

Having been a resident of the Near West Side for a few years prior to attending high school, Earl experienced enough to know how to handle threats and affronts from other people. He knew that gang pressure was not handled by talking rationally with his antagonist. His response to the challenges made by other youths was prudent and deliberate, given what he had come to understand as the right way of handling business on the Near West Side.[17] His foremost concern was eradicating a threat efficiently without surrendering to his challenger. Consequently, Earl's actions in stabbing his antagonist reflected not a poor value system, nor an ignorance of the law, but an orientation to life—a habitus—that involved taking certain decisive actions when the time called for them.

The actual consequences of Earl's violent actions were grave. After being expelled from school, he drifted into a series of illicit activities that caused him to lose focus on school altogether. This route trapped him in a life of petty crime and delinquency:

> [Later on] there was always a chance for me to go to school. . . . I didn't pursue the chances. Like from there I got caught up in the things around me, you know what I'm saying, the neighborhood, and I start selling, messing with, selling drugs, selling reefer, which was all out at the time.

Succumbing to the increasing pressure brought upon most young black men, Earl eventually did join a gang. This move facilitated his involvement in a series of illegal activities. In 1992 he was arrested for narcotics distribution. He was paroled in the spring of 1994, a few weeks before our first discussion.

Earl's story illustrates the danger of being immersed in the kind of habitus that circumscribes the lives of urban, low-income people. The quest to do what others may regard as the right thing—call the police, turn the other cheek, or try to reason with the people that are creating the conflict—essentially has no legitimacy in these communities. While some may pursue these options, the great majority of residents never consider these choices viable. Turning the other cheek or running away from the problems may result in their endless recurrence, because one then gets identified as a "soft" person in the community. A vicious circle takes hold as that kind of label increases the prospects of being confronted again.

Another option is to get others to confront one's problems, or stay close to others who can provide the right kind of protection. Recall that this was Casey's situation (he was the younger brother of a gang leader). Such was the case for Joseph as well. He said that he stayed out of gangs throughout his life. This did not prevent him from moving about ABLA as much as he desired. Joseph had some measure of mobility and security in the neighborhood because his two older brothers were high-ranking gang members. Their status kept him safe from recruitment efforts, while also allowing him to benefit indirectly from the stature and prestige awarded to his brothers. The respect that his brothers garnered continued to do much for Joseph as he went about his everyday life in the neighborhood. Because both of his brothers were in jail when we spoke, he was the only son living at home and charged with taking care of his mother, whom he described as suffering "from Alzheimer's or something like that."

For many, relying upon others carries its own set of risks. One becomes indebted to those who grant favors. This relationship can be problematic depending on what kind of reciprocity the individuals demand. Gang solidarity is predicated on reciprocity. The beneficial side of this arrangement is the provision of mutual protection and support. The risk is that sometimes one must take actions that threaten one's own security, health, or comfort. Finally, a remaining option for dealing with conflict is exactly the one taken by Earl, who handled his business on his own. In the end, he owed no favors to anyone, but still had to suffer the consequences of his violent actions.

As an organizing mechanism for individual and collective life, habitus simultaneously operates at the conscious and subconscious level. In short, people reproduce both patterns of behavior and ideas about themselves and the world around them without being completely cognizant of doing so. Consequently, what eventually appears as the inevitable aspects of social life and individual experience (in Earl's case, the approach toward handling repeated personal affronts and threats) becomes routine because it occurs as regularly as the changing of seasons. Earl knew what to do when threatened because his action was a common, socially legitimated way of handling that particular situation. Over time, such actions by people who live in similar circumstances renders that behavior the common-sense way of doing things. This cycle reveals how such action is directed, regulated, and legitimated by the social environment within which it is produced.[18]

In arguing that habitus is durable, Pierre Bourdieu intends to explicate how regularities in thought and action endure throughout one's life. However, he also argues that individuals may expand their repertoire of responses in light of new experiences because, as a product of history, habitus contains an "open system of dispositions" that is subjected to, and therefore can be altered by, new experiences (Bourdieu and Wacquant 1992 p. 133). Thus, Earl could have veered from the routine response and called the police, turned the other cheek, or tried to reason with his persecutors. If such actions resulted in a positive outcome, and were subsequently modeled by others facing similar circumstances, then a change would have occurred in at least one aspect of the habitus of Near West Side residents. Such a heroic pursuit was not on Earl's mind at the moment of his confrontation with the gang members (probably because of the risk involved in each alternative). Instead, Earl did what was normal to do in the time and space circumscribing his situation, and within the confines of the resources available to him.

This does not mean that all or even most of the violence in communities like the Near West Side results from innocent parties trying to defend themselves with the paltry resources at hand. We do need to consider this kind of situation, however, to fully comprehend the dynamics of this community. We must think more carefully about how and why people make choices that may seem corrupt and extreme to those who do not live in their social world. It also means that in order to better understand the complexity of the lives of people in poverty, one must acknowledge that even those who, for whatever reason, commit remorseless acts of violence on certain days may also commit justified violent acts on other days with the aim of defending themselves in the only way they imagine to be possible.

Earl was not alone in linking his experiences in and around school with violence. Devin, Roy, Larry, and Anthony each left high school without earning diplomas because of their involvement in one or more violent encounters. Roy had been expelled from a Catholic elementary school for fighting. He transferred into a public school. Here he was challenged by classmates who sought to know how the former Catholic school student would respond. His reactions to these challenges became increasingly more violent. This resulted in his becoming a problem case for teachers and staff in his high school. In high school Roy was involved in a major altercation that resulted in his being expelled yet another time. Roy's temper continued to cause him problems throughout his youth. Eventually, as a young adult he ended up having to serve time in Cook County jail for disturbing the peace.

In another scenario linking school and violence, Anthony quit school after finding out that a rival gang had put a contract out on him. At first, this news did not bother him. After all, he had experienced quite a lot of violence while growing up. When Anthony was a child, one of his sisters was thrown out of a public housing apartment window to her death by her boyfriend. He also had an older brother who, as he said, "Had a nice little time on hisself," after being sentenced to prison for his involvement in a gang-related shooting. Anthony explained that a lot of challenges were made in high school between rival gang members, and that he felt secure about distinguishing real from bogus threats. He began to take the situation more seriously shortly after members of a rival gang drove up to a friend and gang associate of his, and tried to drag him into their car. Knowing that going to school could be dangerous, he and his friend decided that it was best to take a break from school. They never returned.

For those who successfully avoided the violence in and immediately around school, there still remained the need to negotiate threat and danger on the walk between home and school. Ted attended elementary and high school just north of the Near West Side. He explained that throughout his elementary school years he had to meet up with his siblings and cousins at a corner near the midpoint of their homes. Together they crossed the gang boundaries that separated their homes from their school. In thinking about his school experiences, he said:

> I can't really, you know, remember [what I valued about high school] because my mind was stuck on coming to school and going home from school. So I don't remember nothing, you know, happening as far as teaching that was there, but, you know, school is school.

Like most of these men, Ted was not a stellar academic performer. A safer route to school would not have ensured better academic performance. However, the fact that the absence of a safe route to school was his strongest recollection of his school years reveals that this extra burden affected his relationship to the schooling experience.

The men did not have to be actors in school-based violence to feel immersed in that milieu. For most of them, stories concerning violence were invoked in an almost casual manner whenever they talked about school. Years before leaving for Texas, Lester went to elementary school near his home in ABLA. He remembered:

> I liked everything about that [Suder Elementary] school except everybody in there wanted to fight man. By me living in that rough neighborhood everybody was fighting everyday, everyday.
> *What do you think caused that?*
> Gangs, that's the only thing that causes it man, gangs.

Even those men who found school to be a safe place once inside were not emotionally protected from the external conditions. The lack of protection pushed learning further down on the agenda. For instance, Barry explained that he stayed away from gangs while growing up in Henry Horner Homes. For him, safety was the point of emphasis in discussing anything that had to do with the positive aspects of high school:

> See when you're inside [the school building] it was like secure. . . . That's what I liked about school was the security of being inside, to me, you know. But when you go outside . . . no security out there. You know when you're in school you, you know, you're with somebody else, there's a group of you all talking and laughing, learning, ain't got the violence, and you know, when you're in school you ain't thinking about that. But when you get out there then it's changed. So basically I liked . . . getting out of the streets. . . . I was there [high school] just to get from out there [the streets].

To understand how school fit into the lives and consciousness of the men of the Near West Side, one only has to reflect upon the extent to which school was talked about in so many ways that have nothing to do with the classroom-based learning experiences. Depending on the particular school, classroom, or year of attendance, it was a place for some of the men to work out gang conflicts if they were members, or to try hard to avoid them if they were not. It is easy to read these accounts of schooling as indicators of a bastardized culture of masculinity that was formed in a specific institutional setting. These stories may make it seem as though young black men are somehow innately aggressive and hostile. It is difficult to argue that these are not salient elements of social life for poor black men in urban communities. A careful reading of these men's accounts shows, however, that these traits, even if internalized by some of the men, do not constitute the entirety of their social being. As their conversations with me show, they are not simply reactants or contributors to a tumultuous social milieu, but individuals who can step back from the social landscape and demonstrate an ability to frame, interpret, and evaluate their actions within it.

The power of the habitus of which they are a part, and which includes the social forces and conditions shaping their experiences in school, prevents them from functioning as fully free actors in that setting—in part because their habitus denies them the capacity to imagine other forms of efficacious action. Thus, there are limits to their ability to frame, interpret, and evaluate. That condition not withstanding, their testimony conveys that these men think about themselves and their experiences with a greater complexity than has previously been recognized. As their remarks make clear, schooling was an institutional sphere that was ill equipped to help them choose a variety of paths. Without the luxury of choosing the best teachers in the Chicago school system, or even being able to turn down many of the worst, Near West Side schools did not stand out as models of educational excellence. Putting all of this together, it is clear that school was a formative experience for these men, but usually for reasons that had nothing to do with the pursuit of a formal education.

Entering into Adulthood

Throughout the interviews most men emphasized that having moved past adolescence and into their early twenties, they were beyond the most intense period of crisis for black men. They considered the teenage years to be the high point of gang involvement and susceptibility to acts of random violence. (I present this not as an objective measure of violence in their community, but solely as the men's explanation of the tribulations of their adolescent years.) Despite their continued acknowledgment of unpredictable and pervasive violence in their communities, the men felt that they had reached a point in their lives where things appeared as if they would begin settling down. If not more materially rewarding, their post-adolescent years at least were less volatile. Believing that they had minimized their exposure to life-threatening circumstances, they began to accept that they might be around longer than they had imagined at earlier points in their lives.[19]

The end of high school, whether by graduation or withdrawal, effectively meant the beginning of adulthood for these men. This new beginning did not necessarily mean total independence from the childhood home. Most of the men still considered their home to be that of their parent or defacto guardian. In the course of our discussions the only men who did not give their mother's or grandmother's home as their permanent address were Devin, Butch, Jason, Casey, and Gus, who lived with friends or girlfriends in or a few blocks from Henry Horner and ABLA. For the other men, any given night could find them in any of a variety of places; thus living with a parent was no real indication that they led very different lifestyles from the five men who maintained their own residences. For those without their own domiciles, mothers, grandmothers, and guardians had the most secure and stable addresses. That was enough for these men to call these places home.

Twenty-one of the men were fathers at the time that I met them (seventeen men had one or two children, and four had from three to eight). None of the men was married, and only three, Butch, Devin, and Ted, resided with their children.[20] None of the other fathers had formal custody of their children. By their report, interaction with children ranged from consistent to nonexistent. Those that claimed consistent involvement stated that they visited their children and provided whatever material support they could garner.[21] None of the nonresident fathers expressed intentions of marrying the mothers of their children. These nonresident fathers also reported that their interaction with them ranged from congenial to turbulent. Of the men who did live with their children, only Devin expressed any intention of marrying the mother.

The men reported that fatherhood mattered significantly for establishing key aspects of their adult identity. They reported that the birth of their children (usually the first child) encouraged them to think seriously for the first time about how better to take charge of their lives and figure out how to support themselves and their children.[22] Conrad talked about how becoming a father made him see himself in a different light: "I realize that I ain't just living for myself no more. I got my daughter and my son to live for, you know." Conrad did not know much about his own father, and he did not want this same situation to be duplicated for his children: "I don't want to be like my father was to me. I never want to desert my son or my daughter." Conrad portrayed himself as a bit of a hell-raiser during his youth. He had been raised by his grandmother because his mother suffered from severe drug addiction and could not effectively care for him. The grandmother's best efforts did not prevent him from a career in petty hustling and other forms of trouble throughout his youth. These activities left him with a criminal record and a stay in Cook County Jail prior to becoming a father. The thing to do after becoming a parent, he thought, was find work. Conrad proclaimed, "Nowadays, you know, people are dropping like flies. And I feel like, you know, if I go I want my son and my daughter to have something, you know, to collect something from me, because if I go now they ain't going to get nothing, you know what I'm saying."

His comments were not atypical. Fatherhood encouraged the men to think about what it meant to be a man, and what it meant to be one in the midst of poverty. However, broader notions of fatherhood (relations with the mothers of their children, myriad ways of interacting with and contributing to the development of their children, etc.) were talked about with considerably less frequency and detail. This is consistent with research that indicates that men in low-income contexts often lack the social and material resources needed for developing collective strategies (with peers, family members, the mothers of their children, etc.) for child rearing in nonmarital contexts (Sullivan 1989). Thus, the men's responses to becoming fathers indicated how they thought differently about themselves more than how they might relate differently to the women and children in their lives.[23] Their remarks about their children conveyed a sense of strong emotional attachment to them, and the hope that they could become positive adult models for them later in life.[24] Otherwise, the men spoke little of formal family obligations or involvements in their present-day lives. Their brief involvement in the children's lives was much like their involvement with work: neither was a major daily preoccupation.

The World of Work

Whether they possessed a high school diploma or not, the men entered their late adolescence and early adulthood with extremely marginal prospects for work. The downturn of the Chicago economy in the late 1980s and early 1990s has already been documented. The structural transformations of the municipal and local economy, and a lack of preparedness for anything but manual labor, were primary factors for the lean work histories of these men. In looking at the varied aspects of their pasts, their formal work experiences make for the shortest story of all. They had very little consistent or long-term employment. Other than Jordan, who worked at a funeral parlor for two years, at the time of the interviews none had held a job for more than a few months at a time.[25] This current state of affairs followed some years of piecemeal and per diem work as adolescents. Aside from that, there was little in the way of employment experiences for the men to talk about.

In sharing the accounts of how they acquired and then lost jobs in their past, a number of the men expressed more concern about being respected or appreciated by their employers than about simply maintaining a specific job.[26] This mindset was a virtual guarantee that a job would not last very long. For example, Tito survived a number of gang conflicts in his past, one of which left him with limited use of his left arm after he was shot repeatedly with an automatic rifle. He also had served time in Centralia State Penitentiary, and he talked quite a bit about his knowledge of how to survive on the streets. What he could not survive was working in a warehouse for a moving company:

> I ain't have to quit, but I couldn't accept what was happening in there because the manager's sister came and two days later she's assistant manager. We trying to move up. How she going to get that spot in front of all of us and she ain't been there, you know. So I kept saying something. I was speaking what I had in my mind. I was speaking my mind. . . . I went to talk to the manager. I said, "Can I talk to you about our positions?" He said, "Yeah, yeah, go ahead." "Okay, I want to know how can she be a manager?" "Well I don't want to talk about it." "But you wanted to talk about it before we were. . . ." She wanted to talk about it before she found out I want to talk about her sister, you know. I told her I want to talk about her sister and she ain't want to talk about it. So I said, "Man, you know what, man, I quit," because I cursed at her. I think she would have fired me anyway, in the end. . . . She would have fired me anyway I think.

Racial conflict also was a salient part of the work experiences for other men. Felton gives an example:

> When I was working at Dominick's I just came to work, you know, minding my own business, and you know it was up north, and them people up there are pretty crazy. It was a Caucasian guy, and I'm bagging these groceries, and at Dominick's they tell you to evaluate the load. That means make both bags even in weight. So I'm here bagging his groceries, and by the time he just got his money from the cashier, he just pushed me and said, "Bag my groceries right nigger," like that. And we got to fighting. I mean, you know, I just didn't like what he did. The manager, he's sitting over here. He's looking right at it because there is a little stand that looks like it's short, but it's tall when you stand up behind a counter. The manager had come over there and he was a white guy too. He came over there and he broke it up. He was like, "What's all this ruckus for." I said, "Man, I'm minding my own business. He just pushed me and told me to grab his groceries and 'bag his groceries right nigger.' " And the manager pulled me over to the side and told me the customer is always right. I said, "Fuck you," and got out of there. Excuse my language but that's what I said.

For a handful of the men, brief encounters with work allowed some important exposure to life beyond the confines of the Near West Side of Chicago. Although they were not in positions to access a better quality of life, these experiences enabled them to better visualize it. The images before them were of clean streets, attractive storefronts, and well-dressed busy people hurriedly moving about in the midst of tending to their personal business. Though such images may appear to be commonplace to the non-poor, they were nonexistent on the Near West Side.

This situation concerning work—or more appropriately, the lack of it—is one of the more dominant effects of social isolation. In Chicago, isolation not only consists of extreme social distance from the necessary resources for engaging mobility but also geographic distance. Viaducts, railroad tracks, and landmarks serve as demarcations that define and divide Chicago neighborhoods. The rigidity of neighborhood boundaries has resulted in the persistence of vibrant ethnic enclaves well past the days of the initial ethnic urban ghetto formation of the early twentieth century.[27] However, for the people of the Near West Side and other impoverished communities, such geographic segmentation promotes a very durable parochialism that makes the consequences of social isolation even more severe. It was no light statement when Larry said, "I look at people that's been around there [Henry Horner Homes] all their life, ain't probably been downtown, don't know how to travel downtown."

While some of the men in this book made it to downtown and a few other places, many were not even remotely familiar with places other than the Near West Side. The unfamiliarity of places outside of their immediate community made it all the more difficult for these men to relate effectively to the outside world. The men who were fortunate enough to experience even low-skilled work in other communities had the rare opportunity to see how people functioned in other places. Dennis provides an illustration:

> [*On working for McDonald's*] It really encouraged me to try and advance because I worked up north for them on Chicago and State [streets in downtown Chicago], and, you know, all the people that you see come back and forth and the way they dress, how they look, and the way they carry themselves, they make you want to dress and look and be like them, you know. I was, you know, I used to see all kinds of walks of life as being out there, then you see the homeless, people that ain't got nothing, and then you look at people that got everything. . . . And that's what made me look like "What I'm doing in a McDonald's job when I could be doing the work they doing," you know. I don't know what they doing but I know whatever it is it's an honest living, you know. You see them come in there every morning or every evening for lunch. You know, I know they doing something honest, dress nice, and, you know, that's what I'm saying. Ain't got to sweat. That's what made me look at that.

Dennis was one of the few men who spoke of having any kind of regular interaction with business people, even though his was restricted to interaction across the service counter at McDonald's. As sparse as his exposure to the white-collar professional milieu was, it allowed him to create a sense of that world far beyond what most of other men could contemplate. This exposure becomes especially meaningful for understanding some of the arguments that he and others make in the following chapters.

Crime, Vice, and Incarceration

For a lot of these men, placement out of the formal labor force was counterbalanced by involvement in illicit activity. These ventures were the closest that some of the men ever came to consistent wage-earning activity. Over half of them indicated that they engaged in such affairs. Most of it, they said, was restricted to petty thievery and hustling. The others who were involved in illicit activity sold narcotics.[28] None of the men involved in such activity ever gained long-term financial benefit from it. Instead, they reported that the major consequence of their involvement was a higher susceptibility to violence in their lives. Barry, for one, said that drug dealing was more of a problem than a solution to his financial woes:

> First I wasn't even paying no attention to all of that [the violence associated with the drug trade and the possibilities of going to jail], just, I got this money. Now I ain't got that money, and that's, ah, I wish I had never started. I know that much . . . I didn't get nothing out of it. You know, not what I was [hoping for]. I don't know. It just tricked me, you know. . . . As fast as it came, as fast as it went.

Barry never served time for dealing drugs. That was not the case for most of the other men who reported drug dealing. Tito, Travis, Anthony, Devin, and Earl each spent some time in state penal institutions, including juvenile detention centers. Arthur, Dennis, Roy, Lester, Casey, and Conrad each spent from a few weeks to a few months in the Cook County Jail for their activities, which included possession of illegal substances, thievery, and disturbing the peace.

In fact, almost all of the twenty-six men I interviewed had been detained at the local police precinct for one incident or another. As for many black men of their socioeconomic status, jail formed a bigger part of their lives than did work. Spending time behind bars did not always lead to a conviction; often the men were just detained by the police. Detention was talked about as if it were a common event in their lives. Conviction was a close second. Nothing created as great a stigma for them than the possession of a criminal record. Each knew very well that a record was a severe detriment to finding work. As in other aspects of their lives, however, they accepted that this was their predicament, and nothing could change it.

For those that experienced it, prison was an important learning experience in its own right. Incarceration exposed the men to one scenario that
was universally regarded as worse than anything on the Near West Side.
Anthony, who served time for stealing a United Parcel Post delivery truck
in the hopes of selling off its packages, had the following to say about his
experience:

> I served a year. . . . They sent me to Mount Sterling Penitentiary. That taught
> me the biggest lesson in the world boy, that I don't never want to go back there
> . . . it's like they got you in a cage. It's like a mother-parent thing all over again
> but only thing it's worser. It's the guards, if it ain't the guards it's the niggers
> that's in there. So the one thing you're doing is you got to watch your back in
> there and then you got to hope you don't do nothing else to get in trouble to
> stay in there even longer.

Travis was incarcerated for robbery. Throughout the course of our interaction he repeatedly claimed that he was falsely charged, and that claim
served as his overriding point of reference for everything that he had to
say about the poor quality of his life and his hopes for a better future. He
served time in Joliet Correctional Center, one of the most notorious penal
institution in Illinois. As he recalled:

> Man, [it was] chaos . . . just like being in a time bomb. I mean you could just
> explode at any time . . . it was so much tension in the air, brothers, I mean you
> just bump your shoe they want to kill you. I mean if you ain't hooked up you
> ain't got no rights, you know. And guards see this. The security that's suppose
> to be your protection, they see this, you know what I'm saying. If I'm not
> hooked up I ain't got me no rights. I got five minutes on the telephone. What
> could I say in five minutes? If I want to talk to my family, my mother, what
> could I say in five minutes? I got five minutes on the phone, but gang leaders
> and gang members get thirty or forty minutes on the phone. Come on man, you
> know what I'm saying. But if I open my mouth I might get busted in my mouth,
> now where's justice there. I still getting bitter. I'm getting even bitter and bitter
> about this, about the situation. Then if I lock up [go into protective custody]
> I'm a puck, you know what I'm saying. It's messed up man. And I was trying
> to talk to brothers, "Man, what's wrong with you all, man. We in the same
> boat. We in a white man's jail and you all still want to act silly." Man, listen, I
> just couldn't believe it.

Incarceration provided a new and unique perspective on life. The horrors of prison were worse than those of the Near West Side.

As much as being incarcerated created obstacles to finding good work
once back out on the streets, for some of the men the experience enhanced
their own sense of their ability to simply get by. In recalling how this

occurred, Ken, the man with a factory job who was much better off than the twenty-six men included in this study, said:

> Man, me getting out [of prison], you know, in one full piece, I still got my eyes. A lot of people when I was there, you see their eyes, it's one eye, you know. Motherfuckers done try to tear their eye out their head. I've seen that. You know, fingers, limbs, you know.

The completion of a prision sentence also brought a renewed sense of the value of the freedom to move about daily. It also is easily imaginable that some of the men who went to prision learned more about how to commit crime than they did about how to better their life prospects. The latter lesson is not one that prisons deliver in any meaningful sense anyway. Altogether, life prospects were thought about a bit differently by the men who possessed a criminal record—and almost always in terms of how much more problematic getting ahead would be.

Other Places and Other People: Life Outside of Chicago

> I liked it. . . . The population there, it was more white. I mean this was a new experience for me. I never went to school with, you know, I heard about Martin Luther King saying blacks and whites should come together, you know what I'm saying [but] I had never saw it. I would never figure me from the vicinity I come from and the area and all this, crime area and, you know, high infested area, and I'm here [in Iowa]. I mean I ain't got to look over my shoulder all the time. I ain't, you know, no scars, no gunshots. I mean it was clean. I mean, you could hear birds whistling. I mean this, it was hard to believe this.

This was a part of Travis's recollection of living with a friend for a year in Iowa. Looking for a place to "clear his head," he went there with a friend who enrolled in a small school near Davenport, Iowa to play basketball. When he came across this other way of living, Travis was struck by all that contrasted with his everyday reality in Chicago. He saw and participated in congenial interracial interaction, and he got a taste of life in a rural community. While talking about Davenport and neighboring East Moline, Illinois, Travis also told a lot about what he knew as normal life on the Near West Side:

> And then there was interracial relationships, you know what I'm saying. I saw this with my own eyes. I never saw it before in Chicago. I never saw that, but I saw it in East Moline [*while Travis accompanied his friend for a basketball game*]. . . . I'm like wow, you know what I'm saying. . . . I learned from the experience, so then as far as the racism side, I mean it happened. You know, brothers do mess with Caucasians and Caucasians do mess with Blacks, you

know what I'm saying. I saw this. I mean it was, to me it was like a new experience. I never saw this before.

On the west side of Chicago, a major part of living in social isolation meant standing firmly on one side of the racial divide. Davenport, Iowa, brought Travis to the other side. What he saw as new and intriguing would appear as quite common to those who do not live in the context of racially isolated urban poverty.

Despite the new insight on the world that Iowa brought to him, Travis came back to Chicago after a year. What he returned to was exactly the same kind of life that he had left. When asked why he chose to return, he said, "I don't want to be no bind on my friend, you know what I'm saying, I'm out of here." His was one of the few experiences that the men had with environments far from, and very much unlike, the Near West Side. If serving time in prison was the most confining of the social experiences that these men encountered, perhaps the most liberating were opportunities (outside of prison) away from the Near West Side. Experiences such as these introduced the men to alternative ways of living, giving them the chance to develop something of a different outlook on the social world (the full significance of this will be made clearer in the following chapters). The experiences exposed them to people not commonly found in their neighborhoods, and to lifestyles that were foreign to those in the Near West Side.

Twelve men spent substantial time in communities other than a low-income neighborhood in Chicago. Two went away for periods of less than six months (Peter went away to college in Alabama for an academic term, and as a teenager Joseph had the opportunity to travel one summer throughout the Midwest with a neighborhood-based drum and bugle corps). The ten others who spent some time outside of Chicago did so for periods ranging from one to six years.[29] Travis, Dennis, Earl, Lester, Jason, Arthur, and Kurt temporarily relocated with their families or specific family members, or were born elsewhere and migrated to Chicago with their families. Jordan and Butch spent some time in the Job Corps (in Illinois and Indiana, respectively). Lastly, Gus served in the army (which eventually brought him to the Middle East during Operation Desert Storm in the early 1990s).

Lester's family was one of those that relocated for a few years: for reasons that we have already documented, they moved to Texas. Lester returned to Chicago without his family shortly after his parents' court case. He took up residence with relatives in the ABLA housing development. After all was said and done, he recalled his time in Texas as an uplifting and inspiring time, despite its coming to an end on negative terms:

Man it was open space, fresher air, you be more relaxed. . . . And you know they're like, they ain't too prejudiced cause they [the families in his new neighborhood] in the service [armed forces] anyway. They mingling with other, you know, races. So everybody was like, and down there everybody has kids. So all the kids used to play on the streets, play football, used to go to the gym, then you used to go to teen clubs, then we used to play cross-fire with bee-bee guns and camp out in the backyard with a tent. We had some fun out there. It was a good experience though.

He explained what this new-found exposure meant for people from the inner-city like himself:

If you're in a rough neighborhood you're going to grow up being rough, you know what I'm saying, but [my father] didn't want us to be in that environment. You see, everywhere you move it's different environments. It make you think different. It will change you, all for the better or for the worst though. In our case it changed us for the better.

Change for the better only meant the chance to acquire a broader vision of life's possibilities. As already discussed, Lester's family circumstances eventually made things much worse for him. Yet, by explaining what was appealing and interesting about Texas, his account illustrates exactly how much constraint and confinement there was for the men who never left the Near West Side. Going to new places meant acquiring new understandings of community, security, and serenity. Moreover, for many of them it was their first encounter with interracial interaction aside from encounters with police officers, civil servants, or other governmental figures. Thus it was the first opportunity to experience relations across class and racial lines in nonhostile or nonconflictive ways.

The absence of extensive interracial and interclass exposure is the normative condition for the Near West Side. People there live in a virtually all-black, low-income social environment. This severely limits their capacity to envision other forms and patterns of living. The following chapters will continue to explore the significance of their narrowed perspective for their visions of personal and social mobility and opportunity in American life. As we already know, the men who experienced something other than the Near West Side were unable to put these experiences to use in the pursuit of secure upward mobility. Consequently, the experiences became little more than emotionally enriching or eye-opening encounters. Yet those encounters allowed the men to acquire a broader and richer basis for comparing, evaluating, and interpreting their present circumstances. As they had little other capital, they were unable to make these experiences mean anything more for them in terms of mobility prospects.

Conclusion

This overview of the life histories of these men in no way conveys the full complexity of their experiences. Its more modest aim is to make two related points that form part of the new cultural analysis of poor African American men: to show how developments in key spheres of life such as family and school situate the men in their positions of disadvantage, and to provide some historical context for understanding how these men make sense of American society with respect to mobility and opportunity, their place and stake in that society, and whatever future possibilities they could imagine for themselves in it. In the course of pursuing these objectives, some important insights have emerged regarding the culture of urban-based low-income African Americans.

By drawing upon the notion of capital as a product of social experience and a resource for meaning-making, the foregoing discussion assists in the development of an improved cultural analysis of poor black men. This analysis opens up a new perspective on how these men learned to read their immediate social world, and how such readings led them to make choices regarding family, school, and social relations. In brief, the relationship between life history and capital accumulation on the Near West Side reveals that deficiencies in certain forms of capital feed upon each other such that it is hard to ever begin accumulating the right kinds of capital for personal stability, much less social advancement. The importance of this deficiency cannot be overstated. Deficits in capital do not only disempower people to take action, but they also limit their capacity to imagine or construe alternative possibilities for action.

Recall the fact that so many men were told that a high school diploma itself would lead to stable and meaningful employment. Their acceptance of that idea grounded their initial approach to schooling. Part of their approach included the incapacity to realize early in life how to think beyond high school in forming an educational agenda. At school, a series of other developments (gang pressures, peer influences, etc.) also influenced how the men both approached schooling and located it in their lifeworlds. It was not that schooling was deemed unimportant. The problem was that once in school, the men had to expend all of their energy dealing with nonacademic issues such as handling violence and threats.

Family members often attempted to help by offering basic messages about the importance of schooling. Yet, as we have seen, these messages were too simplistic and did not contain more provocative ideas about how the men might overcome the formidable obstacles of their environment and better navigate their daily experiences in the school building. Indeed, some of the men found that their energy during the school day went mostly toward getting to and from school safely across gang boundaries. The challenging experiences that began in the early school years created additional difficulties for the men as they grew into adulthood.

If better sense is to be made of how and why the men acted as they did in the past, the analysis cannot rest on their presumably flawed values, but on precisely how they came to understand what opportunity is and how it should be pursued given the social and material qualities of their communities. In other words, we must focus on how interpretations of the social world and understandings of appropriate action within it are affected by social isolation. For many of these men, an effect of being socially isolated was that they could not benefit from the people and resources that could help them to better understand how their actions and beliefs would negatively affect their long-term economic well-being.

While the overarching task of this book is to convey an understanding of how these men make sense of issues and concerns about mobility, a secondary task is to make better sense of the efforts of their families. Surely, it is essential that one has a fairly clear vision of a better day in order to actually live that day at some point in one's life. Without the vision, the attainment of a goal occurs only by chance. Yet, that vision, even when fostered by parents, grandparents, and others in the family setting, is not enough to ensure that an individual can overcome the actual barriers and obstacles that stand in the way of a better life. Dreams must be supplemented with resources, or what here has been called capital. Otherwise, those dreams will eventually whither with frustration.

Traditional analyses rest on the notion that the norms and values of individuals provide the key for understanding their behavior. We have seen, however, that understanding behavior necessitates a more complex cultural approach that takes the notion of capital into account. People can share the same basic value and normative system, yet possess very different repositories of capital. They draw from those different repositories in order to understand the environment in which they function, as well as to plan courses of action in it. The concept of capital allows the researcher to better attend to issues of access to different kinds of information in order to understand why people respond as they do.

Capital is also a conceptual device that helps create a level analytical field for assessing individual and collective experiences, reactions, and behaviors. Rather than starting from the position that people have different values, and using that logic to explain what is presumed to be foreign or unwarranted behavior, we should rather view people as accumulators of capital. The accumulation process unfolds in different ways and with different consequences. Values and norms are imbued with particular meanings to individuals in conjunction with the process of capital accumulation. In other words, whatever people find to appreciate or disdain about the world around them (and whatever becomes their aspirations) are concretized out of the images and information about social life that are provided by other people. Social capital, then, precedes value formation. This does not mean that values, norms, and psychological dispositions have no significant place in the analysis of social experience. Rather, focusing on capital lends some insight into why people behave in different ways and why they develop different understandings about those around them.

As this chapter has shown, the men of the Near West Side actively made sense of their world within life histories that left them without many of the raw materials needed to prepare for upward mobility. The capacity of people to identify and interpret particular aspects of the social world has a great deal to do with where they are socially located in the first place. It also has to do with their history of social interaction and social exposure. The types of people with whom these men associated established further boundaries on their capacity to make sense of their immediate environment as well as the world beyond the Near West Side. Each man grew up in the same kind of social and cultural milieu. Each faced very similar, if not identical, structural impediments to personal mobility. For example, all of the men were faced with mounting unemployment rates from early childhood through adolescence. The lack of jobs became the norm rather than the exception. Coming up in the Near West Side, the men faced choices and options that were more pernicious than promising. More often than not, their reactions to these circumstances reinforced their already crippled prospects for advancement. Sometimes their behavior was calculated; other times it was impulsive. Almost all of the time it was detrimental to a quest to improve their life situations in their early adulthood years. The circumstances that led the men to a virtual dead-end station in life were also those that gave them whatever basis they had for conceptualizing a possible future, and for understanding how other people might do so as well.

Central to modern industrialized American society are its highly regulated and ordered patterns of daily living. People plan their work, and carefully arrange times for play around their occupations. By contrast, for many residents of the Near West Side, daily life is characterized primarily by immobility, stagnation, and idleness. It may seem like a far stretch, therefore, to have asked these men to talk about social processes and social organization in parts of American society from which they are so far removed. Nonetheless, acquiring this information is essential for understanding more deeply and fully how they conceive of mobility and opportunity in American life. Their conceptions of the social order in American society (or even whether they believe one to exist), and how they think that other Americans approach getting ahead, provide the template from which they build arguments about themselves and their personal prospects. What they do and don't perceive about American life, and what they can and can't figure out and articulate, is the foundation for how they make sense of their own future. Having lived similar lives of disadvantage and constraint, they may appear alike to those of us from other milieus. Yet, as we will see, these men think very differently about how the social world operates in terms of mobility and opportunity.

Part Three

WORLDVIEWS

Chapter Four

Framing Social Reality: Stratification and Inequality

I FIRST MET Barry one spring afternoon in 1994 when he came into the Near West Side alderman's community office. Barry was tall and lean, but not in an athletic way—lanky is a better description. He also had a haggard look on his face. I had long ago stopped thinking of this look as unusual for a twenty-four-year-old man living in this community. Barry told me his life story, all of which unfolded squarely within the boundaries of the Near West Side.

As a child Barry took very few trips downtown. Because he had no friends or family outside of the neighborhood, he had no opportunities to travel to other areas of the state or country. Barry was born in the Henry Horner Homes, attended one of the local grammar schools, and then enrolled in Crane High School. Getting to school involved no more than a short walk through certain sections of the neighborhood. We have already mentioned that Barry was determined throughout his youth to avoid associations with gang members. Like some of the other men, Barry regarded school as a safe space in the midst of what otherwise was a neighborhood full of turbulence and threats. Although he was far from a stellar achiever, high school was especially good for him because gang members left him alone:

> They [gang members] know which one ride [with one faction], which one ride [with another faction], so they just stayed to theyself. They wouldn't like recruit people, making them be in this. So we were straight there [in the school building]. They knew who they wanted to gangbang with, you know. So pretty much they didn't bother me.

Barry's narrow physical frame and shy demeanor—the haggard face notwithstanding—presented a perfect complement to his disposition toward avoiding conflict. Barry did not appear threatening in any way. Rather, he looked as though he would be more of a liability than an asset in the heat of a battle.

Barry completed high school and received a diploma. Like many young black men, he thought that military service would be an avenue toward a better life. As it turned out, he never made it into the military. Instead, Barry drifted into the drug trade during the summer after he finished high school: "What happened was that when I started using drugs I started selling drugs. And the fast money led to other shit and before I knew it I ain't never been back to school or work." It began for him, as it often does for others, as a quick way to make some pocket change. Barry explained that his desire to get into the business emerged as a result of thinking about the quality of his mother's life, and the deprivation that he experienced while growing up:

> When I was coming up I could never hardly get hardly what I wanted or didn't hardly have no money. 'Cause my mother was like, she was on aid, and then sometimes she did a little security [work]. So we, we struggled. So when I got out of high school [I thought] like, "Man I could get, you know, expensive gym shoes now and all that." It psyched, it tricked me, you know. That fast money tricked me and I regret it now.

Barry began his involvement in drug sales by doing some delivery and lookout work for other people in the business. He said that these people considered him to be a safe person on the streets, since his physical appearance and his temperament didn't draw much attention. These attributes, coupled with his increasing eagerness to get further involved in the drug business, made him an attractive recruit: "I was always around it and seeing it, and seeing what [my peers] was getting out of it, the ones that was lucky, you know. Thought I'd be lucky too and shit, like that."

In short time, Barry began his own small-scale distribution activities. He worked hard at it, operating seven days a week. For a short while he did quite well. A good day's work brought him over a thousand dollars. A bad day's work brought him no less than five hundred. In thinking about those days, he said, "It seemed like fame man, fame and fortune." He also did a good job of spending the money. "As fast as it came," he said, "as fast as it went."

Barry told me stories of how he spent his money on "women, cars, and family." He said, "It went. I wasn't selfish, definitely I wasn't selfish with it." He also said that a portion of his income went into supporting his own habit, which began shortly before he started selling the substance. Barry could not say enough about how much he enjoyed the fast life that came with selling drugs, " 'Cause like I said I went to doing drugs and working, you know, selling the stuff. And the drug thing, I liked that excitement, that tension, that's why [I did it]."

Within a year's time his career in the drug trade was over. A number of events led him to begin thinking about stepping away from the business. Finally, he was forced out:

> Well, my grandmother died, and she knew before she died I was doing it [selling drugs] and she's telling me that I wasn't going to last and that she could see

bad vibes and all that. And then when she passed it seemed like things started happening, police was, I wasn't going to jail but they was on me. And people all of a sudden want to stick me up and beat me up for the stuff. So I just stopped, you know. . . . It got violent. That's what happened.

The people in pursuit of Barry were gang members who ran more elaborate drug operations. Not being a gang member meant that Barry could not benefit from the protection and support that a gang provided. Functioning as a lone wolf kept him safe and out of trouble when he was younger, but it left him vulnerable when he was a little older and out in the streets trying to sell his wares.[1] Rather than risk getting hurt or incarcerated, he got out of the business. Barry never worked a legitimate job in the three years between his leaving the drug trade and our first meeting. Instead, he got his best meals and a place to sleep from his mother. Whenever the chance presented itself he also hustled around the neighborhood, trying to make ends meet. He appeared melancholy in assessing this phase of his life:

> The key is coming and seeing how everything is going and that ain't no future. First I wasn't even paying no attention to all of that. [It was] just, I got this money [from selling drugs]. Now I ain't got that money. . . . I wish I had never started. I know that much. . . . I didn't get nothing out of it. You know, not what I was [hoping to get]. I don't know. It just tricked me, you know. If all that [the money and the fame] wasn't there I wouldn't [have been in it]. I probably be asking you these questions that you're asking me, you know, just sitting better than what I'm doing now.

Although specific events and circumstances differ, Barry's story is replete with many of the same elements of tragedy and failure as many of the other men's. Yet, when our discussion moved away from his past and toward his vision of future mobility and opportunity, Barry's responses began to diverge from those of many of the other men who faced similar life situations. Our discussion of mobility and opportunity began with my asking him a series of questions on the role of social differences and hierarchies in American society. When I asked him if he thought that people were treated as equals in society, he said after a pause, "I don't know." After another, longer pause he said, "It don't seem like it." It became increasingly clear that Barry could not explain or interpret the same social issues that many of the other men appeared to grasp clearly. His lack of articulateness regarding the workings of society was evident from the start of our conversation on the topic. I sought to delve deeper into his thinking by asking him what made him feel the way that he did. He replied, "Because if you ain't got it, you ain't got it, you know. That ain't equal, I mean that ain't treated right. You know, that's like you ain't having a chance. . . . When you ain't nothing, you ain't got nothing. When you got something you got something, you know."

While Barry was certain that there were "haves" and "have-nots" in American life, he stopped short of stating what kinds of people fit into either category. As a black man living in urban America, I assumed that he might have something to say about race in response to my line of questioning. When I asked Barry whether he believed that race was an important social issue in American life, he said: "It ain't important. . . . To me it's within the individual in order to get along. To me it's up to the person, you know. I don't think it's a racial thing. Everything's possible, I don't think it's racial. [There are] people that will say that. [But] I believe it could be worked out."

Saying a Lot with Few Words

From the outset of my project I maintained one simple premise regarding my goal of uncovering how these men framed notions of stratification and inequality. I believed that if I simply listened to their responses to my queries, the men's understanding of the social world would become perfectly clear to me. I thought that my interviews would capture the kind of talk that occurs in their everyday lives (which had not been analyzed as systematically as it might have been, given prior researchers' predilections to look more specifically at behavior, interaction, or socialization). I also assumed that any differences between the men in outlook or perspective would come across clearly in their commentary. It turned out, however, that documenting such differences was no simple task. Many men did speak about the impact of racism and classism on the ability to get ahead in American life. However, far more men than I anticipated had little or nothing to say about these broader social issues. While aware that discrimination or disadvantage had some social import, men such as Barry could not dissect these issues, nor articulate any rich sense of how such forces shaped American society. These men had a kind of intuitive sense that discrimination existed, but they lacked the ability to explain it in any detailed way. Jason and Lester gave responses very similar to Barry's:

JASON: I think that [*pause*] I think African Americans, they have been treated unjust for a while. But I guess within time everything will straighten out.
Do you think that different groups in society get along very well or they don't get along?
[*Pause*] Well I don't really worry about it, I would just like leave it alone. What are you going to do.

LESTER: Yeah there are different groups, but ah, as far as I really don't have too much to say about, that's all, all that is basically I think is, well, politics and all that. I think it's just politics man. As far as, you know, [*pause*] everybody, they just, see I don't really know how to put it, you know.

During the first few months in the field I wondered whether something was wrong with my approach to interviewing. Was I asking the right questions? Was I somehow asking the wrong men? I found it odd that men who could talk in a matter-of-fact style about the violence, conflict, and deprivation that was a part of their past and present-day social experiences were the same who offered so little about barriers or obstacles to employment and upward mobility that came with life on the Near West Side. By the middle of my stint in the field I began to reflect more systematically about what was going on with those men who had little to say about obstacles and barriers to mobility.[2] If some had so much to say, why did others—men who also shared a life experience on the Near West Side— say so little? Eventually I came to the conclusion that there was nothing necessarily wrong with these men. Rather, what was wrong was my early conviction that words were the main avenue to discovering what people think about an issue. My experience with these men showed me that often a great deal of what people think is communicated by what they do not or cannot say. In other words, I began to take seriously the crucial role of silences and the "I don't know" response for unraveling how people make sense of aspects of the social world around them.

The "I don't know" response poses a challenge to social-scientific inquiry inasmuch as it interferes with the development of concise patterns in data coding and analysis. In survey research it is often placed in a residual category alongside other responses that have been determined to hold little or no relevance for the research initiative. In an effort to sanitize the "I don't know" responses, researchers sometimes replace every "I don't know" or blank reply with what they determine to be the average response given by respondents to a question. Other researchers conclude that the "I don't know" responses reveal that the respondents simply did not commit to any of the options presented to them.

These common methods of assessing the "I don't know" responses rarely, if ever, point to a key finding in the study at hand. Yet, I remained convinced that the "I don't know" and the silent responses revealed something of importance regarding the worldviews of a subgroup of black men from the Near West Side.[3] I eventually determined that the men who frequently uttered "I don't know" or remained silent on certain issues were illustrating the effects of their lack of consistent access and exposure to people, resources, or encounters outside of the Near West Side. What they did not encounter or experience through the course of their lives became precisely that which they found difficult to talk about. An important step toward making sense of how these men interpreted their social environment is to account for where and how they remained silent in the course of a discussion.[4] Differences in the outlooks of these men become more distinct when attention is paid not only to what they said about issues such as racism and class barriers, but also to what they did not say. The distinctions among the men appear most vivid regarding matters about which some men spoke passionately, while others did not speak at all.

Because Barry was the first of a number of men that I encountered who downplayed the social significance of race in mobility processes, I was especially intrigued by his responses. After hearing him say "I don't know" or otherwise provide very short replies to my series of questions about stratification and mobility in American life, I asked him to comment on whether he believed that he ever faced discrimination on racial grounds, and if so, what the circumstances were and what the experience felt like. "Naw," he said, "I believe you discriminate yourself man. I don't think I've been discriminated. I did that to myself" (referring to the events in his life experience). Echoing the language of the "American Dream," Barry went on to say that America was a land of opportunity because "you just try to be what you want to be, that's it." The ticket to reaching that end was "not accepting 'no,' that's all."

In short, these comments delineate Barry's theory of social organization and the means for individual upward mobility in American society. I paused for a minute to digest what Barry was saying. Before me was an African American male, a man born and reared in urban squalor and an ex–drug dealer, who had never held a legitimate job in his life. And, yet, he did not indict society for his situation. He did not lash out at the more privileged as contributors to his predicament. Instead, he maintained that his actions constituted the central cause of his present-day circumstances. He also maintained that not much beyond his own motivation stood in the way of his getting ahead.

The Effect of Social Isolation on Talking about
Stratification and Inequality

One might be tempted to stop here and draw the conclusion that, unlike many black men who share his social world, Barry made no excuses for obstacles such as racism, and took personal responsibility for his own actions. In this context, Barry's remarks seem to provide ample evidence for claims that public intervention and social support programs are misguided. Indeed, one could conclude from his words that even the most downtrodden realize that mobility is a personal matter, that little else other than personal effort has anything to do with getting ahead. However, there is another, more fruitful way of interpreting Barry's words. The best clues to this alternate interpretation are the series of "I don't know" answers and silences in response to many of my follow-up questions. In earlier parts of our conversation, Barry downplayed racism's relevance to much of what happens to people in the mobility process, without uttering "I don't know" more than once or twice. But then the "I don't know's" proliferated at the moment when I imagined that he would communicate more fully his rationale for his initial claims—by responding to questions about personal encounters having to do with race. When I asked him "Do you think you are treated fairly in society?" he paused for a moment and then said, "I guess so. I guess I'm treated fairly, I guess." I waited to see what else he might say, but nothing was forthcoming. After some gentle prodding Barry told me that he "just didn't know no white people," and that was why it was so hard for him to say more in this part of our discussion.

I moved on to issues concerning public perceptions of race. My question was, "Do you think that white society has an image of you in any way?" His reply was, "Naw, I don't think so," followed by silence. Pushing further, I asked him whether he believed that being a black man had anything to do with his own chances for getting ahead. He struggled with the question for a minute and finally said, "I don't feel like I'm recognized to them" (white people), as he shrugged his shoulders. Another lengthy pause ensued. I then asked him three more questions. The first was, "Do you think that you're in anyway at an advantage by being a black male?" After pausing a few seconds to think, Barry said, "No." Then came the second question, "Are you at a disadvantage by being a black male?" Again Barry paused for a moment and then said, "No." My third question asked, "Are there any groups that have more or fewer advantages than black men?" After pausing a little longer this time, Barry replied, "I don't know." I imagine that he was reading a puzzled look on my face, because after another couple of seconds he responded, "I really don't know no white people. That's it. That's it."

It took a moment for the gravity of Barry's replies to my queries about race perceptions to sink in. At first, I interpreted his final remark to mean that he had no close white friends or associates. I assumed that surely he must have known some white people during the course of his life. It took only a few more minutes for Barry to make it clear that he had experienced no significant encounters with whites to draw upon as a young man. Although there were times when he had money in his pocket that would have allowed him to venture outside of the neighborhood, Barry said that he always remained close to home. He claimed to socialize only with people that he knew in the neighborhood, and strictly in neighborhood establishments. He had no friends who lived beyond the Near West Side, and had only had a few scattered contacts with community figures like police, parole officers, and social service providers. In other words, Barry lived a life of extreme social isolation. His situation made much more sense to me months later, after I had heard so many other men report the same lack of interactive experience, not only with whites, but also with anyone other than the low-income African Americans that made up the communities of the Near West Side.

As if he had finally figured out something that he wanted to say earlier in our conversation but could not find a place to do so, Barry then offered, "I know it's there but I don't know what it is." He was saying something very meaningful for him, but I was not exactly sure what it might be. I discreetly responded, "What makes you feel that *it's* out there?" Barry said, "'Cause it got to be out there. It's out there. 'Cause just like the whites is having it, I mean it's out there. People that you see that's doing better than you, it's out there. It had to be out there, they, you know, they all right. It's out there."

Tables 2.2 and 2.3 succinctly convey the reality that these men rarely experienced cross-racial contacts. The comments of men such as Barry supplement these figures by revealing what this lack of contact means in terms of how the men apprehended and framed certain notions of social reality. The experience of minimal to no contact with members of other racial groups left these men without the grounds to talk about race as a social phenomenon. This explains why they followed up their initial, quite lucid, statements about race not being an important social factor, with less assured claims about how race mattered in their individual experiences. The most definitive commentary they could offer on these matters was "I don't know."

Altogether, Barry's presentation included some lengthy remarks, a few short and direct answers, some puzzled expressions, and some slightly imprecise utterances. In between these remarks were a stream of "I don't knows" and dead silences about how race operated in his personal life. These kinds of responses constituted Barry's framing of how the world works with respect to mobility processes, the structure of opportunity, and the significance (or lack thereof) of race-based and other obstacles. He conveyed his thoughts much by what he did not say, or had trouble saying, than by what he did say. Some weeks after I left the field, I looked over Barry's transcript, paying most attention to moments where he had very little to say. Reading over the other interviews with Barry's silences in mind, I realized that about one third of the men followed the same pattern and were unable to articulate a complex understanding of obstacles and barriers for mobility in American life. It became clear to me that these men's lack of access to people unlike themselves left them with very little basis for apprehending racial inequality or other forms of externally produced constraint.

Barry's life history involved extreme social isolation not only from labor markets and other institutions relevant to upward mobility, but also from some of the most mobile and connected people in his own neighborhood, such as gang members, college-bound athletes and other students, and other individuals who maintained social ties beyond neighborhood boundaries. Barry's lack of social ties denied him much-needed experience with people in different positions along the social hierarchy of American life. Barry's social world included few people other than the low-income residents of the Near West Side. These are the same people he went to school with, sold drugs to, and lived amongst. The scantiness of Barry's social networks paralleled the narrowness of his views on mobility and opportunity. Thus, it is essential to consider not only what Barry said and did not say in response to my questions, but how his life experiences shaped those responses. What is significant about Barry's comments is that they were articulated in a social context that was void of contact with more privileged people. He could not recall encountering racism or discrimination; therefore he did not blame his plight on it. He could not articulate exactly what white Americans—or more well-to-do black Americans, for that matter—thought of him because he had no experiential basis for forming an opinion on the issue.

Barry's statements alone do not prove that racism or other forms of oppression do not pose major obstacles for his life prospects. A particular power of oppressive forces is that people sometimes do not recognize them as such.[5] The point here is not to assess the validity or legitimacy of Barry's claims about the world, but to explore how they relate to the specific social contexts in which they were produced. My discussions with these men regarding race and class-based issues provoked a wide range of responses. In emphasizing the role of the individual to the exclusion of external structural factors, Barry stood at one end of the continuum representing the men's views on racial and class barriers to mobility in American life. At the other end stood the men who viewed race and class as overwhelmingly decisive in the mobility process.

Each man I interviewed made clear at some point in our discussions that equality was not a reality in American life. Some made this point in the context of lengthy expositions, others did so in only a few words. Recall that Barry was unable to articulate whether and how people got along with each other, and whether race or class were important factors in that process. He did say, however, that some whites had "it," whereas people like himself did not. All of the men argued that wealth and social status created important social distinctions. Each also implied—if at times indirectly—that skin color correlated with wealth, power, and prestige (or the lack of it).

The key difference among the men was the extent to which they could explain how hierarchies were formed and maintained, and the extent to which they saw race- and class-specific factors as part of the causal mechanisms of stratification and inequality. The differences concerning their worldviews were based upon the degree to which these men were exposed to social institutions or individuals that provided them with vivid images of social power, authority, and social hierarchies across race and class lines. These images often were accessed either by experiencing life outside of the Near West Side for a substantial amount of time, or by extensive encounters on Near West Side grounds with people who occupy positions of greater social power than the average community resident. The people in and around the community who seemingly possessed the greatest social power included civil servants, social workers, and the police. These kinds of people controlled important resources that had a direct impact on the freedom and maneuverability of these men. The more the men had direct and consistent contact with such people, the better they were able to say who had social power and influence, who did not, and most importantly, why this was the case.[6] The only other way for these men to acquire such insights was through social experiences that brought them outside of the Near West Side, where they could observe different models of social relations.[7]

The Extremely Isolated: One End of the Continuum

Like Barry, Larry led a very restricted life during his years in the Henry Horner Homes. However, Larry is much bigger and more physically developed than Barry. It came as no surprise to me, then, when Larry said that a good amount of his time as a youth was spent avoiding gang recruitment efforts. Often, he succeeded in fending off would-be attackers by getting violent with them. In fact, it was his violent encounter with a gang member that got him thrown out of Creiger High School. Ironically, perhaps, Larry's lack of association with gang members translated into a lack of prospects for forming friendship ties with neighborhood peers. Hence, like Barry, Larry did not experience much of life outside of the extended neighborhood. He had a few close friends, his three older brothers and one older sister, and occasional relations with women in the neighborhood. Like Barry's, his was a situation of reinforced social isolation. He was isolated not only from social networks of regularly employed people (true for all of the men), but also from the larger friendship or interactive circles that came from gang involvement or social ties beyond the Near West Side (and which also brought some regular interaction with police officers or other figures of authority and social power).

In our discussion about how the social structure of American society and social relations within it might affect people's access to the resources for mobility, I began by asking Larry if he felt that equality was a reality in American society. He said, "No, not really. . . . There's going to be something, there's going to be something up in there that just ain't right. There's going to be something that ain't right." I attempted to push him on his thinking about what that something was. My efforts were met with headshakes and replies along the lines of "I don't really know," and "I just can't say no more on that."

We moved onto a discussion of his position on whether equality could ever come about. He paused for a while and then said:

> Well, it depends on the way they [the powerless] feel about it, my man, you know. And maybe it's the way they carry themselves. They could make themselves equal if they wanted to be, you know. So it's up to them to be equal or not, you know. That's the way I figure, you know.

When pressed to explain whether he really felt that equality could come about, he said, "No, I don't think so. I don't know man, I just don't think so."

Larry knew full well that people occupied different places in social hierarchies. The problem was that he could not say exactly why this was the case and how it could be altered. He also knew that race was meaningful in American society. He simply had a hard time trying to specify its meaningfulness. His inability to explain precisely how race might matter in social life was matched by his difficulty in discussing how people took stock of him as a black man. At one point I asked him, "How do you think American society looks upon you as a black man?" He paused for a long time, looking as though he was struggling to find some words to say. He finally said, "Man, I really can't say man. I mean break it down to me, explain it to me right so I can understand what you're trying to say."

Searching for other words, I asked, "How do you think, you know, you are looked at by others as a black man?"

Feeling a little more secure with this phrasing, Larry said, "Oh well, as a black man, me? [*changing to a slightly more authoritative tone of voice and speaking about himself in third person*] 'Well that Larry, you know, he all right, you know.' " He went back to his normal voice and continued to speak. "I ain't no gangbanger or nothing, so they look at me like I'm not into all that, you know gangbanging and stuff like that. So they can look at me and say, 'Well that's a nice young man right there. . . .' "

Here Larry was unable to reply to a direct question about how his being African American might matter to others. He struggled with having to consider whether his racial identity had any social relevance. Little in his life had prepared him to think about these issues. This lack of experience helps to explain why he exhibited more than a little consternation over this line of questioning. He could not point to any past experiences that led him to consider the issue of race. Similarly, in responding to a question about whether he had ever encountered discrimination, Larry simply said "Nope." He said the same when asked about the extent of contact that he had with nonblacks in Chicago. He had experienced some casual contacts in the past, mostly with teachers in school, but nothing that had led him to feel that he knew much about people who did not live on the Near West Side. I closed this line of questioning by asking him what he thought the disadvantages and advantages of being a black man in American society were. He said:

> Well I'm black, I mean I can't change that jack, so, I could be down, but I mean, man. I got advantages being black man 'cause the black man can do as much as the white man can do, any man. I'm not prejudiced or nothing, you know. I mean it's all up here in your mind, if you put your mind to it you can do it. . . . [Black and white men] they all men so, just color [is the difference]. Man I'm not into no, you know, racial stuff, you know. A man is a man.

Larry and Barry are just two of the many men who encountered extremely little of the world beyond the Near West Side. The men whose lives were shaped by a similar social isolation and who responded in this manner included Jake, Joseph, Jordan, Jason, Lester, Conrad, and Butch. Each man was equally void of confidence or clarity in asserting that racism or class-based factors significantly affected America's social stratification scheme.[8] These men, who had virtually no sustained social exposure outside of their community were unable to register a strong sense of how race or other factors operate as social forces. Their commentary lacked confidence and clarity in attributing any significance to racial injustice in the processes of social stratification. The social dynamics and structure of "the neighborhood" was all that was familiar to them. Accordingly, nothing substantive was said about that unfamiliar terrain—American society at large.

Lester was the exception in this group in that he spent some time in Texas, where he went to school with Hawaiians and encountered other types of people across racial and ethnic boundaries. Lester resided there with his family for four years, living in a town near a military base. His memories of his time in Texas made it seem like a racial oasis. He said, "They ain't too prejudiced 'cause they in the service anyway. They mingling with other, you know, races."

The years spent in Texas made Lester appear to have more social integration than did the other men who fell along this end of the continuum. His interaction with people of ethnic backgrounds unlike his own clearly makes that case. However, Lester's consistent remarks about life near the military base as being a period of racial harmony and positive interaction indicate how, like the other men at this point on the continuum, he recalled no serial experiences with racial hostility or overt discrimination. Hence, although for a considerable amount of time he lived in conditions that were vastly different from those experienced by the most socially isolated men, the effect of his experience was quite similar; if he witnessed race-specific conflicts in Texas, he certainly did not see them as central to his life there, and he had no sustained interaction with legal or governmental authorities that he regarded as unfair, unjust, or discriminatory.

Other than his Texas interlude, Lester's life experiences took place almost exclusively in the Near West Side. He could recall very few stressful or conflict-ridden cross-racial encounters. Like most of the others, he had a criminal record, but not a history of regular interaction with the police. He explained that his criminal record came about not because of violent activity or conflict, but because he was in the wrong place at the wrong time. One evening, the police were doing a small-scale sweep around parts of ABLA. They were looking for some men who had looted some contents from what appeared to be an abandoned store. Although Lester said that he had nothing to do with this incident, one of the men in the group he was standing with had merchandise in his possession that matched the contents of the store. That meant that all of the men on the corner were in trouble that night.[9] This was Lester's only encounter with the police. Even his parents' problems with the law did not appear to him to have specific racial overtones. Thus, in his mind, whatever was wrong with society was due to dynamics internal to the Near West Side; he could not elaborate about social problems in a larger social context.

Lester and the other men in this subgroup understood that people in their community were not as well-to-do as were some others. They also knew that some other neighborhoods had bigger houses and provided a better quality of life. Similarly, they realized that others had more money as well as more social power and influence. What they did not know, or could not clearly articulate, was how prestige and power functioned in structuring opportunity in American life, and what role barriers and obstacles external to the individual might play.

In short, compared to the others in this study, men such as Barry, Larry, and Lester had amassed almost no social and cultural capital relevant to mobility. They had little or no involvement in venues that could have afforded them social experiences beyond the Near West Side. The men in this subgroup held fewer jobs than the other men, and, other than Lester, experienced no schooling in integrated settings. They also had little or no involvement in gangs. We have seen that gangs not only often served as a basis for some outer-community exposure, but also afforded the men vivid and up-close encounters with conflict, hierarchies, and the complex workings of power relations. Gang involvement also usually meant encounters with police officers and the penal system. Such encounters necessarily exposed the men to the external structures that shaped their lives (usually by restricting their actions). Indeed, the men most likely to encounter power differentials on a consistent basis were gang members (who experienced the greatest range of social interaction in the community), and those with more than a casual or short-term involvement in illegal activity (because they were likely to meet authority figures on a regular basis).

Conrad's views on the importance of race in American life were very similar to Larry's and Barry's. Conrad argued that different ethnic groups possessed different degrees of social power, but he could not elaborate upon how such differences were established or maintained. I asked him whether there were any groups that he thought had fewer advantages than black males. He paused, as he customarily did throughout my questioning. After about ten seconds he said:

> I don't know. I think Hispanics. I think they worse than us. They worse than black folks, you know. That's what I guess, you know, because, it's just like I guess we're all in a race or something, you know. . . . Whites, Blacks, Hispanics, it goes in that order. If you're filling out a form or something they have "white" first. . . . That's just my opinion. I don't know how it really goes, you know. I just feel like Hispanics got it worse than we do, you know what I'm saying. It's harder for them I guess than for blacks. I don't know. That's just how I feel. That's the way I see it. . . .

Conrad was cognizant of race as a salient feature in the social organization of society, but he could not elaborate further. The neighborhood was the sole social context that he could draw upon, as it was for Barry and Larry. As we know, whites were not even a minimal presence in that environment. I asked him if he thought that American society was divided into social groups in any way. After pausing he replied: "I really don't know cause as far as my life go it's right here [in the neighborhood], you know what I'm saying. I don't know."

Conrad continued to offer "I don't know" answers to many of my questions on race relations. I asked him the inverse of the earlier question on black men: did he think any groups have more advantages than black males? Getting slightly frustrated with his inability to be clear about this, even to himself, he responded, ". . . I can't tell, you know, I really haven't been nowhere to experience things like that. Like I say, I'm just here. Different groups [*pause*]. It's [*pause*]. I don't know."

Conrad's inability to discuss white Americans reflected his social distance from them. When asked to comment on any perceived differences or similarities between himself and whites, he paused for a while and then said:

> I don't know. I never hung around a group of white people before. Like I say, it, to me it seems like white people got it made, you know, better than we do. Like I say, I might be wrong. I don't know, you know. I might be wrong.

His views on the importance of race in modern life conveyed the same lack of precision and depth. When asked to assess the possible changing significance of race over the past few decades and into the future, he said:

> I think in the past it was worse than it is now. It's kind of like, it's kind of like, it ain't like it was from like the things I see on TV in the past, and hear about how racism was then. I think nowadays ain't no white person going too quick to walk up on a black person and hit them, especially from no projects. You ain't. No, uh uh, ain't nothing happening like that. . . . [In the future] I don't know. I guess it's all going to, I don't know. I can't really say about the future, you know what I'm saying. I can't say what's going to happen in the future as far as racism goes.

Twenty-five-year-old Butch spoke in a similar vein. A little taller than Barry, and thin like him, Butch was about two shades darker. Both possessed the haggard look of beaten-down men. Butch offered the following remark to the same questions about social hierarchies and the relevance of race:

> Different people [make up different social groups in American society], you know, and they got these gay people, straight people, you got all that. It's divided in such a way, it's different though, you know. Like it's just divided, you know, I can't explain.

Also in a similar vein, twenty-three-year-old Joseph had this to say about social divisions in American society:

> American society, I don't know. I don't know too much about American society. . . . I mean me, myself, like I say if they ain't bothering me I don't care. I mean gays got they group, lesbians got their group, whatever. You see what I mean? . . . No not all groups get along in society like they should. . . . No, they're not all treated equal, but I think I do believe that every human being on this earth is equal. . . . Some probably are treated worse than others, I don't know. I don't know for sure.[10]

Even the few men who could offer slightly more substantive arguments about how and why social stratification emerged focused on the neighborhood context as evidence for their claims. Lester made this clear:

[*on social divisions in American society*] Yeah it's divided. . . . Well it's divided like in the community, like this community, like everybody might be in ABLA, like it could be like Robert Taylor [*another large public housing unit, located on the south side of Chicago*] is just like ABLA, but everybody is doing their own thing in they community. Like they might have block parties over there, and we might not have block parties over here. Then they might have a softball team over there, and we might not have one over here.

When pushed to think about these issues as they pertain to American society rather than to public housing in Chicago, Lester continued his argument on the social patterns that he saw in ABLA public housing, which, in the absence of having other experiences to draw upon, became his referent for the way things happened in the rest of the country:

Yeah there are different groups, but ah, as far as I really don't have too much to say about, that's all, all that is basically I think is, well, politics and all that. I think it's just politics man. As far as, you know, [*pause*] everybody, they just, see I don't really know how to put it, you know. Everybody is thinking for themselves. And then once you're in one area you're going to try to think about that one area. You don't want to spread out. A lot of people, they don't want to, you know, they don't want to spread out and just help one another. Everybody want to be just equal in the same area, like you got this state right here, then you got this country right here, you know what I'm saying. Everybody don't have that unity like they suppose to have.

Jake shared this parochialism:

Naw I can't say nothing about that [social divisions in American society]. I don't know. You saying do I think American society is separated?. . . . You know, we [black Americans] always had it bad, you know. I mean I, it's, you know you hear things and you don't hear things, man. I try not to, you know, worry myself about that man. It's about getting yours. And I guess by getting yours you don't worry too much about what somebody else is trying to do, you know. I don't know, that's something I never did, never. I mean you hear stuff about the racial discrimination and stuff with us and everything. You know that's evident. It's going on. I don't think I have ever ran into it myself, you know. You just hear things about what other people are saying, "Well, man, it's hard over there. They won't do that." But I guess I never, maybe it did happen to me and I just didn't know it was happening, you know what I'm saying. So like that man, you know, I just, to me that's negative, all negativity man, you know.

However, Jake certainly was not totally oblivious to differences in wealth, nor did he believe that equality was a feasible prospect for the future:

Not from what I've seen man [*on the possibilities for equality*]. . . . I mean well, it's just things you could see that, you know, it's just like it can't be right or whatever, you know. But then again it does not, I try not to deal with it, you know, I mean anything that's having to do with like racial, you know, people against people, you know what I'm saying. All I see is people, man, you know what I'm saying. And I feel people ought to be people and just leave it alone. But you know, obviously you know that's not, I mean you know, I'm not in a cave or nothing, you can hear things and you can, I don't know man. You can feel certain ways of, I don't know. You hear other people talking, people that you respect talking about stuff like that, then you be like, you know, "Maybe it is going on," or "Maybe it ain't." But it's like what I'm saying is I haven't actually ran into it myself so I maybe can't elaborate on it too much about what is going on and what is happening, you know what I'm saying.

In the majority of cases the men believed that stratification existed. They knew that poor people and wealthy people led very different lives. They also usually associated black Americans with poverty and white Americans with wealth. More than anything else, though, race was used as a descriptive measure in their commentary about stratification; it was almost never talked about as a causal force. The men either had few ideas about how to explain any deeper relevance of race, or explained it as irrelevant because exposure to racial conflict was not a vivid part of their everyday lives. They did not feel secure about talking about race beyond the local context. The neighborhood was their main reference point for formulating their worldviews. However, the neighborhood experience was a limiting one inasmuch as the men had little or no meaningful inter-action with people of other races and classes. Hence, the men had few tools to understand and deconstruct the broader issues of the uses and abuses of power, and the social organization and placement of people within social hierarchies.

Some may wonder how men who grew up in a community that thirty years ago was home to one of the most visible Black Panther Party chapters in the country, and that hosted Martin Luther King during one of his cru-sades for racial and economic justice, could appear so unreflective about race in American society. One response is that the 1960s were very different times. A major difference between the 1960s and the 1990s is that the latter period saw a gradual waning of emphasis on race matters in mainstream national discourse.[11] Social organizing around racial issues became less common than in the 1960s. The 1990s also saw few, if any, politicians and mainstream figures giving legitimacy to claims about racial injustice or an

American race problem. Thus, most of these men lived without frequent and visible confrontations around race issues. In addition, there was very little public discourse about race and social inequality to help nurture their ideas about social stratification, inequality, and related issues.

The geography of the city of Chicago also served to shape the men's framing of race issues. Chapter 3 documented how physical and symbolic boundaries around the Near West Side disconnect it from other parts of the city. This geographic isolation results in curtailed access to and knowledge about jobs, and limited access to people unlike those found in the neighborhood. The radical separation of neighborhoods that leads to a lack of access or exposure to people of different racial or class backgrounds is in many ways particular to the city of Chicago. Sociologists Douglas S. Massey and Nancy Denton (1993) argue that Chicago is one of the five most racially and residentially segregated cities in America. When one takes class into account, as William Julius Wilson (1996) did, the African American poor of Chicago pretty much live in complete isolation in certain areas of the city. They must venture into other community areas to come into contact with African Americans of higher socioeconomic standing. In other cities, such as New York, black men like those in this study would probably have experienced more casual contact with people unlike themselves. For the men living in the Near West Side in the 1990s, geographical and social isolation made up the dominant social reality. This isolation meant that they were cut off from broader public discussions of racial inequities as well as grassroots mobilization efforts. This social context shaped what these men had to say, and did not say, about the role of race and other external constraints in creating social stratification and inequality.

The Marginally Connected: Making Different
Sense of Stratification and Inequality

A second subgroup of the men had more to say about race and inequality: those who had more contact with people outside of the Near West Side or with people who ventured into the community.[12] This contact with the external world was through short-term schooling experiences outside of the community (usually in predominantly white public institutions), or brief spells of employment in a workforce or neighborhood that was predominantly white or more socioeconomically secure. Their work experiences did not last long enough to provide the men with much of a basis for improving their lives. However, even short-term employment provided them with access to a wide range of people. The contact taught the men something about how people in different social and cultural milieus manage their lives. Consequently, these men spoke much more assertively about the existence of a stratification in American society; they were also more emphatic about how and why social stratification endured.

Donald worked a few odd jobs throughout his teenage years and early adulthood. His work experience included sweeping floors in restaurants and delivering packages. While the work was neither exciting nor promising, it did allow him to witness business people and other professionals going about their usual activities. He was in no position to have serious conversations with them, but he was well situated to observe them on a daily basis, an experience that the first group of men rarely, if ever, had. Donald saw these individuals sitting at tables in the restaurant, at work inside office buildings, or moving about the streets. In each of his short spells of employment he was positioned close enough to them to learn that they talked about things that he and his friends did not. He soon learned how much their social world differed from his own, and what some of its key characteristics and traits were. The biggest lesson that he learned was that the richer and more powerful acted in ways that people from the Near West Side neither did nor could. With this kind of exposure, it was no surprise that Donald did not hesitate in responding positively to a question about whether social divisions exist in American society:

> Absolutely. . . . Ah man, you can see it out here right along with racism and this and that. It's out there clear to be seen. . . . There are all types of differences, sexism, all that. It really can't be divided because they divided already. . . . Okay some have more money, some have less money. Some have better jobs, better education, so forth, so that's a dividing line right there too.

Unlike the men in the first group, Donald was not confused by questions concerning whether different groups got along in society. He maintained that the situation was, "Like a balance, some [groups] do, some don't; some want to, some don't want to."

He was equally forward in discussing social inequality:

> I'd say everybody is not like equal, but everybody has equal rights, cause you know there's always going to be somebody out here better and worse. So I don't know where the equalness comes in, but as far as educational-wise there is a possibility to be equal. You could find somebody to be equal to. [However] everybody is not going to be equal. You can be equal with the individual in the same category, but different categories, it's going to be unequal . . . that's just a shot of reality.

Donald took a more critical position regarding the equality ethic inherent in the notion of the American Dream. His exposure to varied populations, viewed from his perspective as a subordinate worker, convinced him that people had different skills and resources or else were treated differently on a number of other bases. Consequently, Donald believed that it was nonsensical to talk about equality as even remotely attainable. He elaborated on his views on social inequality, arguing that both "fair" and "unfair" social practices produced it. When asked whether social inequality was fair or unfair, Donald said, "It balances off, half and half. . . . It balances off depending on the individual and what they out there doing. It balances off."

Donald's remarks on American society reflect greater sensitivity and awareness of the matter than we saw expressed by the first group of men. Reflecting on whether true social equality could ever come about, he said, "I doubt it. . . . We'll never have full equality as long as, how can I say, as long as you're going to have a straight bias in life period, in anything." With a wide smile on his face he said, "If I could think of it [a way to create equality] I would. I'd be president!"

Gus, a high school football star in his mid-teens, an enlistee in the military in his late teens, and a cocaine addict since adolescence, expressed a similar point of view. Although Gus's addiction eventually led to the demise of his athletic career, his military and other experiences introduced him to a wide variety of places and people. Gus lived in the South following his military service. While there he hustled and sold drugs before eventually making his way back to Chicago. His exposure to different sectors of society equipped him with the insight to say quite a bit about the racial and class divides in American society:

> You know I look at it a lot of different ways. It's like the people that's doing things, the people that have jobs, nice jobs pretty much [stick together]. Most of the middle-class people stick with middle-class people, you know what I'm saying, and things like that. It's a lot of, it's not a lot of whites and blacks hanging out, you know what I'm saying. It all depends on the, to me it all depends on how much money you got or what you're doing with yourself, you know. So people in the lower class they're just living. It's separated, you know, blacks be with the blacks, whites be with the whites, you know what I'm saying, lower-class, middle-class people pretty much it all depends on the neighborhood you live in and the kind of jobs you have or where you were born. Upper-class people pretty much they just stick with the upper-class people.

Earl's story illustrates that peers who achieved some measure of success could serve as an important source of information regarding the creation of inequality and stratification in American society. A gang member in his youth who was released from prison right before our first meeting, Earl had this to say:

> All people are equal, you know what I'm saying, but in society they don't treat people like they're equal, you know what I'm saying. . . . Because I feel that

people that have got ahead, once they get ahead they feel like they've gone. They don't reach back and try to help the next man out, you know. Maybe some people that got ahead was in the same predicament that the other person was in, you know what I'm saying, they was struggling.

Earl then turned to what these dynamics meant for individuals who were at the bottom and trying to move up:

You know, you just have to have what it takes to bring about equality for yourself. I feel if you ain't got no education or no previous experience or stuff like that it's going to be, it's going to be real hard for you, you know what I'm saying, if you don't know how to go about doing it, or nobody to show you, you can always feel that the world is down on you and you're not going to be able to make a strive for yourself.

Leon's contact with the world beyond the Near West Side came about during his high school years. For two years he attended Whitney Young, one of the most academically competitive public high schools in Chicago. By his junior year he started to falter. He explained that he had begun associating with the wrong people and increasingly doing less of what he needed to in order to achieve in school. The period spent at Whitney Young, as short as it was, nonetheless gave him the opportunity to meet people whom he otherwise would never have met. His experience of social interaction is evident in his remark about whether people from different social groups get along:

If you ask me they don't, they really don't . . . because the poor feels like the rich is a snob, and the rich feel like, "the only thing you can do is, you know, I can find something for you to do for me but other than that I ain't really got no common, I ain't going to have no whole conversation with you because we got nothing in common." "I'm on this level and you're on this level," and it just don't interact. . . . All persons are created equal, but as far as being treated, no. . . .

In offering his utopian strategy for achieving equality, Leon showed that he had an understanding of how different kinds of people respond to each other:

Anything can be achieved if everybody be willing to work together as one instead of sectioning people off as black, white, this and that, rich, poor, you know, if people would stop doing that, but I'll say it can be achieved. [But] I don't think in my lifetime that it will. . . . People of all races, you know, races, different ethnics, rich, poor, you know, whatever category, it needs to get down and get together and you need to like put them together and let them just talk to each other, and you'll find out that everybody's got something in common with one another.

The other men in this subgroup offered similar arguments regarding social stratification. Like Donald, Felton had worked a few jobs outside of the neighborhood. Earlier in his life Felton believed that professional baseball would be his ticket out of the ghetto. His favorite job was working at the concessions at Wrigley Field, home of the Chicago Cubs. This was as close to professional baseball as he ever got. That experience, as well as some others, helped to frame his views on inequality and the possibilities for cohesion across social groups. He merely said, "Nope," when asked if equality existed in America. When asked to substantiate this view, he said, "I think the majority people with the good jobs are white people, and the minority is black. They'll hire just a few blacks just to keep discrimination there."

This second group of men were much more explicit about the significance of race and class in social stratification than were those of the first group. They also were decidedly more pessimistic about the future bringing about any changes in the social order. Donald's and Leon's remarks were typical:

DONALD: [*on the quality of race relations*] It's like no change. It's going to stay. Well, I don't believe it can get worse. It's just there. It's there, just like the moon. It will always be there. Not in this lifetime it won't [change].

LEON: I'll say whites have much more advantage, basically the whites, they got one half of the pie and everybody else is cutting up the other half. See, we got one big pie, white folks half, and all the minorities got to get the leftovers.

Having some experience with social worlds beyond the Near West Side, and seeing more closely the distinctions in power, prestige, and resources, these men formulated rather pessimistic opinions on mobility in American life. They placed greater emphasis on race and class as forces shaping where and how people were located in social hierarchies than did those in the first group. Moreover, they discussed more concretely the relevance of race and class in the formation of boundaries affecting access to positions of privilege.

The Provisionally Connected: The Other End of the Continuum

The last subgroup of the twenty-six men, Peter, Devin, Casey, and Ted, had the most sustained and most proximate encounters with the more privileged and powerful. Their views were quite similar to those of the men just discussed, but they expressed them with a greater intensity. Their increased exposure to social conflict (through encounters with police officers, for example) or to people in positions of greater social power or influence (through schooling experiences in significantly more privileged settings) shaped their more conflict-based view of social stratification in American society. This group of men placed race and racial antagonism at the center of their schemas of how social stratification, constraint, and inequality function in American life. Rather than associating stratification with skills and abilities, as the first group of men had done, these men viewed race and class-based factors as key. They also believed that the American social structure was sustained primarily, and intentionally, by the suppression of black Americans.

Devin's involvement in gang activities, his incarceration, and his multiple encounters with the police were by far the most extensive of all the twenty-six men. Additionally, Casey, Ted, and Peter experienced the most consistent cross-racial interaction of the entire group. A large part of their schooling took place outside of the Near West Side in institutions that they attested were vastly superior to those in the neighborhood. They also developed the strongest friendship ties with people who lived in other communities.

Casey's personal history included repeated aggressive and violent encounters with the police, as well as with white and Latino students. Casey spent four years in a high school that was much more integrated than any in the immediate neighborhood. The intensity of his fractious encounters rings loud and clear in his reply to a question about whether social divisions exist in American society:

> Hell yeah. Hell yeah. Race is the number one issue. Jobs is number two. Living quality is number three. The differences of opinion [that people have] of one another, I'm not talking about just race, I'm talking about in general, you know, that's number four. It's a lot of different reasons, man, it's a screwed up society.

Throughout our conversation Casey returned to his views on racial divisions and what they meant for the American social order. At another moment he said:

> They [whites] got the most advantages in the world, shit. They going to keep it that way. Before they lose it, man, they'd destroy this motherfucker, believe me. . . . [*Pointing back and forth between myself and himself*] I think we [black males] ranked the lowest on their list.

Ted was a close friend of Casey's. He introduced me to Casey a few days after the completion of our interview. They had been friends since early childhood and were high school classmates. Casey was a part of the group of youths that Ted met up with in order to get to grammar school safely. Ted said the following in discussing the importance of race:

If you're white it seems like you get everything to go your way. You can go anywhere you want to go and the police don't bother you. You know, the other thing is you don't get called honkey this and honkey that, but you [*referring to African Americans*] can go anywhere else it's nigger this and nigger that, even in your own community.

Peter was the most erudite of the entire group of men. A short, powerfully built young man, he spoke as if he had been reared in a middle-class African American family in the suburbs. The son of a physician, he had attended an elite private grammar school for the first few years of his formal schooling. His father suddenly abandoned the family when Peter was in the second grade. Peter's mom immediately relocated him, his brother, and two sisters to an apartment a few blocks from the Horner Homes, a few miles west of the near-downtown apartment that was his home at the time of his birth. This relocation was intended to be temporary to give the family time to stabilize itself. However, the move turned out to be permanent, and Peter's family had to live from then on in a state of severe socioeconomic disadvantage.[13] The family benefited from some financial support from relatives, which allowed Peter to attend parochial school for some of his elementary education. He said the following, speaking deliberately and patiently, when asked to comment on how social groups get along in American society:

> American society is like corporate America, a big triangle, and unless you break the mode of that triangle, American society is divided. Let me say this it's upper, upper class, upper wealthy class, upper class, upper middle, middle, lower middle, poor. . . . You're judged by your wealth in America. I don't care what your educational background is. I don't care, people say money is not everything when the fact of the matter is money is all we do. You go to school all your life but when you get out what are going to school for? Money! Money is it. Money represents power. Money represents your life, and therefore you're judged by your money. If you have a lot of money you can live in this [better] neighborhood. If you don't you can't. If you have a lot of money you can go here and buy this. If you don't you can't. If you have a lot of money people shut up and listen to you. If you don't they don't.

Devin, whose early childhood experiences were nothing like Peter's, came to a similar conclusion regarding power and the importance of social divisions in society. Devin went to a state penal institution for juvenile offenders. There, he experienced the effects of social power by being in a highly subordinate position in an institutional setting. He said:

> I figure all whites are Disciples.[14] All whites stick together, no matter what. And I know this for a fact 'cause when I was in jail a Latin Disciple and a

Latin King, both of these is white persons,[15] fought one black brother. Two different gangs, one ride up on the fifth, one ride up on the sixth.[16] They supposed to be fighting each other, but you going to pull up this black brother, 'cause both of you, white stick together. I could say that much. . . . Blacks, we got problems of our own. When we try to get education there is always someone there to knock us down or put us down. We can't go, we might put on a dress, we might put on a shirt and tie and walk up into an office, try to get a job, they look at us because of our skin is colored. "You're black, no, we don't want you. We'll call you." But a white person walk in there with a shirt and tie on, they get the job right then and there. Fuck them. You can't never have no equal rights here.

In their assessment of the opportunities for black men in contemporary American society, this last group of men provided the most lengthy and sophisticated testimonies regarding what kind of changes had occurred over time:

PETER: It's less. I think it's less. Back in the '60s it was less people going to college and more jobs. Now it's more folk going to college and less jobs. If I go to college all these years and spend all this money I should darn need a guaranteed job when I come out. But, it's no guarantees. It's no guarantees in life.

Devin amplified his earlier remarks by making the following point about black-white relations in America:

I think they [white people] look at me as the, not my people, but to the racists, they look at me like the enemy. They feel that we all blacks is out to get them. Which I believe like this here, I'm is out to get them. . . . Yes. . . . Because they getting too much money. We fight for, we fought for the United States, not them. We went to war. We got to stand up for our rights. We not getting treated right. We're not even getting equal rights.

Having lived lives that involved either the most interpersonal conflict or the most intimacy with people of high social status and wealth, it is not surprising that Ted, Casey, Peter, and Devin had the most conflict-oriented worldviews about stratification and inequality in American life.

The Special Predicament of African Americans

This chapter has emphasized the differences in the men's views of social stratification based on distinctions in their life experiences. We have seen that the men who had the most extensive external social contacts were the same ones who perceived most acutely the formative role of race and class in shaping American society. However, when it came to assessing the specific case of African Americans with respect to social stratification, the men were nearly unanimous in painting a bleak portrait. Their common perspective clearly derived from the fact that they all were reared in an overwhelming low-income, African American community. Their views were similar because they were built from the same imagery of African Americans—poor, urban-based, and disenfranchised:

DONALD: In some instances with percentages it's terrible. . . . You can see it out on the street every day. We're losing a lot of black young brothers. We're losing them everywhere. We're losing, losing, losing. . . . We just can't label all of them. Well, I ain't going to say any particular percentages but there's a lot of them, but not all of them. Not all of them.

ANTHONY: We are not looking out for one another. We're trying to hurt each other more than we is trying to help each other. If they all stick together I think we could make it.

LESTER: Like on the streets they just warring man. You can't keep killing your own black brothers and sisters man. You know, everybody wants, that's the saying now, "Well we're going to let the blacks kills theyselves." And that's what we doing, but we need to come to an agreement man, as far as all them gangs man. If all them gang members can come to agree, cause all that drug money, if they use that drug money for the community now it would be better right there. That's what I feel.

BUTCH: [Black men] is against each others, trying to, well they just against each other. They don't work together no more like they used to . . . 'cause all this fighting and stuff, killing and stuff, black on black crime, you know.

The men portrayed black men as responding in the best way possible to problematic and constraining social conditions, though perhaps not always in ways that would benefit them in the end. As the men spoke, the only area of divergent opinion was whether black men were to blame for their condition, or whether social conditions beyond the control of the individual were to blame (of course, a few of the men emphasized both perspectives). The men who experienced greater social exposure across race and class lines tended to emphasize the role of social conditions. The more socially isolated men tended to blame black men themselves for their plight; in their minds, black men largely were the creators of their own demise.

The Case of Black Women

When talking about the African American community, the men's initial reactions were extraordinarily gendered. Black women were brought into the discussion only when the men were specifically asked about them. When asked to speak about the situation of black women in particular, the men almost unanimously indicted the women for their troubled circumstances:

ARTHUR: Well, the young black woman has been trapped, double trapped, and triple trapped—trapped to believe that sex is the only way that she can get ahead and that having babies is the way to get a free check. She's double trapped because she's being pulled by the white man on one end to prostitution because the white man likes her when he's just going for money. . . . She's triple trapped because her identity has been stolen. She thinks she's a prostitute. She thinks she's a welfare queen. And she thinks that if she lives in the projects for the rest of her life she has a place to stay, she can have her children and food. . . . You know the welfare society is saying you can't get a check if you have a man, but there's only $4.50 an hour jobs for you if you ain't got no skills or no education. So what they do is they have babies and they don't have a man . . . [over time] it's a continuation of that same thing.

TRAVIS: I mean they trying to grow up too fast, they getting pregnancy. Teenaged pregnancy, man, it's a mess, man. And it's our population that it's happening to, you know what I'm saying. And people got to talk 'bout the issue, and it's okay if you want to do that just use some precaution for it. I mean you just can't jump in the bed with everybody and do this and do that and then you end up pregnant. So that's what black women, as far as the age bracket that I know, man, it's just outrageous.

DEVIN: Black womens is, they a trip. . . . Black womens nowadays they want a nigger to take care of them. I'm not the one. They'll tell you in a minute there's three things that they want, a car, money, credit cards. If you ain't got that you ain't got no chance. I'll tell you that's the God's truth. . . . Uh huh, that will never change.

CASEY: Trifling, too many kids, not enough pride, most of our mothers nowadays are between the ages of sixteen and twenty-three. It's not like it used to be, between twenty-five and forty. You don't have that leadership qualities no more. You got a girl thirty and her baby is almost seventeen. You know, no years there, no real years. They don't got no respect about themselves.

While these men were clearly also involved in creating these situations, they spoke as if black women were solely responsible. I was not so surprised to find such sexism in their orientation toward black women. The real surprise was that the only time that the men brought women into the discussion of race issues was in response to my specific questions. Gender was almost never implicated beyond casual references to the different positions men and women held in American social hierarchy. The overwhelming lack of spontaneous commentary on women reveals that the majority of the men did not view women as critical participants in mobility and opportunity schemas in American society. When asked to comment on social hierarchies and possible differences in power, prestige, and status, the men had in mind the kind of social actors that have been traditional occupants of privileged positions: men.

Conclusion

In this chapter we have entered into the minds of these men in order to explore their interpretations of power, hierarchy, and social relations across race and class lines. Rather than focusing on mental capabilities and processes relevant to making meaning (i.e., the domain of cognitive psychology), we focused instead on the content of these men's interpretations and the underlying experiential factors. We emphasized both similarities and differences in the men's views of stratification and inequality and explored how differences in personal experience connect to the kinds of interpretations offered. To approach meaning-making in this way is to undertake a project in cognitive sociology. Cognitive sociologists pay great attention to how the organization of society, and the locations of people within it, affect how individuals read and interpret their world.[17] Eviatar Zerubavel, one of the major proponents of this mode of inquiry, has explicated the underlying logic of this approach: "not only does our social environment affect how we perceive the world; it also helps determine what actually 'enters' our minds in the first place" (1997, p. 35).

Zerubavel and other scholars claim that the attempt to make sense of the world is strongly conditioned by social contexts and social experiences. As Zerubavel put it, people are members of "thought communities," such as professional or occupational groups, ethnic groups, or nations (pp. 8–9). Membership in these communities helps to create a shared focus on certain aspects of the complex social world. As members of particular communities, individuals share interests, goals, and reactions to what transpires in those communities.[18] In this respect, cognitive sociologists provide much needed attention to the importance of social landscapes for shaping the resources available for individuals to interpret the world around them. Language stands as the most essential resource; without it people cannot effectively label or speak about a particular phenomenon. Individuals experience various phenomena through social interaction and social experience, but vicarious experiences can serve the same purpose. In the latter instance, individuals can imagine or contemplate aspects of the world that they have not actually experienced. They draw conclusions or inferences by assessing them in comparison to dimensions of the world that they have encountered. Hence, poor people may develop a whole host of beliefs about wealthier people, true or not, by converting the stresses or strains that accompany life in poverty into perceptions of comfort and ease that they presume to be associated with living in wealth.

The area in which cognitive sociology has so far fallen short relates to representations of social inequality. Thus, my analytical perspective stands between the arguments of some cognitive sociologists regarding meaning-making and the framework offered by scholars who have employed survey research to document black Americans' views of social inequality (Hochschild 1995, Jackman 1994, Kluegel and Smith 1986, Schuman et al. 1997, Sears et al. 2000, Sigelman and Welch 1991). While social inequality has been underexplored by the cognitive sociologists, survey researchers do not (and given their methodological orientations, cannot) provide vivid depictions of how patterns of life history and social experience connect with worldviews or frames. The analysis offered here attempts to bridge these two analytical arenas, to allow us to explore how specific differences in life experience, all of which have unfolded within a shared social milieu of poverty, have led to ways of framing notions of stratification and inequality.

We have seen that incarceration stood as the main formal institution in which the men experienced the most extreme sense of powerlessness, and consequently in which they acquired the greatest awareness of the pervasiveness of power differences. Getting away from the Near West Side for schooling or employment provided another important avenue for encountering power and resource differentials. Both the inherently detrimental, and the potentially enriching, forms of social contact gave the men the opportunity to see and interact with people other than low-income black Americans. These opportunities brought the men some understanding of how power and influence operate, and how those with greater power and influence respond to poor black men. The men who had no sustained contact with people or places beyond the Near West Side lacked the capacity to go beyond their limited and prosaic remarks about inequality. While these men did not necessarily believe that everyone had an equal opportunity to get ahead in life, they could not specify, and in many cases could not even recognize, how external constraints factored into this process.

In conclusion, arguments about how patterns of life experience connect to interpretations of the social world are not contingent on assessing the absence or presence of any single event or condition in an individual's life. Instead, how people frame the workings of the world around them is grounded in the length or depth of immersion over time in certain social milieus and networks. Consequently, the casual or irregular contact beyond the Near West Side experienced by some of the men was not sufficient to help them see the world much differently than those who never ventured beyond its boundaries. Sustained exposure to different kinds of people and new social paradigms were what made the difference.[19] The key factor in providing the men with the capacity to express complex views on matters of stratification and inequality was the depth and length of their encounters with the world outside the neighborhood.

Chapter Five ―――――――――――――

Framing Individual Mobility and Attainment

ON ONE AFTERNOON in the summer of 1994 I sat across from Tito in the community office of the 28th Ward alderman. Dark-skinned and thin, Tito was an extremely talkative young man. Whenever he wanted to assert himself or make a special point about something in response to my questioning, he would begin by bursting out, "Yeah, yeah, yeah!. . ." followed by his commentary. Most of this occurred as he was talking about his past, which included intense periods of gangbanging, incarceration, and a very brief period of employment with a moving company. In an extremely literal sense, Tito was a survivor of the Near West Side. His left arm and parts of the left side of his upper body were peppered with large scars (little of which was shielded by his tank top). It was not uncommon for some of the men to have visibly damaged limbs, so Tito's state was not entirely surprising to me. After being in the field for a few months I also came to know that these men usually talked about their injuries (physical or emotional) as minor or ancillary details included in a response to one of my questions.

At some point in the middle of a conversation on his prospects for upward mobility, Tito explained to me that a few years ago he had been severely wounded by gunfire from an automatic rifle. The injuries that he sustained from the shooting resulted in his having surgical pins inserted into his left arm and leg. He told the story of the shooting after I asked him whether he believed there were events, situations, and circumstances in his past that might hurt his chances of getting ahead in life. Immediately upon being asked, he replied, "Yeah, yeah, yeah!" and went on to talk briefly about the shooting, which had been carried out by a member of a rival gang.

Tito was at his most talkative when discussing his own life chances. When asked a series of questions about how people in American society get ahead, however, Tito became more taciturn and reflective. He rarely began his replies to these questions with the usual refrain. Instead, he patiently replied to my first question on the matter, "Which people do you think have the best chances for getting ahead in society?" by stating, very carefully, "People with education."

"And what makes you feel that way?" I responded.

"Because these days you need education, man, if you ain't got the knowledge to do stuff you can't do it."

Thinking that this was fair enough, I moved to the other side of the issue by asking, "And which people have the worst chance?"

"People that's not trying," Tito said. "I ain't going to call nobody dumb, but people who ain't trying. How are you going to get somewhere in life if you not trying?"

In making his case even further, after being asked, "What do you think is the best way for somebody to get ahead in society today?" Tito went on to say, "Work for it. Try, try, try to strive for yourself. You know, do what you got to do. Don't be doing nothing stupid but do what's right, what you have to do."

To bring closure to this part of our dialogue I asked, "Is there anything that people have to know or do to get ahead beyond what you just said?"

He said, "You have to respect others as you want to be respected. Treat people like you want to be treated, cause that's how people are going to treat you these days. You call her a blase skippy she's going to call you one, too. And it might be a little worse. Sometime I think that's why things get all hectic."

And finally, "What do you think holds a person back from getting ahead?"

Tito said, "Himself, only himself."

I asked him what made him feel that way. He said, "Because I feel can't nobody stop you from trying to get ahead, can't nobody stop you from getting ahead if you can get ahead. It's just that you stop yourself. I think you can only stop yourself."

Tito's remarks offer an illuminating entryway into the men's overall perspective regarding individual mobility. Echoing once again the moralism of the language of individualism and the American Dream, all the men underscored individual effort and initiative as the principle driving force behind mobility. Some men supplemented their arguments by emphasizing the obstacles and barriers standing in the way of securing personal mobility. Those who could more fully describe race and class as mechanisms of stratification and inequality in American society at large also were able to articulate a more complex understanding of the processes of personal mobility and attainment. In this chapter, much as we saw in the previous chapter, we shall see that the men who were most socially and culturally isolated (from the world of work as well as from prison or gang networks) employed most extensively the language of the individual work ethic. Being the most isolated, these men were the least likely to speak of the role that external forces play in shaping one's life chances. The men with more work experience, and those who were more consistently involved in social conflicts and relations with authority figures, were much more likely to talk about the formative role of external factors facing the individual.

Endorsing the Language of the American Dream:
A Note on Method

Like many Americans, all of the men professed a belief in individual initiative as essential for successful upward mobility.[1] Like Tito, all of the men appeared to subscribe to the traditional American creed— the notion inherent in the "Protestant Ethic"—that hard work begets positive results for getting ahead. In this respect the men underscored the centrality of hard work, education, and social ties to explain how people move up the American hierarchy.[2]

I employed rank-order questions to help to unearth the men's views on these topics. My intent was to discover whether the men maintained any rank ordering of factors concerning mobility. The scale-format questioning involved ranking on a scale of 1 (extremely important) to 5 (not important) the following attributes concerning getting ahead in life: education, money in the family, racial heritage, hard work, knowing the right people, luck, neighborhood, gender, commitment to religion, and intellectual ability. Each factor was ranked independently; any or all of them conceivably could be ranked as very important or not important. The men were also asked if there was anything missing from this list that should be included. Few added anything new; the remarks they did make included things like discipline, belief in oneself, or other factors associated with hard work. Education, hard work, knowing the right people, and intellectual ability were rated 1 or 2 by virtually all of the men.

Ultimately, the rank-order questions yielded no clear patterns. In the course of our discussions, the men often said things that were not consistent with the numeric rankings they had given, or else said things that provided more clarity than did their straightforward ranking of the factors. They would also invoke some of these attributes during our open-ended discussions as being of critical importance, only to later modify, and still later re-modify, those remarks. Thus, a cautionary note must be offered about any attempt to measure precisely how committed any man was to a specific order or ranking of attributes critical for upward mobility.

Tito's remarks provide a case in point. His comments outlined at the outset of the chapter, which were made during the open-ended part of our discussion, reveal one side of his thinking on personal mobility. His answers to the closed questions, however, tell another story. Here, Tito ranked the factor "plain hard work" as a 3, whereas earlier he had placed hard work as the central factor for getting ahead. When asked to explain this inconsistency, he said, "Yeah because it can be like the most important that you're working hard. Then, on another day it ain't got to mean nothing [just] 'cause you're working hard, you know. It can go both ways."

It is important to recognize that although he ranked hard work as 3, Tito was not asserting that it was less important than the other factors. Rather, his point was that other people do not always realize how hard one is working. Thus, working hard may not generate the benefits that other, more clearly visible factors might. The distinction that Tito made in the rank-order portion of our discussion would not have been registered had he not had the chance to elaborate on his ranking. Similarly, his actual ranking would not have been an accurate indication of what he thought about hard work if we had not spoken further about the issue.[3]

It is not surprising that contradictions and inconsistencies emerge when people are given the chance to explain their answers through open-ended discussions. Contradictions and inconsistencies need not pose an insurmountable problem when trying to ascertain where people stand. Instead, we should view them as clues that help us to form a more accurate picture of people's thoughts on particular issues. Contradictions and inconsistencies are essential features of narrative (Bertaux 1981, Laslett 1991, Linde 1993). Any extended account of an individual's reactions, opinions, and interpretations of complex issues is liable to contain contradiction and inconsistency. In narrative accounts, the analyst is charged with figuring out in which ways these inconsistencies allow the individual to maintain his general worldview on a topic.[4] For example, what might appear to be inconsistent testimony concerning the importance of appropriate social contacts versus family money for mobility is less important than what conditional or circumstantial points are made about each in the course of discussing how they may be relevant for getting ahead in life.

With these methodological caveats in minds, let's return to the words of the men as they responded to questions regarding critical factors, such as education and work experience, necessary for getting ahead in American society:

LEON: [*on education*] A good education is one of the biggest assets towards a good job, because everybody wants to see some kind of paper. There was a time when you could get by with no diploma and get a good job, then a high school diploma required you to get a good job. Now you need even a four-year college or three don't guarantee you a good job today. They talking about Ph.D.'s, what Master's and Ph.D.'s them is what get you good jobs now. So once again it's already down to the point that a B.S. degree don't even help.

JAKE: [*on hard work*] I mean if you want something you should go out there and get it. You can't get nothing if you sit around and think that stuff is just going to come to you. Ain't nobody handing to you nothing on no platter, you know what I'm saying. You know, you got to go out there and work for it, man. You got to crawl before you walk anyway. You know, you can get anything you want if you're willing to get out there and work. Won't nothing come to you by sitting at home twenty-four hours a day doing nothing. [*Pointing to me*] I mean, you yourself, what do you think you can get by sitting at home? You can't get nothing man.

ARTHUR: [*on religion*] It teaches morality and how a person should relate to their fellow neighbor. Not to say that all religion is right, but not to say that all religion is wrong. There's a God in all of them, so in that particular sense I think they're all right. But in the particular sense of how a person chose to worship it's their choice. So basically, you know, I think that it does influence a person and everybody should be involved in some type of morality because that teaches you to think. Religion teaches you how to deal with self, disciplining yourself, then focusing on pushing your way through what you want to do. So I think it's a positive thing.

ANTHONY: [*on social ties*] I think it's really mostly you got to know somebody on a higher step before you can even get there and once that person knows, if you know that person that's on a higher stump he going to pull you up there with him. So if you don't know nobody higher than [you,] you ain't going to get nowhere you fast, unless you definitely do it for yourself.

What is striking when reading these men's words is the fact that each comment reflects some degree of adherence to the individualism of the ideology of the American Dream. The men referred most often to the factor of "hard work," followed by references to the importance of a "good education." Education was emphasized as a credential for granting access to opportunities as much as an indicator of skills and abilities for work. The men also spoke about the significance of social ties, particularly ties to individuals of higher socioeconomic status. Arthur's statement was one of a few that focused on religion. Most of the men argued that faith was important, but not essential, for upward mobility. In the end, we find that all of the men shared the common ground of an adherence to the traditional individualism and moralism of the standard notion of the American Dream.

Not all the men subscribed fully to the traditional formula for success in American society. Like their views on stratification and inequality, the men's views on personal mobility and attainment exist along a continuum. Whereas some men appeared almost entirely committed to the individualism and moralism of the dominant American narrative of getting ahead, other men expressed much more complex ideas about how mobility and attainment unfolded. It is useful to view these men's perspectives as comprising "co-narratives" about how people move up in American society. "Co-narrative" was a term defined by Carla O'Connor in her investigation of low-income African American high school students' views about achievement and getting ahead (1997). In the traditional model, individuals either accept or reject the socially dominant point of view; if they reject it, their alternative version of reality is called a "counter-narrative." O'Connor claims that individuals often neither fully adhere to nor fully reject "mainstream" ideologies, theories, or philosophies; instead, they modify the dominant or widely shared views on an issue with a range of additional claims, creating a co-narrative rather than a counter-narrative.

To cite one example, the traditional, mainstream narrative about getting ahead suggests that one must work hard in school and conduct oneself in accordance with institutional rules of behavior. A popular notion is that low-income students choose not to abide by this plan, arguing that such conduct is irrelevant for getting ahead.[5] Rather than producing counter-narratives about getting ahead, the students in O'Connor's study incorporated parts or all of "mainstream" arguments along with some alternative ideas about how an African American student should interact with teachers and institutional figures, and what constitutes achievement for black Americans. The point of employing the concept of co-narrative is not to imply that counter-narratives are irrelevant or nonexistent. Rather, the notion of co-narrative is crucial for deciphering worldviews that do not run directly counter to the dominant paradigms, but that nonetheless include new ideas alongside the traditional ones. With the model of the co-narrative in mind, we can now return to the men's commentary on mobility and attainment in American society.

The Extremely Isolated on Mobility and Attainment

As noted earlier, those men with the fewest social contacts and experiences beyond the Near West Side viewed personal mobility as almost entirely determined by individual effort and initiative. Their emphasis on individualism is not surprising, given that they could not articulate with clarity or depth whether and how power differentials mattered in American society. Their inability to locate any relevance for race or class distinctions in social hierarchies was matched by their inability to discuss these factors as relevant to the mobility process in America. If they could not delineate the role of discriminatory factors in stratification, then it is all the more understandable that individual-level explanations were all that could be offered for how mobility could be achieved. Barry's remarks illustrates this perspective:

[*on what it takes to move up in life*] Yeah, it's possible [if] you want to do it. . . . To me it's within the individual in order to get along. To me it's up to the person, you know. I don't think it's a racial thing. It's just what they want to do or how they accept one another, that's it. 'Cause somebody could like you and you don't like them, and you end up liking them, you know what I'm saying, so. Everything's possible, I don't think it's racial. [There are] people that will say that. I believe it could be worked out. That's what I'm saying. . . .

When asked whether anybody could get a good job, Barry said, "If they try. . . . Like I say, you just want to do it. You know you can go out and do what it take to get the good job. You know, don't stop, just go all the way. Keep trying 'til you get it."

Having already been intrigued by Barry's perspective on other matters in the course of our conversation, I did not hesitate in pushing him to explain what "going all the way" would do for a person. He said:

I don't know, I understand what you're saying. But everybody don't win. But there is still a way out of it. Something's going to change, something can work out. You can work something out some kind of way. You know, if you probably can't get up there but, you know, as long as you get somewhere you all right.

Conrad followed the same line of thinking regarding which individuals have the least chance to move up:

The people who don't want nothing, who just sit back and wait on it to come to them, you know. You ain't fitting to get ahead like that. You got to work for what you want. . . . Be determined, focused, you know, you got to be focused.

Conrad made no mention of external obstacles or barriers to personal mobility. His remarks focused entirely on individual initiative. He elaborated on what it took to get ahead by remarking, "I don't know, I hear different people say you got to know people in high places, I guess. I don't know how that go." Conrad revealed a similar lack of understanding of the role of external factors when he spoke about what holds people back from getting ahead. After a long pause following a question on that issue, he said, "I don't know, being lazy I guess, cause if you lazy ain't nothing coming to you."

Like Conrad's, Jake's vision of how mobility worked in American society was devoid of an understanding of the role of external factors such as race, class, and gender. The following is his reply to my question regarding how people get ahead:

> You got to always be optimistic, you know. Be optimistic about everything, you know what I'm saying. You never know what could happen. You go out there and make opportunities for yourself, you know, that's how you do that. Just get out, man, you know. Find out what's going on around you, you know what I'm saying. Read things, like read newspapers and stuff. Find out what's happening, look into your field and things, you know what I'm saying. Go out and talk to people, you know, cause you can find friends that got jobs, you know that's the best way to find things that are going on, to find out all kind of opportunities. You talk to people that's doing something and they probably can tell you opportunities where you can go and do this and that, you know what I'm saying, how to go about doing that and stuff . . . I don't know man. [*Long pause*] I think there's opportunity out there. . . . You just got to go get it. . . . I mean if you just stop thinking there's opportunity then I guess you're going about it the wrong way.

Perhaps many would agree with Jake's perspective. The point is not that Jake is wrong, but rather that he could not articulate a more complex understanding of how personal mobility unfolds. Jake had nothing to say about race and whether mobility worked differently for black Americans than for white Americans. He also said nothing about gender and whether men found it easier or harder to engage mobility than women. Instead, as a final comment on how people could improve their lot, Jake returned to the vocabulary of the traditional narrative shared by the more socially isolated men by saying, "hard work, plain and simple man, hard work."

Finally, Lester offered his version of the individualist logic:

> If you set that goal and that person gives you that push, then that person opens that door for you man, I feel like if I'm motivated, okay say [*pause*] say you the vice president of a big corporation. I qualify for the job. So I knew that I had to come for an interview, you know, a week ago. I'm a be motivated. I'm going over my little papers, my files, so when I speak to you I'll know just what to say, when to say it, and answer every question accordingly to the best way that I could, you know, to qualify for that job. See that way you'll motivate yourself. Once you motivate yourself can't nothing get in your way. Plus if you open the door for me, you know I feel that if you invite me in that's a good start right there, you know. As long as you know, a lot of people on interviews they might, they might, you know, tell you "Yeah okay," lose interest in you while you're talking. You know, that's when you know you're burnt up right there. When they lose interest in you man, you can count it out man because they really don't want to have nothing, to hear nothing that you got to say.

The ultimate significance of the comments of Conrad, Jake, and Lester does not lie in what the men said, much of which is both plausible and believable. Rather, the significance of their comments lies in what they did not say, and in how their framing of mobility and attainment differs from the less socially isolated men. The more socially isolated group of men did not talk about barriers or obstacles to personal mobility in any significant way. Instead, they spoke as if the world were there to be taken advantage of by any individual who could muster the requisite motivation and determination.

The Marginally Connected: Making Different Sense of Mobility and Attainment

In contrast to the socially isolated men such as Conrad, Jake, and Lester, the men whom we have identified as having greater contacts (those at the middle of the continuum) spoke more about the external constraints that often stand in the way of one's getting ahead. These men focused on the theme of class and race boundaries, and the myriad ways by which wealthier people attempt to distance themselves from the disadvantaged.[6] Even when they affirmed the dominant perspective on how to get ahead, they also noted that powerful people and certain social conditions play critical roles in affecting any individual's effort to get ahead, usually so much so that they overwhelm whatever initiative the individual adds to the situation. Leon voiced this perspective:

> I'll say you can go from a poor to a middle class, but when it comes from middle class to rich that's a whole different ball game there, because most of the time the rich is going to stay the rich. Even if you do get into their category they still won't accept you because you came from the poor. It's like you're still unacceptable in that type of society. I can give you an instance like Mike Tyson, now even though he's made all these millions of dollars his attitude is from a poor standard and in a way he still carried on as if he still had nothing. I don't care what he was able to buy, his attitude was still like a person that was an uneducated person. It's like, "Hey, I made all this money," but to them he's still as dumb as a person that's walking these streets and still ain't got nothing.

Leon explained that judgments made by others serve as a powerful force impacting any individual's quest to move up the social hierarchy. Unlike men such as Larry, who did not talk about how he might be viewed negatively by those with more socioeconomic resources, Leon stressed the important role that differences in wealth and status play in mobility process. He continued by arguing that the best one could do was try to improve one's lot in life, and accrue whatever may come from that effort:

Go to school and get you a good education, that's the number one. The best strategy, like I say, it's gotten down to the point of who you know, but just be willing to work hard for what you want. That's all I can come up with as far as strategy. Just work good hard work, good hard work. Be willing to dedicate yourself to what you want to do with your life.

Leon also said the following when he was asked if there was anything else that people must know or do in order to get ahead:

Well I don't like to use this phrase but a lot of people can kiss people's behind to get ahead in life. If I want to get to this level I know I got to kiss his behind in order to get there so some people will do that just to try to reach the top, but I don't advise that that's the right way to go because that very rarely last long.

Leon's discussion of what factors might hold people back from getting ahead reveals his greater awareness of holes in the individualistic ethic of the American Dream subscribed to by many of the other men:

They say you got to be your best but get to know different ethnic groups, you know, cause you find out that people are people if you just take the time out to get to know them. But if you confine yourself to your one group then when you come across these different other nationalities, I mean, you know, ethnic groups, and they say something . . . you can take that and blow it all out of proportion because you really don't understand what they referring to.

Leon started out at one of Chicago's most competitive public high schools and eventually flunked out. During his high school years he was exposed to members of a variety of cultures and ethnic groups. Many of these peers were highly competitive academic achievers. Exposure to these wide-ranging social differences created a referential basis for Leon to make his arguments about mobility and attainment. His unique social exposure, in contrast to the social isolation of some of the other men, helped him to form very clear opinions on who controlled mobility processes in the United States:

Well it's always white folks have the best chance for getting ahead because see the way society is, at least here in Chicago. it's not what you know, it's who you know. If I know somebody that's sitting there on top I almost ain't got to know nothing and be white. I just got to know that person and they going to pull me right to the front door, you know.

Men like Leon also were more prone to think a bit more critically about how the well-to-do viewed the less fortunate. Regarding which individuals faced the greatest challenges in getting ahead, Leon remarked:

People with no education, no knowledge of the job market, and who don't know anybody have little or no chance of getting ahead in life unless they willing to take initiative on their own and create something. . . . You see, money don't make the person, see, some people just can't get ahead because they just don't have it, you know. So life keeps kicking them down and then they get to the point where they figure this is where I belong, you know.

More socially exposed men like Leon provided richer analytical frameworks about how the social world operated. Their broader perspective allowed them to speak about societal processes rather than limiting their comments to the frame of their own personal experiences. Donald, a former restaurant worker, provides a good example of this broader perspective in his comment that "Yeah, there's always a way [to move up in society]. . . . Most people try to change their friends, their acquaintances, where they live, the people they be around." As basic as Donald's remarks may seem, one only needs to compare them to the comments made by the first group of men to grasp the extent to which Donald focused on social rather than individual-level dynamics to make his point.

When talking about mobility and attainment all of the men in the second group consistently contrasted their situation to that of other groups in American society. As busboys in restaurants, clerks in fast food establishments, or convicts in the penal system, these men saw how different types of people conducted their everyday lives. These experiences gave them a vantage point to interpret the differences in social functioning between the more and less privileged. They also came to understand better exactly how the more privileged created and made use of distancing mechanisms to preserve space between themselves and the poor.

The Provisionally Connected on Mobility and Attainment

The group of men with the greatest awareness of the complexity of the processes of mobility and attainment in American society were those with the most extensive contacts beyond the neighborhood. Casey and Ted went to high school beyond the northern border of the Near West Side. While Latinos predominated at their school, they also encountered white students. Their ethnically diverse schooling experiences differed dramatically from those of most of the other men. Consequently, these men's views of the social world were very different from what we have seen so far. Casey also had multiple run-ins with the police due to his forays into drug dealing and substance abuse. He continually emphasized race during our discussions of mobility:

You have to work hard. You've got to be willing to step on feet. You got to be willing to take whatever opportunities come about, whether they be legitimate or whether they be illegal, to get ahead. I'm not talking about selling no drugs.

I'm talking about, well, if I can do certain things that would terminate this object to get away from me, or not to compete with me, just to get to my next step, then you do. They [whites] been doing it for years. . . . They [blacks] have to know where they, they have to know where they came from. . . . If I'm the same color of him this is what I got to do to get what he was at, you know what I mean? Experience, you know, you look at other people for strength in your experiences, whether they white, black, blue, grey, I don't care. You look at what they went through to obtain whatever you want to obtain if it's in that particular vicinity, you know. If you want to obtain what he obtained, you have to do what he did to get it, no matter what it was. But if you don't have them opportunities, you have to be dirty. . . . Opportunities, if you don't have the opportunity to do something you can't get it. You can't make it happen. You can't force it to happen. It has to be an opportunity. You have to, you know, somebody has to say, "Well, hey man, we got an opportunity to unite, to start a softball team." Whatever, you got to have the opportunity.

Similarly, Peter's experiences with people of privilege and high status helped him to learn precisely the extent to which the elite can affect the mobility outcomes of others:

What a [less well off] man needs to do is change his ways. If a man would consider his ways and understand, here again, getting an understanding why is this system like this. This is a system. This stuff [mobility processes] is institutionalized. It's a system and understanding the rules [is what matters].

Peter's argument about mobility seemed to be drawn from what he was exposed to in his early years:

Information and environment, the two things I believe really hold people back because you can be in an environment but that environment does not have to be in you. And a lot of it going to be, a lot of the fault lies in the parents because you're suppose to train your child. You're suppose to show your child. You might not have all the money, but you can surely walk through a wealthy neighborhood and certainly show them wealth. You can certainly walk through a wealthy neighborhood and show them wealth. . . . But they've got to be shown. If you don't see better how will you ever know that there is something better? How would you ever have a desire to be better or to do better if you've never seen better? I got a desire to do better and want better because I've *seen* better.

Some of the effect of "seeing better" was that Peter grasped the reality that the powerful get even further ahead than everybody else:

It boils down to this, who do you know. White folk get ahead because their parents know people that own companies. Their parents own a company. . . . White folks have the best chance, the best opportunity. Why? They run the country. . . . White people definitely have the best chance of getting ahead because their families stay together. Number one their families stay together. Number two they invest in, they believe in not working for others. They believe in working for their own self. And that's something that blacks got to get. We got problems internally, but a lot of those problems have been perpetrated and have been perpetuated by white folks.

Working from a similar logic, Devin said that it took "money, power, knowing someone, basically knowing someone," to get ahead in life. His perspective was clearly informed by his lengthy history of directly confronting and interacting with authority figures throughout his life. Like others in this subgroup, Devin's co-narrative included more than just references to the hard work ethic. He added, "School smarts are good but street smarts are the best. . . . That's where you're pressing hard. Can't no one beat you out of anything."

Devin's remarks about the virtues of street smarts were closely associated with his sentiments about race and social mobility:

Blacks are smarter than whites. Blacks learn from experience. Whites didn't. Whites, they can get a job 'cause they know someone. A black person, I bet you can't pay a white person to fix a car because they don't know nothing they're doing. They got to pay thirteen hundred dollars just to go to the school to try to learn when you could have the education by looking, listening, and learning, and watching another person.

As was the case with their views on stratification and inequality, the men fell into three subgroups regarding their views on the topic of mobility in American society. The first group of men, the most socially isolated, maintained a strong individualistic orientation. These men did not have the experience or the tools to locate and interpret the broader social forces and structures that affect how people interact and move up the social ladder. The second set of men incorporated racial and class-based issues in their vision of how people move ahead in society. These men also more readily invoked the importance of establishing social ties and securing certain credentials. Most importantly, these men were more articulate about the barriers and obstacles that impede mobility. The final group of men appeared the most committed to conflict-based understandings of how mobility operates. They were more keenly aware of oppression, and brought this factor into the discussion more often than did the other men. Their talk emphasized aggressive maneuvering and defense of personal and collective interests. They never spoke about black and white Americans as being in anything but a continual state of social conflict. They also saw the rich and poor in a continual state of conflict. These men held that in order to engage mobility from a subordinate position one had to consciously and assertively confront power and status differentials in a warlike fashion.

Mobility and Attainment in the World of Work

So far we have seen that men who shared the same general state of disadvantage nonetheless expressed themselves very differently when pressed to comment about certain features of the social world. The determining factor separating the men's views had to do with the degree of social contact and exposure they had experienced in their lives. While some areas of inquiry brought forth stark contrasts, the men were all in agreement when discussing mobility and attainment in the world of work. While some of the men had direct experience with the penal system, gang membership, or schooling in more integrated settings, all of the men were equally removed from and unfamiliar with the institutional setting of the world of employment. Because the men shared the same status of chronically unemployed adults, their interpretations of this sphere of life are remarkably consistent. Joseph's response when asked about how people go about finding work is typical for those men with the least work experience:

> If you know a place that's applying, taking applications for secretary, and you know you can't type twenty-five words a minute, but you can type some words within a minute's time, I mean what is it going to hurt to go fill out that application. Nine times out of ten you might get the job. They might say, "Well look, we'll find someone to do the typing," or the boss might be able to type better than you. He do his own typing and you could do the rest of the work. See, just do it. That's what I mean.

Joseph's understanding of the world of work is obviously woefully inadequate. Despite the certainty in his tone of voice, even a cursory reading of his words renders his comments absurd. Joseph has held two full-time jobs in his life, as a message courier and as a worker at a McDonald's restaurant near his home. Neither job lasted more than a few months. He left the first job for the second, and quit the second in order to enroll in a training program for security work. Unfortunately, the school that sponsored the program went bankrupt while he was enrolled. The absence of consistent ties to employment prevented Joseph from developing a sufficient understanding of employer-employee relations or a realistic assessment of requirements for employment. His comments reflect the thinking of most of the other men on the topic of employment. These views on finding work convey misguided notions of how the world of work actually operates. More specifically, the men seem unaware of how prospective employees are evaluated and on what basis duties are assigned in the workplace.

Most people have, at best, only a partial understanding of the socioeconomic structures that shape their lives. As victims of chronic unemployment, the men in this study understood even less about the world of work than most people who work consistently. However, they were not com-

pletely oblivious to certain aspects of the modern world of work. Consequently, they knew that finding work was harder for them than for men
of earlier times:

TRAVIS: I think it's more harder now, 'cause I know there is a lot of
           people that's unemployed. I think it's kind of hard now [in
           comparison to the past]. [In the past] as far as my family,
           everybody I knew in my family—as far as aunties, uncles—
           everybody was employed. . . . A lot of people that I've been
           involved with or talk to, they, you know, are looking for a
           job or trying to get a job, or trying to get a better job.

TITO: I think there's less [employment opportunity in Chicago]. . . .
           It's less because it's not, it's like the jobs that was out here
           back in the days . . . because in those days you could be like,
           you could be so much. You could be this or you could be
           that, and get a job easy. But like now, these days, I think you
           need a high school diploma to be a garbage man, you know,
           to be driving out there.

JOSEPH: Ain't no reason nobody should be unemployed, but they say
           they don't have enough jobs for everybody, so. I mean they
           steady building stuff so quit having people come from the sub-
           urbs to the city and working. I mean they making all the city
           money, and they way out in the suburbs. It don't make sense.

It is evident that most of the men could not grasp, much less explain
the reasons behind changes in the employment sector. They displayed only
a vague recognition that changes in the past several decades meant that
their situation was much worse than that of the previous generation.
Some of the men offered more critical commentary about the quality of
inner-city employment, stating, for example, that black Americans in the
city had always been at a severe disadvantage in terms employment. However, such critical perspectives were rarely linked to strategies formulated
to overcome these constraints in order to secure employment.

Some men were convinced that the job situation in the past was better
than that which they confronted. Jordan was such a case. He spent much
of his everyday time associating with people in ABLA's community center,
and he seemed to particularly enjoy conversing with visitors to the facility.
His remarks typified the views of many of the men regarding the increasing need for credentials in order to secure employment in the modern
urban community. As accurate as he may have been, his history of chronic
unemployment left him only partially able to delineate effective strategies
for confronting these new conditions:

There used to be a time, they used to tell you you couldn't sweep a floor, you
couldn't get a job without a high school diploma. Now they tell you you have

to go to school to get a bachelor's degree. Now you have to get a higher degree. And after that you still have to go to school for more, more, more, training. And as you look back on all that money you been spending, all that training you can get, there's still nothing out there at all. Every year they tell you, "Well the market is going up. You need this. You need that. You need this. You need that." And then you're steadily going to school, then the more older you get, and then you get out and apply for such and such a job, and certain jobs ain't out there. And then you're still stuck with that loan. If you don't find a job you're still stuck with it. That's a good way to mess up your credit, and your credit gets messed up the rest of your life. . . . So, therefore, when you get your diploma, your degree, that doesn't mean that job is open in that field, and you're stuck with a piece of paper and you'll be stuck with nothing but the bills still hanging over your head. But they don't tell you that. . . .

Jordan went on to speak of the irrelevance of pursuing higher education given these conditions. His life experience left him unable to identify, or even conceive of, many people who pursued higher education and overcame the dilemmas he described. He had no close friends who had attended, much less graduated from, college. When asked to explain the origin of his views about the value of a college education, he replied that he developed his views from conversations with others in the neighborhood. His remarks indicate the extent to which he and others who shared his views lacked an appropriate vantage point from which to make sense of the employment context in Chicago. While he accurately assessed the increasing importance of academic credentials for access to jobs, he had no awareness of the utility of other aspects of a college education for overcoming barriers to upward mobility.

Jordan is similar to the other men in that his interpretations of the world of work are only partially accurate. Like most of the other men, he could make sense of what was immediately apparent, such as the current requirement of academic credentials for jobs that historically had been available to low-income black men in Chicago. However, he could not decipher the general usefulness of resources such as a higher education for getting ahead in life. In other words, the arenas of life that were neither visible nor accessible to these men (e.g., higher education, skilled labor markets) are precisely those that are most significant for upward mobility in contemporary American society.

While the men knew that academic credentials were of growing importance for accessing even minimally skilled jobs, they remained unaware of other recent developments that shaped their prospects for employment. For instance, many of the men spoke of the increasing importance of technology in the employment sector. For them, the term "technology" meant anything that had to do with the increased mechanization of the workplace. But even the basic developments concerning technological advances in the workplace were foreign to them. Once again, their uninformed discussion of technology conveyed the extent to which their absence from the world of work affected their ability to form accurate interpretations. Jason said the following when discussing the impact of technology on employment opportunities:

> Everybody's going to be the same. . . . It's going to be like first come first serve. That's what things are going to be like. . . . 'Cause the way technology is going, there's more pushing like, everything will be computerized, you know terminals and stuff like that. People will be competing for the same job and you happen to show up a little later and I show up a little earlier I get your job. I think it's going to be more like that. For the person that comes and is eager to work they going to give the job to them.

Gus, a former high school all-city football player, commented:

> Technology has changed and everything, things have changed and all, the more you're willing to work at it the more you have to work with now. They're spending a lot of money on things that are going to help make a difference. All you got to do is want to make a difference.

Only a few of the men displayed even the slightest awareness that such technological advances might ultimately serve to lessen the employment chances of the disadvantaged. Larry's comment hints at the connection between technology and race:

> I think there's less man, you know [of a chance to find work given the rise in technology] . . . because, see, back in the early days it was like easy, but nowadays, man, things are run by computers and all that, man.

These men understood that technological change was important, but most had little inkling as to why. Most of them continued to fit the issue of technology into the framework of the individualism of the American Dream narrative, arguing that individual skill and motivation would override factors such as one's public appearance or social ties in the determination of who gets hired. Needless to say, the evidence of Chicago-area employers' negative attitudes toward hiring black men indicates that the men's optimistic perspective is entirely unrealistic (Holzer 1996; Kirschenmann and Neckerman 1991; Moss and Tilly 2001; Neckerman and Kirschenmann 1991; O'Connor, Tilly, and Bobo 2000). Research has shown that black men are still seen as a liability to a productive workplace. Hence, their racial background makes a stronger statement about their suitability for employment than does their possession of work-related skills. Unfortunately, most of the men I interviewed were not fully cognizant of how much being black men would remain a handicap for employment.

Conclusion

The intent of this chapter has been to encourage rethinking about how low-income black men make sense of mobility and attainment in American society. Our exploration of the men's views on these issues has raised some important points regarding how we can help improve their prospects for advancement. The men of the Near West Side framed their responses to my queries in terms of what they had actually experienced, or imagined, about the world around them. One's imagination is itself preconditioned by firsthand experience. Hence, the men's ability to imagine much about the distant aspects of the social world was circumscribed by what they experienced.

An outsider's conception of inner-city black men navigating a resource-diminished, blighted urban landscape is only a superficial depiction of the reality of their lives. In order to take the next crucial step toward understanding the lives of these men, we must attempt to discern exactly how these individuals describe, interpret, and feel about particular aspects of their experiences. Once we step beyond the superficial level of understanding, we find a great diversity in the men's patterns of interpretation. The men may all suffer from socioeconomic disadvantage, but the fusion of different aspects of that disadvantage with particular life experiences fosters radically different ways of thinking about the world that they inhabit.

Broadly speaking, we have seen that all of the men subscribed to the traditional American ideology of individualism with respect to what it takes to get ahead in American society. As the political scientist Jennifer Hochschild (1995) has argued, many Americans, regardless of their social station in life, adhere to this construct. In the discussions with the men presented in this chapter, it is clear that this traditional ideology is altered by different kinds of life experience. The absence of broader social experiences and encounters left many of the men with little other than the dominant ideology for figuring out the way the world works. The men with broader social exposure garnered the cognitive material for supplementing the dominant ideology with a range of additional ideas about mobility, opportunity, stratification, and inequality.

In this chapter I was concerned with exploring certain aspects of the social world that were not greatly visible to these men, but that nonetheless have great bearing on their lives (demands and expectations of employers, transformations in different labor market sectors, etc.). The men's comments on these broader social issues provides a context for understanding how low-income black men make sense of the structures and processes in their immediate environment inasmuch as they reveal how this immediate locale shapes the men's capacity for comprehending the larger world.

The lack of attention to such matters in the public dialogue about black men stems from a preoccupation with terms like "underclass," which encourage a narrow vision of who poor people are and how they think about their situations. Concepts like underclass draw attention to public behavior to the exclusion of the critical realm of thought processes and how intersubjective and shared systems of thought are formed. The analysis of the men's comments on mobility and attainment offered here reveals that different orientations emerge out of the same social context. There is no doubt that these men face very similar social conditions on the Near West Side. Yet, we have seen that they offered diverse responses to queries about personal mobility and the world of work. The key variable that shaped the men's different perspectives is the degree of social contact they experienced beyond the boundaries of the immediate neighborhood. Those men who were the most socially isolated drew most heavily on the individualistic and moralistic language of the traditional narrative of the American Dream. Those men who had the greatest exposure to the outside world, whether through schooling, work, or incarceration, were most likely to frame the world, and hence their own opportunities, in terms of conflict and oppression.

We have explored how these men framed certain parts of the social world in which they lived. The next two chapters turn to a more precise examination of how they located themselves in that world and how they personally came to terms with the obstacles or barriers that they saw as part of it.

Chapter Six

Looking Up from Below: Framing Personal Reality

If I could get away from the projects you know, maybe it could come true man, you know. If I get away from the projects, man, get away from around them, my friends, you know. I mean I ain't downing them man, but, you know, in a way they is bringing me down too. . . . Man, I don't want to go down man. I definitely don't want to go down. . . . Well, the good life for me man, just like I said, get out the projects. I mean that right there is something like a dream man, like I could talk about it but I know it ain't going to come true, man. I would probably want a lot man, swimming pool, big old house, backyard man, you know.

These words reveal Larry's vision of a better life. His remarks, however, make no mention of the particular kinds of jobs that might act as a springboard to this kind of life. Larry mentioned employment only after I asked him directly about the kind of job that he hoped to be doing in five to ten years; he then spoke in general terms about the possibility of a unionized job with the city of Chicago. His comment about unionized work capped our discussion of his personal hopes and dreams, his failures, his views on job opportunities in Chicago, the resources necessary for finding work, and the skills and abilities needed for effective performance in the world of work.

Talking about the Good Life

About half of the men's visions of an ideal future looked a lot like Larry's. Rather than talking about substantial personal wealth or luxurious homes surrounded by white picket fences, they focused on finding stability and basic comfort. Their remarks centered on three spheres of life: work, home, and individual well-being. Like Larry, the men rarely elaborated upon the nature of the job that they hoped to acquire. Instead, they simply hoped to get whatever fit their definition of a well-paying job.

Having lived without stable work, the men's vision of a satisfying future centered on what were common realities to many people who go to work every day—a sense of freedom and maneuverability, some material acquisitions, and a steady, suitable income. Life did not have to be perfect;

it simply had to offer those things that were currently unavailable. Donald put it plainly in discussing the kind of work that would help him to attain his idea of the good life: "Anything reasonable, you know, that I can make some money at, nothing in particular, you know. Nothing under-down or nothing like that, but just something I can, you know, survive on."

Travis described has desire simply:

> Just to be living man, just to survive without no heartache. I hate to just struggle man. I just hate to struggle. It's happening to me man, you know what I'm saying, but I didn't thought, growing up I didn't never thought it would be this way, but, you know, I'm experiencing this, you know. It's hard man. . . . 'Cause I know there's much more than this, that's how I'm living now. There's got to be more than this.

And finally, Barry said:

> I just want to become able, stable, with a life, you know, a good life. I just want to work man. I just want to work. . . . Yeah I just want to get in and get out, you know. That's it for me, get in and get out. . . . Whatever it takes to live, you know, do it and go on, you know, go on about my business and be set, you know.

Some men did speak much more directly about desiring a particular kind of work situation. Arthur was a recovered substance abuser and an occasional volunteer at the 28th Ward's alderman's office when our paths first intersected. His life story involved doing a little hustling in addition to a fare amount of drugs. His mother had abandoned him when he was a child, leaving him at the age of fourteen to be raised by his uncle. Despite his ordeals, Arthur had not given up on himself. His past difficulties did not stop him from taking advantage of whatever small opportunities came up at the Western Avenue alderman's office to earn some pocket money. When asked about where he hoped to be in the future, he said:

> Whatever God plans for me to do [is what I'll do], but basically own my own business, a shipping business, shipping things overseas. That's what Onassis did, I think. And UPS, that's how they got started. Onassis concentrated on shipping and he just used a boat. And another thing is getting into the music industry like being a concert promoter or something like that. And another thing is opening up a small business. So one of those three things I know I'm a get a chance to do.

Arthur believed that one of these outcomes was possible for him because, as he explained, he was very attentive to how small businesses were run in his community. He told me, "I'm also doing research right now on small businesses, you know. I do things on the side, like I worked for a liquor store and I see how they run the store."

Arthur explained that his work for the liquor store involved running some small errands—nothing that ever amounted to a steady long-term job. While talking about his entrepreneurial agenda Arthur was unable to outline a more detailed plan about how he would take steps to become a successful business owner given his current financial situation. When asked to elaborate on how he would make his dreams come true, he offered, "I'm a hard worker, I'm diligent, and I'm consistent, and I do that on a daily basis because I believe that there is no tomorrow."

Joseph sounded a lot like Arthur:

> The career that I would like to have, it's a . . . it's kind of hard to explain. I want to be the owner of an import-export business. . . . I want to be the owner because I want an office of my own so I could take care of my own business. If I feel like I could just sit down there I can. . . . That's where the money's at, or either stocks and bonds.

I asked Joseph about how he determined these life goals. He said that importing and exporting goods is "where the money is at," and that one could see this from thinking about how many things in the United States were made in other places. He also said that stock and bonds have much to do with the companies that are making these goods, and getting into them would be another means of obtaining some of the money being made in America. These vague ideas comprised the entirety of his explanation of how he would put his plan together. He was unable to say anything more about how he would achieve his goals.

Peter, who also thought about business ownership, offered a little more detail. Still, his remarks reveal that, much like the other men, he had not spent much time figuring out the steps needed to implement his plan. In other words, the intensity of his commitment to business ownership was not matched by a depth of understanding of what might help him to achieve this goal:

> I want to go back to work. I want my own business in mechanics, and I have to find a solid job. I don't necessarily want to go through the rigmarole of prerequisites. I want to get my certification.

You may recall that Peter spent one term in college in the South. Given this experience, one might assume that he was interested in acquiring as much education as possible to help him reach his goal. However, Peter went on to explain that most higher education is a waste of time:

> I think education is just cluttering your head with a bunch of stuff. . . . If you've not gotten it by high school you're not going to get it in two years or four years of high school crammed in two years [of college]. . . . Just to generate revenue, that is the first two years of college.

To further his argument he gave the following example:

> If I'm going to be a social worker what do I need with math? I know how to
> add, subtract, multiply, and divide. What do I need with calculus? What do I
> need with tangents? What do I need with this stuff? It's not related.

Showing that he had no time for things that did not make sense to him,
Peter concluded his argument by talking about people known to him who
found financial success and security without much formal schooling:

> I know a lot of people who have no degrees who have not even stepped foot in
> an institution but they make $50,000 a year. Why is this? I don't understand
> it. And then I began to understand that as long as a man is subject to another
> man or has no vision, he'll work for a man that has a vision. And that's why I
> want to be self-employed. I don't want to work for anybody. I want my own
> economic base.

The approaches to business ownership expressed by men such as Peter,
Joseph, and Arthur reveal glaring inadequacies. Arthur could not elaborate on what he had actually learned at the liquor store that had anything
to do with developing a business plan. Joseph said little other than that
you have to "read up on things" and pay attention to what is going on
in order to pursue your long-term plans. Finally, Peter dismissed out of
hand the role that additional education might play in assisting him in
working toward business ownership. Rather than focusing on the practi-
calities, Peter could not get beyond dreaming about what achieving this
goal would do for his emotional state of being, which was one of dire
frustration with the quality of his life. In each case, the men's words rarely
delved into the circumstances, goals, or objectives specifically connected
to the industries and business sectors of interest to them. It became clear
that they had little insight into specific models of business activities and
practices. Even rudimentary ideas about market research or financial capital accumulation escaped their understanding.

Undoubtedly, their distance from the world of work was a factor in their
inability to provide more depth to their statements. Peter was the only man
who specified the business—mechanics—that interested him. Arthur and
Joseph never mentioned a specific kind of business, but spoke in general
terms about a variety of businesses. In all cases the men's sights were set
far beyond a realistic goal given their lack of resources or precise plans for
starting a business. What appeared to be most important to all of the men
was the status of being a business owner. They appeared attracted to the
autonomy, power, and economic prosperity associated with that status. In
other words, what attracted them to the idea of becoming a business owner
was the social standing it would grant them in the community. As Conrad
put it when talking about his desire to own a construction company:

I ain't got nobody looking over my shoulder trying to tell me how to do it. I can take my timing and do it right, you know what I'm saying. And, you know, I could be my own man, so [why not go for it]?

Conrad's words alone do not convey what his intense and earnest facial expression revealed about his deep appreciation for what he viewed as the prime benefits of business ownership—personal freedom and control.[1] The good life for these men meant achieving the opposite of what they experienced in their everyday lives: a sense of autonomy, power, and material comfort. The avenue they imagined would lead them to these goals was business ownership. Thus, talk about business ownership was not so much a discussion of tangible objectives as much as it was a statement of what was missing in their lives.[2] When taking into account the men's chronic state of unemployment, it is not surprising that the image of the ideal job outlined by these men was not matched by an understanding of the prerequisites for attaining it. Experiencing a life without work might lead one to talk quite specifically about certain career niches, such as owning a business, as a life goal, or it might lead one to focus on more realistic, incremental improvements in one's life situation. Although the two orientations appear very different at the surface level, they are, in fact, products of the same life circumstances.

The fact that some men strove for little more than daily stability while others focused upon far-reaching interests in business ownership and entrepreneurial ventures is one of a wide-ranging set of issues concerning how they thought about their own future. The aim of this chapter is to define and explicate such issues and concerns. We begin with some commonly noted ideas about the life goals and desires of low-income African Americans, which have been articulated quite thoroughly in contemporary research on this population.[3] In short, low-income African Americans want to work at jobs that pay wages that would allow them to sustain their families. They desire appropriate living quarters for their families. Furthermore, they want benefits and rewards for doing good work. They also would like the chance to move up, and to enable their children to move up at least one step ahead of them when they become adults.

While this is the common ground of thinking for many low-income African American men, a wide range and variation in views can be found when their thoughts about the future are unpacked and reclassified according to how the good life is defined, and how aspirations, expectations, probabilities, and possibilities are expressed. These terms point to distinct, but closely related, categories of future-oriented thinking. For instance, comments about the good life illustrate what these men regarded as ideal life circumstances, or the most grandiose of their future visions.

These comments reflect the upper boundary of their future-oriented thinking. Consequently, whatever is not found in expressions of ideal circumstances surely will not be evident in conversations about aspirations, expectations, probabilities, and possibilities. Accordingly, if the ideal is
talked about solely in terms of achieving daily stability by securing a basic
means of sustenance, then other future-oriented thoughts will not be any
further-reaching. Exploration of the content of ideal visions, as well as of
aspirations, expectations, and so on, allows for a more substantive and
detailed analysis of the thoughts of these men. When related back to the
different kinds of life experiences they had, this exploration, in turn, provides important cues for why certain kinds of life goals never appear in
their thinking. In following this logic, and in order to grasp more precisely
how these men think about their personal prospects for the future, a special vocabulary will be applied. After introducing this vocabulary, this
chapter will take a critical look at the men's notions of the ideal, followed
by their aspirations and expectations, and then their sense of the personal
skills and resources they possess for achieving any of these ends.

Rethinking the Vocabulary for Personal
    Mobility and Opportunity

Thus far I have used the notion of "the ideal" to refer to the men's further-
most goals and dreams, irrespective of whether those goals can be realisti-
cally accomplished, or whether the men have any sense of how to accomplish them. For instance, Arthur believed that he would achieve one of
his ideal objectives because he had witnessed firsthand how a business
operates. He believed that he had a workable map for navigating success
in the field he was considering. Even a moderately critical assessment of
his argument shows that neither his map nor the personal resources at his
disposal were adequate to help him reach his goals. Still, Arthur believed
that he could achieve his ends because working in a liquor store gave him
some idea, however incomplete, of how to set up his own business. Neither Joseph nor Conrad spoke of any resources, and neither had even a
basic plan of how to reach their ultimate goals.

I have employed the notion of an ideal to refer to something different
from an *aspiration*. I define an aspiration as a goal that is tied closely to
tangible strategies for attainment. To put it another way, aspirations are
taken here to be dreams attached to a reasonably clear understanding of
how they can be achieved. These conditions are not to be confused with
whether the men feel certain about achieving them, which, as we shall
see, is a prerequisite for an expectation. An aspiration necessitates only
that one have some coherent idea of how a goal might be achieved, thus

making it a tangible pursuit in life. On the other hand, an *ideal* represents the most grandiose of one's desires. An ideal may not be grandiose in and of itself, but only in relation to one's other desires, hopes, expectations, or probabilities for the future.

Ideals and aspirations can converge, when individuals have a clear notion of how to achieve their most desired goals. An example would be a skilled college basketball player who aspires to the National Basketball Association. The end state may be as much of an ideal for him as it is for a teenager with severely limited basketball skills. In the case of the standout college athlete, however, the ideal and the aspiration converge because the athlete is better equipped for attaining the end goal. The athlete has the relevant skills and other resources at his disposal (i.e., coaches, sports agents, or other social contacts to facilitate connections to the NBA).

Both ideals and aspirations differ from *expectations*. An expectation is that which is almost certainly achievable in one's estimation. Its achievability is due to its being rooted in a clear sense of how it can be attained. Let's take the case of the collegiate All-American basketball player who would like to get drafted into the professional ranks and make the roster of a team. This individual *aspires* to that ideal, which means that he has some idea of how he can make it possible. Given his status as an All-American, he *expects* to get drafted and sign a contract with an NBA franchise. In this case, then, the three parts of the individual's future orientation—ideals, aspirations, and expectations—converge.[4] A successful convergence of the three elements is contingent upon the realistic nature of the goal given one's resources, abilities, and imaginative capacities. Whatever the individual case, it is analytically important to note that each of these elements refers to a place in a hierarchy of future interests and goals. Moreover, one's ability to form distinctions among ideals, aspirations, and expectations will shape how one approaches and reacts to future life circumstances.

Some may argue that this is a highly overdeveloped terminology for what are, in reality, fairly simple social processes. I contend, however, that traditional scholarly assessments of mobility present an oversimplified view of what people think about their future prospects, due to a lack of conceptual precision.[5] The concept of aspiration, for example, is usually applied to a wide array of phenomena, ranging from anything that is slightly more ambitious than an expectation to that which typifies the grandest and boldest of dreams. The revised and extended terminology utilized here places more precise boundaries around the thoughts that an individual may hold regarding his future prospects. For poor black men, whose perspectives are sometimes assumed to be more alike than is actually the case, the greater precision in vocabulary helps to highlight the true diversity of their views.

The goal for the next part of this chapter is to explore the men's explanations of mobility, opportunity, and future life chances. All three frames of thinking—the ideal, the possibly attainable, and the probable—help constitute these men's conceptions of future life chances. The story told here will not just relate the content of these men's images of future prospects, but will also address how they plan to take steps in those directions. Thus, having begun with a discussion of images of a better future, the chapter ends with attention to what the men view as their resource base for engaging mobility.

The World of Work and the Good Life: Aspirations and Expectations

On the level of ideals, whether concentrating more on daily security and stability or on business ownership, the main point of men's preoccupations with both the world of work and the good life was clear and simple—the goal of establishing materially and emotionally enriched family lives. As for aspirations, the men aspired to nothing more than a toned-down version of the ideal. In this regard, Earl said:

> Well like owning my own home, you know, providing for my own family, and just having the nicest things in life. . . . Well for me personally I would like to be married, to get married, you know what I'm saying. I believe that a man need a good partner behind him, you know what I'm saying, to be, not necessarily to be successful but to share things with all through your life.

Anthony added:

> I would like to have all the money in the world, but you know, I know that ain't going to happen, but the necessary income for me, I would like to make a good, man, you know, I would like to at least make $18,000 a year. . . . It means a whole bunch because if I got a comfortable life I know then my kids would be happy with the life they got too. . . . I always wanted a family, I got a family, so I wouldn't say that would be the only thing. The next thing would be, I don't think I got everything out of life. I think I could have a little more, you know, if only, there goes that word, the "J" word again, is a job, and so I think I could make it from there.

And finally, Lester said:

> Well my goals now is to get a job that pays well so that I can, you know, save a little money, put a little money up in the bank, get me a little car, you know, and take care of my little family man, 'cause I got two kids. And you know, I'm a be a father to them. I just want to be a father in the right way, to have a job,

you know. . . . [It's] very important because if I can get, if I get a good job then I won't have as many problems as I do have now as far as, you know, right now if I had a good paying job, I'd be working as hard as I can, you know, and my goal, I'd set a goal each time. Like my goal would be to get a certain car. Then I get that car, my goal would be to make my payments on it, and once I paid that up, my goals would be getting my kids this and that. You know, you need money for that, things like that . . . having a little money put up in the bank, just in case something goes wrong, you need a little money, and having a vehicle, having a TV, kitchen appliances and all that, food on the table, clothes that go on they back, you know just the basics. . . . If you got a strong family, man, and everybody loves one another, basically you can accomplish almost anything. . . . If you got a strong family and everybody got a lot of will power, man, then you going to have food on that table everyday, everyday for them kids, everyday man.

Those who did not say much about family restricted their remarks to desires of attaining an easier life. Donald said:

All I need is a steady job, a nice apartment, nothing big, and a car. . . . Money ain't going to make me happy. As long as I got God and Jesus, you know, and a little female here and there, you know, I'm all right. . . . Basically all I just need are the necessities in life, an apartment or house, a car. I'm not asking for much. I'm not asking myself for much.

The men's aspirations for the good life appear to be what more financially secure people would categorize as a decent life. The men viewed greater wealth and more freedom and control over the circumstances of everyday living as part of the idealized good life. Their comments also included the more attainable aspirations of a stable family, income, and residence. In these cases, then, the men merged their aspirations and ideals. However, unlike the earlier example of our NBA-bound basketball player, the convergence of aspirations and ideals cannot be ascribed to the men's heightened abilities to attain the ideal state outlined, but rather to their inability to see much beyond their current situations. These men held no loftier ideals precisely because their thinking was so constrained by the pressures and problems that they faced on a daily basis. Consequently, they could not imagine an ideal more than a level or two higher than their current situation.

The limited nature of these men's ideals is closely tied to their state of perpetual material deprivation. The men I spoke with were no longer children, and for some of them, taking stock of their situation and the possibilities for the future meant stifling the imaginative capacities that they maintained during their early years in order to take more seriously the realities of their present lives. The men with much smaller dreams—

so small that they do not appear "ideal" in any way—were actually indicating the extent to which long-term disadvantage had abated their capacity to think about the future.

The majority of the men said that they were prepared to take advantage of whatever legitimate employment might come up. A minority spoke of specific employment options that they were in the midst of pursuing. Their comments made clear, however, that they did not believe that potentially meaningful employment opportunities really existed. This pessimism about job opportunities clearly shaped what the men had to say about the world of work.[6] When asked about the more realistic and accessible work options to which they aspired, the men outlined their desire for jobs that not only paid a decent salary but offered fringe benefits and union membership. In their thinking, anything less than this did not amount to a real work opportunity. They often claimed that getting a benefits package was more important than the nature of the work itself. Barry argued:

> [A] job like, benefit jobs, jobs that have benefits, not all that you have to be a doctor or policeman, but benefits, you know. . . . It take a lot of load—it's take a load off of you when you know you got something to back you up if you get sick or something, you know.

Additionally, Earl offered:

> There are a lot of good labor jobs, a lot of jobs like working for the city, and just like construction jobs and the good paying jobs, like, well there's a lot of jobs where you don't find a lot of education but a lot of skills, you know what I'm saying. Like I'll say like a bricklayer, you know what I'm saying, you don't need to be, you don't need no computer to lay no bricks, you know, but it's a good paying job.

The men were most interested in steady and stable jobs, like those in city government. They also aspired to working in a large factory. The men made it very clear why these jobs were so valued. A small store could close at any time. Small businesses also meant dealing with a single boss (usually the owner), who established rules that could be changed at any point. Such a boss was also unlikely to provide a benefits package, and was unlikely to treat employees as important members of the enterprise. Additionally, whether one got along well with the boss or not, upward mobility in a small operation was virtually nonexistent. On the Near West Side in particular, working in stores and small shops often meant doing whatever the boss needed for that day. Upon completion of those assignments, there might be work for the next day and thereafter, or there might not.[7]

For the most part, then, the men aspired to a "career" rather than just a job. They did not actually use the term "career," but their comments made clear that this is what they had in mind when talking about work aspirations. A job was work that needed to be done for the moment or for a short period of time. A job might yield some needed income, but also risked the potential for a lot of abuse from superiors. In contrast, a career led to economic stability and security—it was real work with real material returns. Most importantly, a career was what adult men did (or wanted to be seen doing), as a statement of independent functioning and well-being. Jobs were either for adolescents or people with no real commitment or preparedness to making their lives better. Although he used the term "trade" in place of "career," Dennis made the distinction between the two in the following comment:

> I'll say any trade job I think is good. . . . There's a lot of factory jobs and everything. I ain't talking about those little temporary jobs where they halfway work you to death. I mean, you know, something where you can be stable in, financially set if you work everyday. . . . Yeah a trade job, or factory machinist, mechanics, fireman, policeman, every, every trade job I think, you know, not cleaning floors and washing dishes. That ain't no trade, you know. It's a job, but it's not no trade for making money. As far as advancing to me it's not.

Dennis told a story from his past experience to sustain his argument about what was and was not good work:

> You run around here and they talking about three dollars and fifty cent an hour. One guy told me he was paying thirty dollars a day to paint. I said, "Is you nuts?!" Thirty dollars a day! My skills, I think my skills are worth better than that. He said, "Well I'll have to see." [I responded,] "You ain't got to see nothing. My skills is way better than that." If I'm a lay a roof or do a shingle roof for you, you think you're fitting to pay me thirty dollars you're crazy. You must going to pay me thirty dollars, you know, just to do the roof, and it better not take me no more than four hours. That's how I feel my skills is. . . . I ain't went back. I worked a half a day and left. . . . Hey, if you want me to pick up the paint after they [other workers] get through or move paint cloths for thirty dollars that's about all I'm a do. I ain't going to pick up no paint brush and a roller talking about painting if you only talking about giving me thirty dollars. . . . I'm telling you these people is ignorant these days. I feel that is really stupid. . . .

Many of the men shared Dennis's view that refusing to work was preferable to unfair compensation. While each man stated that he desired to work in a secure and stable job, each also said that he would accept any available job that could provide him with what he felt would be an appropriate salary. Although views on what constituted appropriate compensation varied, most of the men claimed that per diem or informal arrangements were unacceptable. The closer the men got to observing the inner world of work, the more convinced they became about these standards.

Having worked at a downtown McDonald's restaurant, Dennis was one of the few men who spoke of his interactions with business people. As sparse as his exposure was to the white-collar milieu, it allowed access to a world that was far beyond what most of the other men could imagine. While at work Dennis caught glimpses of what business people talked about while getting their food. He heard them discuss vacation plans, activities on their own jobs, and other things that were far beyond the purview of most people from the Near West Side. Much of what he had to say about what is out there in the world in terms of getting ahead came from observing and listening to what these people already had. At another level, however, Dennis's situation exemplifies a major conundrum for the few men who had some meaningful work experience (that is, something more than per diem or short-term work), or who possessed some tangible manual skills. The problem was that many potential employers regarded them as an excellent source of short-term, extraordinarily cheap-to-hire labor. However, most of the men were adamantly unwilling to accept those very kinds of opportunities.[8] What employers saw them as best suited for interested them the least.

The type of work in the neighborhood most visible to many Near West Siders remained the underground economy. The men expressed a wide range of feelings regarding whether such pursuits were worthwhile. Again Dennis argued:

> I can't knock a person for selling drugs, I cannot, 'cause if you ain't got a job to go to, you can't get one. People got to survive. And then everybody say "Well it's so wrong, to stick up [commit robberies]." Yeah I think killing is wrong, but it's hard out there, it's hard. Some people say, "Yeah, well get out here and work." . . . Yeah, you're getting out here. Man, I get disappointed all the time, you know what I'm saying.

In the course of our conversations most of the men expressed an understanding as to why individuals would pursue illicit activity. Indeed, over half of them said that they had done so themselves.[9] However, even those who reported being involved in illicit activities maintained that while monetary rewards were plentiful at certain periods, they had begun to question whether a long-term commitment to these endeavors would provide them with the emotional and physical security that could be provided by other forms of employment.

The men also knew that such involvements could not guarantee a consistent income. In making this point they stressed that violence was ever-present in the underground economy. Robbery attempts or reactions to territorial encroachments (over drugs or gang boundaries) were common. Furthermore, the men risked incarceration. Violence and incarceration both worked against a steady flow of income. These caveats did not mean that the men were immune to being caught up in that life (or that all had fully left it, for that matter), but that they were beginning to realize that it was a risky involvement over the long run.

Involvement in the fast life also posed a threat to the men's aspiration to remain "in good health"—that is, free from injury. Freedom from injury might appear to be such an obvious aspiration that it would not even feature prominently in their discussions. However, it was mentioned more than any topic other than finding suitable work and caring for their children. In many respects, it stood as the centerpiece of their discussions of the good life. The men resided in communities riddled with random violence. Some of them were intricately involved in its production. It makes perfect sense that a desire for "good health" would be mentioned so often, because in a community where threats to one's health were abundant—and resources for preserving it were remarkably scarce—it could not be taken for granted.[10] This is all to say that the pursuit of the fast life was losing whatever glamour it had as the men aged, even for those who continued to pursue it, because the risks involved in it were seen as ultimately outweighing the benefits.

Good health also was an essential for good employment, especially for the kinds of jobs that most interested these men. Jobs in government or in manufacturing sectors seemed stable and secure. This was the kind of work done by their mothers, fathers (for those that lived with them), and guardians, at least those with the better jobs.[11] Hence, these men knew that such jobs existed even if they were not equally knowledgeable about the specific job duties or prerequisites. These associations account for why the men valued and talked so much about various kinds of work with which they had no firsthand experience. Lester proved this point well when he talked about jobs with the post office and city government, neither of which he ever had actually ever held:

> I'm thinking about the post office. I'm thinking about ah, [*long pause*]. Basically my main thing is I want to go where the money is, that's the post office. The post office is like city jobs, jobs that are dealing with the city. They pay a lot, you know.

When asked about jobs and work opportunity, Larry said much the same: "I wouldn't mind working for the city or something man, you know, a real job, something I could really call a job where I could be in a union, you know, or something like that, where I could really be making some money." Making sure that I fully understood his disposition toward certain kinds of work, Larry added, "But you know what, I ain't choosy neither, I mean whatever job comes that's a good paying job I'm a jump on it. I ain't choosy. I mean it ain't got to satisfy me, as long as I'm working, man, taking care of myself, it's all right. I don't care what it is."

Four men knew exactly what they wanted to be doing in the next five years. Butch aspired to become a medical assistant. Earl and Gus both wanted to become x-ray technicians. Damon wanted to become a data entry clerk or some comparable position in an office setting. These were the only men whose comments detailed specific career interests when asked about what they thought they might be doing in the near future. Each of them had intimate ties to people in those lines of work, or had relatives who were able to suggest how to get training in those fields. Each also said that he was preparing to pursue such training.

When asked about what they might be doing in five years, the rest of the men were much more vague. The closest they got to the specificity of Butch, Earl, Gus, and Damon was by mentioning "a city job" or "a job with the government." When prompted, the men talked of undefined positions at the post office, the parks department, or elsewhere in the city government. Here again, their comments had little to with specific types of jobs, but rather with the broad features and qualities of the jobs they wanted to acquire.

Although the men had little to say about specific jobs, a lot can be culled from what they said about their general orientations toward the world of work. The ability to talk about the world of work with great clarity and depth comes from being well immersed in that world. Without having experienced much of that world, people who want to work are prone to think more about the virtues of finding satisfactory work, and less about the myriad characteristics and duties associated with a particular job. The chronically unemployed person, as we have seen, can easily misapprehend much about the realities of work. More crucially, people without work may have great difficulty in knowing exactly what to expect regarding finding work in the future.

The men's situation of chronic unemployment also shaped the difficulty they had in answering questions about what they expected to be doing five or so years into the future. The men found it particularly difficult to talk about the future in concrete terms because it demanded a well-honed sense of realism. Asking them about where they hoped to be in the next five years demanded that they include in their thinking some sense of the attainable as well as the desirable. Many of the men responded to my questions about the future much the way Larry did when I first broached the subject of job prospects: he paused for a little while and then said, "But I ain't really gave that no thought neither man." Eventually he said, "Sometimes I think I'll go back to school man. That's what I've been thinking about a lot man."

Another important finding concerning the men's employment aspirations relates to their overwhelming preoccupation with manual work. Whether the men spoke of owning their own businesses, working for the city government, or being employed in a factory, they all emphasized work that allowed them to build, construct, model, or assemble with their hands and bodies. Jake said:

> I want to own my own, my little I guess you call it construction, little construction business, you know, but start off doing like little contracts with people around that you knew, you know and stuff. And that's how you go out and try to break into it. You do the work yourself, you get you somebody that know what they doing, and you go into the process of doing little things first, dry walls, a little plumbing, and stuff like that, you know. Cause like, you know, that's something that I can do. I ain't got nobody looking over my shoulder trying to tell me how to do it. I can take my timing and do it right, you know what I'm saying. And, you know, I could be my own man.

Anthony gave another example. When I met him he had been back on the streets for a couple of years after serving time for stealing a UPS truck and attempting to sell its contents. He had no success in finding work, and felt that his criminal record stood as his biggest obstacle. None of this prevented him from talking freely about the kind of work he desired to do:

> The jobs that I really know how to do is janitorial and I can do roofing, I can do body work, any three of them jobs, I would do them real good. But any kind of other job that would teach me how to, learn me how to do it, I would take it.

As the men spoke about the kinds of employment they felt best suited for, it seemed as though they would have flourished in mid-twentieth-century urban industrial America. They were most interested in unionized factory work and moderately skilled municipal service. Conspicuously absent from their remarks was the quest for inclusion in the white-collar service arena, which was one of the fastest growing employment sectors in modern America, in general, and in Chicago in particular, in the 1990s (Israilevich and Mahidhara 1990). Only Joseph, Devin, and Damon offered more than casual remarks about aspiring to work in this sector, and this was by way of briefly mentioning how data entry, mail clerk duties, and similar kinds of work stood within their reach. Of these three, Damon was the only one who talked about pursuing a training program (in data entry techniques).

The narrowness of the men's perspective on potential work opportunities sheds light on another effect of social isolation. The aspect of the world of work that was most desirable to these men was one that was in actuality diminishing as these men came of age. The industrial-to-service-sector transition in urban employment has been a topic of considerable interest for urban poverty researchers (Bluestone, Stevenson, and Tilly

1993, Kasarda 1995, Wilson 1996). It was not such a hot topic for these men, however. The men seemed not to grasp what the growing service sector might offer them. Instead, they remained fixated on manual work that got their hands dirty and made them sweat.

In early- to mid-twentieth-century urban America, manual labor was closely tied to masculine identity as the popular imagery circumscribing men centered on strength and vigor, the kinds of traits most useful in the manual labor arena (Bernard 1992, Kimmel 1996). For the men of the Near West Side, the model of masculine work dovetailed with both mainstream and low-income community-level conceptions of masculinity.[12] These men grew up with the model of employed men as those who went off to factories and did manual work. The men's understanding of that history, however primitive it was, helped crystallize their sense of what was appropriate for men like themselves to do for a living.[13]

The negative image of black men held by most Chicago employers meant that there were few opportunities for work other than that which required a college education.[14] Thus, the severity of the employment problem for the men went far beyond a lack of adequate information about work opportunities. For one, employers would have to begin thinking of these men as resources rather than as liabilities. The complexities involved in how this transformation might unfold deserve appropriate attention that cannot be given here. It is enough now to state that the problem with poor black men and work goes beyond the behaviors and attitudes of these men.

We have seen that the men's aspirations regarding future employment appeared fairly modest. When we turn to their *expectations* we find a greater degree of despair and caution. We have defined expectations as encompassing an individual's sense of base-level achievements for the future. Nearly half of the men believed that they would definitely find some type of job in the next five years or so. The four who had the most focused career interests (Butch, Earl, Gus, and Damon) said that they expected to obtain the specific jobs they had mentioned earlier. It was impossible to guess whether they would achieve their goals; each was planning to enter a training or certification program, but at the time of our meeting, none was anywhere near the start of formal training. Nonetheless, their faith that their goals were attainable allowed them to couple their expectations with their aspirations.

Butch, Earl, Gus, and Damon were able to merge their expectations and aspirations because they had been shown a means toward their desired end through access to information about training. Rather than relying on guesswork, hope, or intuition, their consolidation of plans for personal mobility was based on access to concrete information about how to improve their personal situations. Accordingly, these four men could articulate ideas about how they would pursue personal prospects with a clarity that escaped the other men.[15] Here we see how access to capital (in this case, ties to individuals who provided connections to these programs) helps determine whether and how these men were able to construct certain end states.

The other men spoke in less certain terms about the types of jobs they would acquire, although they all believed that they would find some kind of work. Eight of them said that they expected some type of employment to come their way in the near future, though they offered little in the way of precise explanation as to how this would happen. For instance, Felton said, "I think my chances are just as better as anybody else because [of] the way I feel, I want it. And I'm going to get it [a job]. So my chances are just as better as anybody else if they want it." Peter said:

> I believe that I'll be somewhere with the state. The state and the city are full of jobs that do nothing but make plenty of money. A lot of jobs are like that. Over the next five years I'll probably be out working for somebody and before long and then I'll be working for my own self. I'm deadly serious about that. I get my own business and my own corporation set up here. I'll go global with it.

The remaining fourteen men were thoroughly unsure about what the future held for them. When asked about expectations, all they uttered were vague statements hoping for something better than their current situation. The men's "I don't know" replies to questions about expectations reflected the same restricted social situation that led them to reply "I don't know" to my earlier questions about mobility and opportunity in American society.[16] While never going as far as to say "I don't know," Anthony's statement is typical:

> Well now that I done settled down I figured it's going to balance. It's got to happen sooner or later. So all I can do is just keep going out there trying to put in applications or just stay away from the bad guys that want to bring me down, and that's no more troubles.

Much like the "I don't know" remarks, this statement is an indication of how much a life experience in social isolation leaves someone without much ability to explain how his future will pan out, even if he dreams at least a little about a better future.

In the 1960s, anthropologist Elliot Liebow looked at how men who associated on a street corner in Washington, DC, responded to the types of jobs available to them. He noted that:

> The streetcorner man wants to be a person in his own right, to be noticed, to be taken account of, but in this respect, as well as in meeting his money needs, his job fails him. The job and the man are even. The job fails the man and the man fails the job. [pp. 62–63]

The disdain for bad jobs that Liebow found in the 1960s was still present for the men I interviewed. Many black men today, however, are faced not only with poor quality jobs as with the absence of employment prospects altogether. This makes the contemporary discussion not so much about men and their jobs as about the removal of poor black men from positions where they can make even rudimentary sense of the modern world of work. It is this context, not the question of whether or not men want to work, that demands the attention of those who aim to help these individuals secure better lives.[17]

The men's ideas regarding opportunity and possibility were two critical products of their efforts to make meaning out of the world around them. Most importantly, ideas of opportunity and possibility set the context within which poor black men's values about work and reactions to work opportunity are formulated. The men desired the kind of work that does what employment is supposed to do—provide people with the means for sustaining themselves and their families. It is critical to understand that this search for security and stability stands at the center of their attitudes toward work. When this core element is not taken into account, many observers mistakenly ascribe to the men values regarding work based on little more than casual observations.

The men's beliefs about the world of work did not emerge from a vacuum, but rather were built from experience. As we have seen, the experiences of these men resulted in the accumulation of forms of capital that were deficient for situating them in upwardly mobile positions. The men had little exposure to social network ties, and few attachments to social institutions that facilitate mobility. Thus, they gained little access to information and resources, and they were blocked from acquiring sufficiently intricate understandings of how the world of work is structured. This gaping lack of social capital regarding the world of work meant that the men could not even begin the process of adapting its structures to their own lives.

Taking Stock of Themselves: Inventories of Skills and Resources for Getting Ahead

The men's lack of social capital relevant to the world of work was compounded by deficiencies in their human capital of strategic skills and talents. In the contemporary world of work, education and certification credentials, often taken to be indicators of brainpower and skill, are some of the most essential resources for success. Strength and physical stamina generally have little importance in the white-collar environment. Advances in technology including the computerization of the workplace have changed the image of the successful modern working man. Corporate leaders dress in suits, possess advanced degrees, and join professional and social networks whose participants communicate with a vocabulary comprehensible only to those who function in their milieu. Other than professional athletes, surgeons, and artists, those who work with their hands and sweat a lot are generally doing work that falls at the bottom of the social hierarchy.

Earlier, we saw that the ideal state for some of these men was to acquire positions alongside the leaders of the work world. When talking about their personal skills and resources for getting ahead, however, all the men referred to attributes associated with lower-level manual laborers. For most of the men, bodily strength was, in fact, their main resource for work.[18] A strong and healthy body was extremely important in the men's vision of themselves. In the Near West Side, as in all urban, low-income communities, the healthy and able-bodied already had a great advantage over the sick, injured, or weak. However, the men's obsession with body image also reflected the fact that they did not possess any other resources, such as connections or credentials, for obtaining jobs.[19] To be sure, the body is an important personal resource for poor and rich alike. Most people value their bodies in some way or another. Yet, for these men the body played a particular role in their worldview. Focusing on the body allowed the men to highlight the single aspect of their lives that they could control and potentially master in the quest for upward mobility. Their body represented all that they could bring to the world of work to counterbalance the paucity of formal skills, credentials, or symbolic resources that could benefit a place of business if they happened to be hired.[20]

The body was seen as a personal resource. The men who professed to have some formal skills in manual labor talked about their bodily abilities in terms of what they could fix, build, erect, or construct. Some of the former high school athletes, like Gus and Felton, viewed athletic ability as one of their best assets. In contrast, the men with less physical prowess focused almost exclusively on sociability as their most important resource. These men saw themselves as especially skilled at getting along with people. To their mind, their sociability was a key asset for building and maintaining a positive work environment. A few of the men claimed to be good both with their hands and with interacting with other people.

> JAKE: I could relate to people man, you know cause I'm a funny guy or whatever, you know what I'm saying. And humor will always get you, you know, somebody with a little humor, then you know, you hit them with the big stuff [other skills].

The men who talked about being skilled with their hands did not have a lot to say about how they acquired their skills. Some of what was learned came from high school vocational programs, the rest in ad hoc work opportunities.[21] Lacking the formal certification that would validate their abilities did not stop them from asserting what they could do if given the chance:

> JASON: Carpentry, woodwork, electrician, plumbing, I could do all that. I need to go to school to achieve more. I just need to go back to get that degree. That's it.

> DENNIS: Like now I'm versatile at any, any field. I can do almost anything, almost. I ain't going to say I'm, you know, but right now I can do almost anything, like construction, roofing, laying floors, carpentry, I can do it all. I can do it all.

Eighteen of the men made mention of having some kind of manual skill.[22] Manual skills included heavy lifting, basic construction, painting, custodial work, and light machinery operations (e.g., printing machines). Ted, Casey, Lester, Jason, Dennis, and Peter stood out from the others by using much more technical language when describing their skills. These men claimed to be trained in carpentry, welding, plumbing, and car repair; however, none had any trade school or other formal training in these areas. Like the other men, what they had learned came from day labor arrangements or other informal work opportunities. Butch, Barry, Anthony, Damon, and Travis each spoke of having some artistic drawing or typing skills, which they learned in high school.[23] Devin never mentioned a concrete manual skill other than in a passing remark about typing. "For me, I could do just about anything," he said. "So it really don't matter cause I'm good with my hands, thinking. Anything that got to do with fixing I'm real good."

In contrast, Leon, Conrad, Kurt, Jordan, Felton, Arthur, Larry, and Donald focused on their social skills when addressing the issue of gaining employment.[24] The general lack of work experience was most apparent with this group of men. They had precious little to elaborate upon when talking about what they could bring to the employment sector. Yet, they often spoke at great length about their social skills. There is a logic behind this. If you can weld, saw, mold, or drill, it does not take a whole lot of words to say so. Moreover, if you really believe that you can do these things, saying so only goes so far. As the men with manual skills constantly reiterated, one has to be given the chance to show what one can do. By contrast, the dialogues about social skills were more open-ended and lengthy because the act of talking was a large part of the proof of the men's abilities. Some of the men believed that their best skill was the ability to get along well with people. Donald captured the spirit of this when he remarked, "I'm fairly good at working with people on a social basis . . . talking to people, listening and learning."

None of this is to downplay the importance of social skills. Certainly traits such as being friendly, humorous, talkative, and receptive to others are valuable supplements to formal skills or abilities in the workplace. Rather, the point is to emphasize the men's exclusive reliance upon good social skills for finding and keeping good work. Moreover, in the absence of other skills and talents, touting these traits may even diminish one's standing in the eyes of potential employers. Yet for some of these men, social skills were all that they had to work with.

In attempting to offer more detailed statements of what they had to offer to the work world, Gus, Jordan, and Joseph captured the flavor of how most of the men labored to present themselves as positively as they could despite being short on the kinds of resources that would matter to most prospective employers:

JORDAN: My skills and talents is to help people and doing all that you can and just being yourself. And once you're yourself you can get in on with what you can, and you give it your best. . . . I think if you know what you're talking about and you can walk and talk like you have a whole lot of degrees on the wall when you don't have to have anything at all. You just go by your personality, you know different things. . . . You just have to know. If you know you can do the job to the best of your ability, then you just give it your best. I learned nine out of ten that people aren't looking at how many diplomas you got, how many stuff you got up on your belt. Most of the time people are looking for talent, your attitude, your credibility, how can you do different things, you know.

JOSEPH: Certain talents or skills? I feel as though right now there's nothing out there that I can't do. There isn't. I mean I could work at a steel mill if they put me at a station and they show me what they want done and how they want it done, that's the way it should be done. [*On what kind of jobs he can do:*] Right now it don't make a difference, whatever the job consists of. There's nothing that a person can't do. The only thing he needs is for someone to show him the one time, or tell him how he want it done. That's it. Go do it.

GUS: I'm just a normal person. I think I have good common sense, pretty much. I do spend time thinking about things before I say it, little things like that. I think I'm a normal person. I don't think I'm too much smarter than nobody. I don't think I'm too much dumber than a lot of people either, but I consider myself being a pretty average guy, you know what I'm saying. . . . I think I'm a fairly hard worker. Compared to others I do believe that I'm willing to work hard. I know that if someone is doing the same job that I'm doing I am willing to do it, to work hard. I do know that. . . . I'll do it 'til I can't do it no more. . . . I'm a good listener. I know if I hear something I might need to be doing I know that I will spend that time listening and I hear and I'll do it. . . . I believe I have a great body. I have a short-term goal of starting to maybe getting into modeling or something.

The statements reveal the difficulty some of the men faced when attempting to offer a precise picture of what they could bring to the workplace. Each man struggled—and ultimately failed—to convey some formal or concrete ability relevant to the work world. Gus, the former standout high school football player, ended his monologue about skills by returning to his physical attributes as an affirmation of what he could offer. Ultimately, his body represented his most important resource. Consequently, the closest thing to a specific job that he said that he could do was one that depended almost entirely on physique.

Leon and Larry were the most tragic in their struggle to identify any personal skills. Leon named his social skills as a last resort effort to mention something in the way of personal resources. "Particular skills at present?" He said when asked about the topic. He then paused as if he had never really thought about the issue before. "That's a hard question to answer because I'm not sure what my talent is. I know I like working with people in general. That's about the best skill that I could say that I do have."

Larry was, perhaps, the worst case. He admitted that he had never before thought about what skills he possessed. "I never gave that no thought neither, man," was all that he had to say. Withdrawing for a moment, he looked as though he was trying hard to think of something else to say; but he never offered anything more on the topic.

Conclusion

The exploration of the men's descriptions and perceptions of their own skills reveals that, barring additional training, most of the men would remain equipped for only the most minimally skilled service-sector positions. The men with acquired manual skills faced a labor market in which appropriate jobs were rapidly disappearing. The men without manual-skill working experience had virtually no skills to help develop work prospects. Still, these lesser skilled men seldom considered job searching in the lower-echelon service sector. Even had they done so, they would have found that these jobs provided far less remuneration than they were prepared to accept in the long term, and minimal or no benefit plans. Maybe such jobs would have been appealing to the men in their adolescence. However, as young adults the men held that such opportunities would not suffice.

The men who lacked manual skills were in the worst predicament of all. Because they could not talk about working with their hands, they were left with only their social skills to talk about. Their lived experience had taught them something about the importance of knowing how to deal with people. Indeed, on the Near West Side, such knowledge could have life-or-death consequences, depending on the people one encountered. Yet, these men remained far removed from the types of opportunities and experiences that could lead them to adapt and broaden their people-centered skills. Even as they touted these skills, it seemed to me that the men knew that much else was needed in order to get ahead at work and in society. They did not, however, elaborate on what else was needed. Had the men been more familiar with the world of work, they would have been aware of the importance of qualities other than basic people skills. Social isolation had left these men struggling with how to build arguments about themselves in the absence of the right kinds of human, financial, social, and cultural capital.

The men's comments on the world of work reveal a host of subtleties and complexities related to the concept of skill. The preceding discussion demonstrates that skill is both a kind of capital and a product of capital. More specifically, skill is both embodied by and produced from human and cultural capital. Human capital translates into perhaps the purest form of skill. This form of capital has to do with what one is capable of doing, but perhaps most importantly, what one is formally certified to do. As we have seen, many of these men had manual skills but suffered from a lack of formal certification to do much of anything related to their hopes and dreams. Some of these men also commented that their skills simply did not matter for the kind of work they were seeking. The dilemma was even graver than for those with manual skills but who lacked certification. It is important to emphasize that all of the men suffered, whether or not they were aware of it, from the negative image that employers have of black men, an image that stood as an additional and formidable obstacle to the men's quest for stable and satisfying work.

We have seen that chronic unemployment and a lack of familiarity with the world of work was the critical formative factor underlying all of the men's experience. The men's alienation from this world is all the more evident when cultural capital is introduced into the analytical picture. Many of the men viewed themselves as possessing an important facet of cultural capital—a sense of when and how to act in specific social settings, or knowledge of what to say and do. As those who are fortunate enough to have good jobs know, for cultural capital to be employed most effectively in the kinds of jobs to which these men aspired, it has to supplement other resources.

This chapter explored these men's ideal desires in life, and their aspirations and expectations. It then uncovered what they believed to be their skills and resources for attaining these objectives. The men's objectives can be thought of as destination points in the course of their life-long journeys. The skills and resources can be thought of as fuel for those journeys. The final piece of the travel plan is a road map, which in this case is made up of ideas and strategies for reaching desired destinations. The topic of the next chapter is what these men conceive of as road maps, given their desired destinations and the kinds of fuel they believe themselves to possess.

Chapter Seven

Getting There: Navigating Personal Mobility

LEON: Like I say, you only get out of it what you put into it. . . . The only thing
         I could see that can, the only obstacle in my way is my own self. It's
         what I'm doing or not doing. That's the only obstacle. Now what hap-
         pens further up the line once I get started, now that I can't determine.

DEVIN: Work on it, keep working for it. . . . Oh there are always going to be
         some problems, no matter what.
         And how do you think you'll handle them?
         Working it out.

TITO: I'm a do all I can to make it better, you know, do everything I can to
         make it better, man. I've got to work harder. I know I've been working
         hard, I've been doing, I've been trying to do things hard. I been trying
         to do things more, as hard as I can, but I ain't been doing it. I've just
         been sitting back and saying, "Man, I ain't doing nothing." I ain't
         been working hard as I can. That's why I feel if I work hard as I can
         now, then things are going to be accomplished better now. . . . The
         best strategy that I could use is just the common strategy, the common
         strategy. I ain't got no game, man just be yourself . . . be myself.

When speaking about what they needed to do to get ahead in life, the
men of the Near West Side said the kinds of things that one would expect
from any citizen of modern-day America: they appropriated the standard
public script of the American Dream by emphasizing factors such as hard
work, discipline, motivation, and education. The men counted a high
school diploma as essential; beyond that, they believed that the only useful
education was training directly tied to one's career interests.

The men viewed education credentials, human capital characteristics,
and appropriate attitudes about work as constituting the bare essentials
for finding the right kinds of jobs, and the good life more generally. The
men saw education as important as a mechanism not only for certifying
competence, but also for learning how to perform certain jobs (i.e., the
dual dimensions of human capital). Their discussions of their failures in
school prefaced their comments on the need for additional educational
training to get ahead. Over two thirds of the men stated that insufficient
schooling was a major impediment for them. While placing varying de-

grees of emphasis on the further education needed, each man remarked that returning to school was essential.[1]

Most men also viewed working hard as a key element in the cultural tool kit for personal mobility in American life.[2] Hard work stood out as an important concept for the men, due to its clear and concise meaning. When someone is identified as a hard worker, the implication is that he is doing well and acting as a productive member of society. The discursive value of the term "hard work" can outweigh its utility as an accurate depiction of effort or strategy, however. For instance, there are surely people who do not actually work very hard, but have gotten very far in life. Yet, due to the men's social isolation and lack of awareness of the various ways people find success, they assumed that most successful people in American life were hard workers. If hard work does not always accurately identify the path to success, the men certainly turned to the term often in describing themselves. Identifying oneself as a hard worker reinforces one's sense of moral worth, thereby enhancing one's legitimacy as a social actor (Lamont 2000). This explains why the men made hard work a staple of their narrative outlining what they must do to get ahead. It also explains why these men echo the standard American script when talking about hard work and success in life.

The men stressed a positive attitude and orientation to work almost as often as they spoke about schooling and hard work. The men defined discipline, focus, and determination as important traits to embody and employ in order to move up in the world. Once again, these terms reflect the men's appropriation of the standard American ideology of self-advancement. As we have seen, the men did not have the requisite employment experience that would have allowed them to associate these terms with actual jobs. This lack of experience did not, however, stop them from employing these terms liberally as they spoke about what they needed to do to get ahead.

One might question the extent to which the men actually believed in the individualist logic of the American Dream. Cultural sociologists and other scholars have shown that people regularly appropriate all sorts of public scripts for varied personal aims and interests, including the goal of presenting positive public selves (Mills 1940, Orbuch 1997, Scott and Lyman 1968). It is probable that the men said what they did because they were aware that it was the appropriate thing to say regarding personal advancement in the world of work. At the same time, we cannot discount the possibility that they had also internalized some of this discourse. Certainly, for the most socially isolated of the men, the articulation of the individualism and moralism of the American Dream grew out of their lack of consistent access to people who held alternative views regarding how mobility works.

These men had very few examples of people who had succeeded in moving far up the social scale. Aside from former associates or distant relatives who made it in the sports world, they knew few people who had radically changed their life circumstances.[3] Thus, the men had little to rely on besides the conventional understandings of how mobility unfolds. Greater exposure to people who have followed different mobility patterns would have offered them room for making more complex arguments. This exposure also would have given them grounds for speaking against some of the conventional narrative that places so much emphasis on individual initiative.

Most intriguingly, the men viewed their failed circumstances as offering poignant counterexamples to the standard American ideology of mobility. Indeed, the fact that they saw themselves as not having lived up to the standards of the Dream is the best proof of their sincere belief in it. Many of the men talked about having not done the right things in terms preparing themselves for upward mobility. In the absence of short-term work or other unusual opportunities, these men spent a lot of time on the corner talking with each other and passing the days. In this respect they had a good amount of time to assess their lifestyle. Sadly, in terms of social status the men most often judged themselves to be losers in the game of life (or at least they were convinced that others probably saw them in this way). When a man does not work everyday, it is easy for him to indict himself, and the people like him who surround him, for their life situation, chastising himself and them for not having worked hard enough, been disciplined, and so on.

In looking at how these men framed personal approaches toward getting ahead, we want to pay special attention to whether and how the men grasped any limits and boundaries affecting their life chances. We want to consider self-induced inhibiting forces such as laziness, poor work habits, or substance abuse, all of which weaken the capacity to do good work or take advantage of opportunities. We also want to consider external factors that are beyond an individual's direct control, like racism, sexism, or other forms of discrimination. To the men of the Near West Side, the self-induced factors were more visible and less complicated to explain. Hence, it is not surprising that the men who had little else to draw upon for interpreting their social predicaments dwelled mainly on these issues.

We have seen that the men expressed a great diversity of views regarding obstacles and barriers for social mobility. The men were divided in their capacity to talk about the significance of socially enforced impediments to mobility. These differences provide a template for assessing how the men strategized about personal mobility. In short, the men derived their sense of the social processes and circumstances relevant to their mobility prospects from their articulations of how social mobility unfolds.

Whatever they saw or did not see as relevant in the social context held for their interpretations of the personal context. Their discussion of personal mobility began with a common ground of overcoming self-initiated barriers and obstacles. We will first explore this common ground before moving on to explore the differences in their responses.

The Personal Impediments to Getting Ahead

All of the men acknowledged having to confront personally induced barriers and obstacles. In fact, those men that had suffered from the effects of narcotics, alcohol, or other infirmities were the most explicit about the role of their own agency in bringing about their current circumstances. Damon, Gus, Jason, Kurt, Arthur, and Casey each talked about bouts with substance abuse and the problems that it caused for them:

DAMON: What do you think may be stopping you or working against you? Me, me. . . . I ought to put the beer bottle down and go back to school . . . and go get me a job.

GUS: If things wouldn't go right I'd get down about it and pretty much start drinking beer and start drinking, going out to party, and getting high again. You know, once I'd get high then I'd just get high and just get out of the mode of working, you know what I'm saying. I really wouldn't be thinking about working and stuff, you know. I'd get caught up into it [drugs] until I just get tired. But I really feel that it's out of my system. I don't have the taste for it anymore. I could be around, like I could walk past people, you know, I can have money in my pocket now and I could walk down the street and people selling drugs, or I know people that got drugs and stuff and I don't think about it. . . . I'm just trying, you know, to get my head together and take it one day at a time, you know, just try to work at maybe getting a job whereas I could have some kind if income coming in, whereas I could have a place to stay, and eventually I am going to go back to school.

JASON: I have flaws, I'm not perfect. Ain't no one perfect, but I have flaws. I been known to stay up a little late, drink, run around with the big crowd, hoop and holler, but I do it all up to a point.

Additionally, all of the men who had been incarcerated (Arthur, Travis, Tito, Anthony, Devin, Earl, Dennis, Roy, Lester, Casey, and Conrad) discussed the difficulties that possession of a criminal record causes for trying to find and take advantage of work opportunities. This same awareness held for the men who were active gang members.[4]

Lastly, many of the men were quite frank in discussing the role of what they believed was their own laziness or misguided efforts in preventing them from advancing in life. As Conrad stated, "I don't know about no obstacles, it's just me being lazy, you know, just wanting everything to come to me instead of me going to get it. . . . It's just, I'm just tired of sitting around, you know, waiting on things to get, they ain't getting no easier, so." Felton said:

> I didn't work hard enough earning it in my years. I didn't work hard enough. So, like I said, if you want it you got to go get it and it's not going to come to you. . . . [I must] just go out and do better than what I did in the past . . . as far as being lazy, not showing the effort to want it. That stops a lot of people, you know. Not just the white people being in control in the high positions, but it's got a lot to do with people not just making the effort.

Roy shared that sentiment when he said, "I could strive to get more, do better as a person, you know. I think I let a lot of chances slip by me that I know I could have grabbed. That's the way I feel about that."

Finally, Dennis said, "If I had one [obstacle] I created it myself. That's all I can say." Their willingness to talk about these issues, and more so, my writing about them, might appear to reinforce the social condemnation of the urban poor as unmotivated and lazy. Needless to say, it is far from my goal to reinforce these stereotypes in bringing these men's words to light. I believe that the men shared this part of their life experience with me because they were honestly acknowledging a part of what stood in the way of their advancement. Their testimony reveals that personal agency maintains some importance in any discussion of disadvantage and limited opportunity. However, their comments should not be taken as a denial of the relevance of the structural conditions circumscribing their lives. They were born into and grew up in an environment with limited choices and multiple obstacles; their own actions form only one part of the multitude of reasons why their lives have turned out the way they have.

It is hard to gauge whether lower-income urban residents actually embrace self-destructive behavior more than do other people. Mainstream America tends to associate such behavior with the urban poor. Surely, the men of the Near West Side did a number of things that were not in their best interests. Unlike wealthier people, though, these men lacked the resources to hide or diminish the impact of those engagements on their public identities and on their prospects for mobility. For instance, an alcoholic or drug abuser appears more visible, and consequently more indecent, when he or she is standing on a street corner due to joblessness than does an employed white-collar professional suffering the same afflictions. Professionals can shield themselves from the public or disguise their conditions much better than can the person on the street. Indeed, the white-collar professional may not even have to confront being publicly labeled as a drug addict. Wealthy and famous "substance abusers" may garner more public sympathy than the poor "drug addicts." This comparison does not diminish the role that drugs and alcohol played in keeping the men of our study down. It does demand that we think more critically about why they made the choices they did, and how they are evaluated in the public eye.[5]

Of course, wealthy Americans enjoy myriad advantages over the urban poor in navigating mobility and managing everyday life. While they might articulate some of the same arguments about what it takes for people to get ahead (i.e., the American public script about personal mobility), they would also have much more to say about their specific situations. Those who are better off can talk about navigating their particular occupational niche (e.g., how to make partner in the firm, how to move from staff member to manager). They may talk about how their particular educational backgrounds may matter for the goals and objectives that they have designed for themselves. They may also draw upon unique resources that are unavailable to others (family trust funds, a parent's contacts in an employment sector, participation in alumni networks).

For these reasons, creative ideas about personal mobility come easier to those who have some capital to employ in the first place. That capital can take the form of money in the bank, ties to people in employment networks who can provide relevant and appropriate advice on getting jobs, or work experiences that reflect good management of human capital. The men I interviewed had access to none of this kind of capital. Thus, they had much less ability to construct personal ideologies about getting ahead. Instead, what was available to them was the standard ideology of the American Dream. The men were not really sure how they came to hold these principles to be true; they just held them to be so. We have seen that the concept of "co-narrative" helps us to understand the men's process of modifying, supplementing, or altering aspects of the "mainstream" ideology in ways that better reflect their personal experiences and vantage points on the social world. Just as their readings of macro-level processes and patterns were expressed via co-narratives, so were their assessments of how to personally navigate mobility.

While the men knew little about how to formulate more specific strategies for navigating the world of work and attaining better lives, they had intimate knowledge of the hardship of living on the Near West Side. Consequently, when they discussed hard work and maintaining focus, the men also spoke about having to avoid further succumbing to the dangers in the community. In this regard, the men held that getting away from the neighborhood would be a positive step in and of itself in helping them to focus on improving their lives.

The lack of more sophisticated strategizing about how to move up was due in no small part to their chronic unemployment and limited schooling. Instead of more elaborate strategizing on how they planned to mobilize resources and skills for attaining their goals and dreams, a good number of the men dwelled on how much their neighborhoods served as a barrier for their getting ahead. This preoccupation reflected their lack of sufficient capital for minimizing the pernicious effects associated with their neighborhoods. Many of the men spoke of the need to "stay focused" in order to effect upward mobility. The situation of life on the Near West Side gives special meaning to the notion of staying focused. Leon stated:

> The environment around me is not, if anything the environment smacks you upside the head like, don't you want to get away from this? Ain't you tired of looking at this kind of a lifestyle? Don't you want to move up? And still there's still that pause, it's like you know it's going to take hard work, when is you going to get up and get started, you know, like you're beating yourself over the head, knowing what you need to do but you ain't got up and done it yet. What you waiting on?

For Leon, as for all of the men, it was hard to avoid succumbing to the hazards and impediments of the streets. The men had a difficult time pointing to any effective buffers against the detrimental aspects of the neighborhood. One possible buffer—organized religion—was discussed only after direct inquiry was made about whether they felt religion could serve as a positive force in their efforts to get ahead. You may recall that most of the men said that they had gone to church when they were younger, but had drifted away from it by mid-adolescence. Therefore, it was no surprise that religion was talked about with reverence, but without any intentions to commit to it in any formal way.

Sixteen men made explicit comments about the importance of religion for their attainment of future desires. Peter said, "The best way for me to get ahead is to, number one, stay with God, number two is to get a good job, a job making some money thereby I can live comfortably." The others who spoke of religion were no more specific in their remarks. Religion, or more specifically, the importance of recognizing a Higher Being, was underscored. The men did not clarify its utility in any concrete or definitive sense.

> DENNIS: Yeah, I tried on religion but right now I'm not into it. I'm not going to church or nothing, but it's important to me. . . . I believe in God. I believe a person should go to church every Sunday. [*pause*] I believe in religion. . . . Religion is a part of [finding success in trying to get ahead]. I'll say that. If you pray enough and do the right things God

will answer your prayer. And I believe in that. I know that for a fact . . . you know I get on my knees and I pray to God every night, no I ain't going to tell that. I'll say I get on my knees sometimes and pray to God, and no matter what I say, sometimes I ask God for different things, you know, and He answers. You know, it might not be a, what *I* want as an answer, but the Lord will answer your prayer. . . . In many of ways I have to go to religion for help, you know. In my life, specifically saying, no I can't say specifically, you know. But in many ways, you know, God helps in mysterious ways, so you, sometimes you might think it's the end of the world and the Lord will bless you in something, you know, will give for you.

Living in despair seemed to make it easy to talk about religion. The key tenets of religion—salvation, redemption, and forgiveness—seemed to be highly valued, though conspicuously absent, in the lives of these men. Having gone to church earlier in their lives, they were familiar with basic religious practices and doctrines. The men asserted that a commitment to a Higher Being would amount to not much more than a small help toward attaining better lives. In this regard, religion was always directly tied to their problem-ridden life circumstances:

BARRY: I know it [religion] should matter. I don't go to church, I don't pray, you know. I ain't going to just lie and say I pray and all that, but naw. I don't pray but I know I need to the way my luck is, you know. . . . Because somebody got to be with me, they say. Somebody got to be.

ROY: Yeah I think I need to get in church more now. . . . Just seeing everything that goes on around me, you know, seeing all the killing and shooting and drug dealing going on. I think I need to be in church more now to get from around, you know, this type of setting.

FELTON: Yeah it [religion] matters, cause I don't have it in my life now, and I think if I would have had it in my life earlier I probably wouldn't be sitting here having this interview now. I'd probably be out of town playing baseball right now.

Conceptualizing and Confronting Obstacles and Barriers: The Special Place of Race and Class

After discussion the issue of personal mobility with the men, I moved on to ask them about the role of external obstacles and barriers beyond the immediate living conditions of the Near West Side. Recall that in the discussion of macro-level obstacles and barriers, the men fell into three subgroups along a continuum of perspectives. The same split occurred when the men were asked to speak about obstacles and barriers at the personal level.

In chapter 4 we saw that Jake, Larry, Barry, Joseph, Jordan, Jason, Lester, Conrad, and Butch had very little to say about the effects of external barriers and mobility processes in American life. The same held true for their remarks about the relevance of these factors for their personal mobility. There was little recognition on their part that being black men, in and of itself, might pose a problem for them in getting ahead. Instead, they ignored the racial issue and focused once again on the themes of hard work, discipline, and focus that they believed would carry them through. They were asked directly about whether they would be evaluated differently because they were African American males, and, if so, whether that might help or hinder them in achieving their desires and objectives. A few denied outright that they would confront racism. The others reacted to these questions with bewilderment and uncertainty. Even the few who seemed to have some primitive thoughts about how race might be significant for shaping access and opportunity in American life, could not articulate how to handle this in their personal lives. It was as if this situation was so far beyond their apprehension that it had escaped their immediate consciousness altogether. As Larry put it:

> Well I'm black, I mean I can't change that jack, so, I could be down, but I mean, man. I got advantages being a black man cause the black man can do as much as the white man can do, any man. I'm not prejudiced or nothing, you know. I mean it's all up here in your mind, if you put your mind to it you can do it.

Larry could not talk about external barriers because they were never made vivid enough to him by experience. Therefore, he returned to his focus on himself as the only relevant consideration for navigating personal mobility:

> If you want a good job, you know, you got to have that knowledge. You got to, you know, strive on getting that, you know. So you, you know, got to go through a lot to try to get there, you know. . . . You got to have a decent education and, ah, high qualities on things. And I guess you can get a good job from there, you know.

Larry and the others in this subgroup were unable to articulate clearly, if at all, how their status as black men might have mattered to their quests of upward mobility. In Barry's case, this was evident in the comments he made following his inability to talk about whether his race and class status was a factor in his pursuit of a better life. When asked whether anything beyond his own efforts might impact his future outcomes, he said, "Like I say, you just want to do it. You know you can go out and do what it take to get the good job. You know, don't stop, just go all the way. Keep trying 'til you get it. . . ." For Barry the only thing that could stand in his way toward moving up was himself.

The views of these men contrast starkly not only with the less isolated men in the group, but also with many African Americans who have regular social contact across race and class lines.[6] Studies have reported that many African Americans consistently, and sometimes obsessively, think about the effect of race on their lives. Strategies for navigating race are often better thought out and enacted when one has a sufficient stock of capital to employ (Young 1999). These strategies can take a number of forms, include interactive styles (e.g., overt friendliness or polite distancing, depending on the situation at hand), ideological convictions (e.g., "those 'other' folks just cannot be trusted"), or psychological dispositions (e.g., the "angry black man" archetype). All of these approaches provide African Americans with designs for mitigating the effects of perceived racial disadvantage.

The lack of awareness of and sensitivity to racial issues expressed by the men of the Near West Side stemmed from life histories that did not offer them enough direct experiences with the realities of racial stratification in American society. Lacking the capacity to define exactly how the external social world might matter for their lives, the men emphasized personal initiative. Having experienced lives filled almost exclusively with people who shared their race and class status, these men were never positioned to witness, experience, or understand how certain forms of structural constraint might be embedded as obstacles in their paths, toward better futures. The effects of extreme social isolation amount to more than being removed from important resources and opportunities necessary for attaining a better life.

Ironically and tragically, the worldview expressed by the men of the Near West Side that emphasizing the individualism of the American Dream narrative to the exclusion of an awareness of external forces such as race and class, is produced precisely by those same circumstances of radical inequality. At first glance, it may seem like a contradictory argument to suggest that the existence of race and class hierarchies serves as the primary force shaping the men's lack of awareness of these same social forces. Yet, social locations can have the effect of putting blinders on people in their apprehension of social life. Consequently, we must take into account the blindness of individuals to important dimensions of life situations unlike their own. For example, wealthy neighborhoods lack the severity of the social problems and circumstances confronting the men of the Near West Side. Other things being held constant, performing well in school is less of a problem in neighborhoods where schools have more funding and there is less threat of violence. Yet, when performance stands as the sole point of consideration, these others matters fade from the analytical landscape. Student conduct and academic performance are given priority over the more hidden structural factors that affect student behavior. Accordingly, when the voices of these men become the sole point of attention, many assume that they are solely responsible for their lack of social mobility. When their voices are analyzed in the context of the kinds of social contacts they have experienced, and when, in turn, they are compared to men who have had different experiences, it becomes much easier to see the formative role of structural factors.

Recall that the same men who said little about race and class factors were those who did not have sustained interactions across race and class lines. The best test of their commitment to these views would be found by exploring whether they would say the same thing if brought into consistent contact with wealthier people and/or those of different racial or ethnic backgrounds. Not having had the opportunity to explore this scenario, we cannot know what these men might say in such situations. However, we do see a different perspective on race and class when we turn to the men who had more contact with people across race and class lines.

Donald, Anthony, Arthur, Tito, Travis, Dennis, Damon, Roy, Felton, Kurt, Earl, Gus, and Leon fell along the midpoint of the continuum regarding their perspectives on race, class, and personal mobility. These men viewed race and class as highly relevant in their plans to navigate personal mobility. They were convinced that they would have to contend with and maneuver around these factors in order to move up in the world. Donald and Leon spoke about how they believed they were viewed as black men in American society:

DONALD: Well, like I say, it depends on who's viewing you. Others can view you as just a black dude. Others can view you as a valuable person. In society, like I say, you never know, you never know until you get to that situation. . . . Of course, we've been discriminated against since we was born, but you don't let that bother you, though. You just keep going. . . . We have advantages. . . . Because of the things we have been through, not to make it a racist statement, the black man is very strong, and can strive if he wants to. . . . The disadvantage is a lot of people would say the disadvantage is the color of your skin.

LEON: Well they just view me as an inferior, I say it like that. They feel like black people's birth is not, they feel like black people is more or less incompetent. They feel like they is missing more brain power than anybody else in the nation. So I think we're the most, they look at us as the least likely to succeed in society, so we just, to them we're like some garbage, you know. . . . I feel the reason I've been discriminated against is because I did go out for a job, you know, and I can see from the person interviewing me, he already decided in his mind that he didn't like me, just from us holding the conversation, you know. And he kind of like showed that "Hey, nigger I'm only doing this because I have to do it. It's not because you going to get no job." And he said to me "Don't worry about it. Don't call us we'll call you." I'm like "Okay." I already got the message. He done told me, "Nigger you ain't getting nothing, so you might as well just, you better go out there and keep on searching."

This subgroup of men argued that being both black and male was particularly detrimental for their mobility prospects. They expected to confront these obstacles in life. Unfortunately, they offered no detailed or precise strategies to overcome these obstacles. The absence of insightful techniques or ideas for handling these circumstances reveals the limiting effects that a shortage of capital has on one's capacity to take action. We have stressed that these men had neither the social ties nor resources to facilitate their developing strategies and techniques. Their social experiences gave them only a rudimentary understanding of the external barriers and obstacles. Although they did not know exactly what to do about these obstacles, they knew that they had to forge a strategy if they were ever going to achieve better lives.

The last subgroup of men, Peter, Devin, Casey, and Ted, expressed views similar to those in the middle of the continuum. However, their words were more volatile, and they clearly had a deeper understanding of the great obstacles they faced as black men. In their pasts, both Devin and Casey managed life in the streets and spent a fair amount of time in jail—Devin as a gang leader and drug dealer, and Casey as a substance abuser, petty thief and hustler. The two men had the following to say about how they imagined themselves to be viewed by the general American public:

DEVIN: I think they look at me as the, not my people, but to the racists, they look at me like the enemy. They feel that we all blacks is out to get them. Which I believe like this here, I'm is. . . . Because they getting too much money. We fight for, we fought for the United States, not them. We went to war. We got to stand up for our rights. We not getting treated right. We're not even getting equal rights.

CASEY: I don't look at no disadvantages [from being a black man] cause my personal opinion is I just say fuck them. They ain't no better than me. They can kiss my ass with all that shit that they talk. I know who I am. Regardless of my situation I know exactly who I am. . . . [What white people say] doesn't make me no difference. I got life. I got a family now that I love [his children and his girlfriend, their mother].

> I'm a real person. I feel like I have emotions and I'm not scared to say it. I'm a black man in a white man's world. I don't have that fear, you know. And it's their world, believe me.

As we have seen, the last two subgroups of men went far beyond the individualistic ethos in discussing their understanding of the relevant factors for navigating personal mobility. To be sure, these men also stressed that hard work, determination, and other attributes associated with the individualistic ethos were essential for getting ahead in life. These men's co-narratives developed out of one or more of the following experiences: incarceration, being arrested or detained by the police, overt public conflicts with police and authority figures such as parole officers, or exposure to more privileged individuals in American society (usually non–African Americans). This pattern of experience provided them with insight into how those with more social power and influence can affect individual mobility, either by protecting their own positions or by regulating entry into them. These men spoke not only about the existence of these barriers, but also of the necessity to actively and assertively confront them in order to get ahead.

Another key point dividing the responses of the three subgroups was the extent to which the men could talk about the probability of securing successful outcomes in the future. The men who explicitly acknowledged the challenges posed by external constraints were more likely to state that personal mobility would be very difficult for them to achieve. In contrast to the more socially isolated men, these men could better explain their conclusions. For example, Devin argued that personal mobility was virtually impossible for him due to the public image that he had cultivated throughout his adolescence and early adulthood. While speaking about future prospects and his need for a job, Devin said, "Yes, that's something I definitely need . . . because I have a family."[7] However, in discussing his chances of getting a good job, he said, "Very bad . . . because where could a guy like me with the background that I carry get a job in five years?"

It was at this point that Devin began assessing his life history and present situation in Chicago. He offered that years of gangbanging and involvements in violence had left a tremendously negative impression upon his neighbors, and more importantly, in the local police precincts. He believed that this image would prevent him from moving ahead, at least as long as he lived in Chicago. When I asked if there was anything that he could do to improve his situation, he said, "It won't do it no good." Devin argued that the police considered him such a well-known threat and public menace that redemption in Chicago would never be an option for him. His problems began with his early involvement in a gang, and were intensified by his rapid rise to a leadership position. Gang affiliation was one public identity that was as durable as it was problematic for those that were so labeled. As Devin explained, "If you was to walk down the street me, in my neighborhood, and another car ride past and see you hanging with me, they'll say that you a Vice Lord, and you ain't nothing. That's just the way, that's the way people think. That's the way our community is."

Devin believed that he might find a better future in Mississippi, a place that he knew nothing about except that it was the birthplace of his mother. His mother's account of it allowed him to imagine it as the opposite of everything that Chicago had been for him throughout his life. All that was negative about Chicago for him—and that was plenty—could be replaced by the positive image he had constructed of Mississippi. As he explained:

> And once I get off these [probation] papers I leaving out of Chicago and start over in Mississippi. . . . It's better down there for me, I don't have to hear that confusion that's going on now and I ain't got to gangbang. It's a country part where I could build like I want to live and do what I want to do. . . . It's just like a second life.

One consequence of Devin's gang involvement was that it left him with a vision of impenetrable obstacles, even as he moved up within the gang itself. More importantly, gang involvement became a point of reference for his understanding of how race was tied to collective social power and control. The gang experience also shaped his perspective dealing with his broader social environment over issues concerning personal mobility. We recall how he explained his racial logic to me:

> I figure all whites are Disciples [a rival faction of gangs in Chicago]. All whites stick together, no matter what. And I know this for a fact 'cause when I was in jail a Latin Disciple and a Latin King, both of these is white persons, fought one black brother.[8] Two different gangs . . . they supposed to be fighting each other, but you going to pull up this black brother, cause both of you is . . . whites stick together. I could say that much.

Due to his multiple personal encounters across racial lines, many of them in prison, Devin came to view racial solidarity as a powerful social force affecting many social conditions and concerns, but especially his capacity for upward mobility. He was clear about not expecting to get ahead.

Devin's situation contrasts dramatically with that of men like Larry, who spoke very little of future prospects. As we saw earlier, Devin knew full well what was keeping him back, and he had some ideas about how to overcome it. His strategy was not a simple or easy one, but in explaining it he showed his awareness of how much the odds were stacked against him. Men like Larry were just as despondent while talking about their situations, but remained clueless about why improvement seemed so hard to come by. Had they been able to get outside of the Near West Side, or to be in touch more regularly with different people, they might have found themselves further frustrated, as they would have certainly confronted a negative response to their status as minimally skilled and economically deprived African American men. Still, such responses, while negative, would have helped them to better understand the external forces of class and race that impeded their attempts to move away from the Horner Homes. Such experiences also might have led to the formation of crude strategies for getting ahead, similar to Devin's, rather than leaving them wallowing in despair.

It cannot be emphasized enough that the degree to which the men of the Near West Side were exposed to the external world was the key to their ability to frame strategies regarding mobility as a social process. The men's personal strategies were constructed out of what they saw as generic patterns in the larger society. The men held the same general goals, and had similar skills and resources, for getting ahead. In certain ways, their notions of what to do to get ahead were quite similar as well. The differences lay in the degree to which they were aware of the role of external constraints that lay in their paths. They all agreed that it was crucial to remain focused and directed, but they differed on what external obstacles they expected to confront in the outside world.

Conclusion

In this chapter we have explored a key aspect of how these men look at themselves as social actors. We considered how they locate themselves in that very social world that their words opened up to us in earlier chapters. The theme of social isolation has emerged as a leitmotiv throughout the chapters. Relative degrees of social isolation shaped the men's views on the social world and how they saw themselves as participants in that world. Actual proximity to those with social power and influence gave the men a more focused and detailed understanding of how these factors needed to be confronted at the individual level. Alternatively, those men who were more socially isolated saw few external barriers or obstacles, and articulated little beyond their own motivation and effort as necessary for achieving success in life.

Social location does not merely isolate individuals from better prospects. It also creates a barrier denying them the capacity to interpret that which lies beyond their social milieu. The men framed a vision of desirable work by connecting what they saw as positive about themselves (skills with hands, body strength) to the kind of manual labor undertaken by their male forebearers. Their limited perspective helps to explain how partially accurate understandings are formed from specific social locations. The men also had access to some information about advances in technology and the disappearance of work in the community, and images about what work was like in the past. This information helped them to portray the world of work with some accuracy. However, because of their chronic unemployment, they knew of very few people who worked regularly. This situation allowed them to construe inaccuracies and to remain confused about the realities of the world of work.

In chapters 6 and 7 we have uncovered some important details that can assist us in expanding the cultural analysis of low-income black men, especially beyond that offered by the normative and value-centered mode of inquiry. First, these low-income black men continued to be ill-suited for the contemporary urban work environment, especially as it has been transformed over the past two decades from an industrial to a service-sector arena. More importantly, these men appeared insufficiently aware of these transformations. Although they knew that the work situation had changed for the worse since their early childhoods, they could not detail the specific changes, nor explain how these changes actually bear upon their own lives. Instead, the men clung to aspirations relevant to a disappearing world of work. Very few of the men had anything to say about the emerging service sector, and what they did say made it clear that this sector was undesirable to most of them.

The men were also resolute about not accepting long-term employment in the most menial occupational niches in the service sector. Having just begun to view themselves as adults with the potential for a long life span, they did not see these jobs as providing them with the financial capital that would help them navigate their lives over the long haul. Essentially, what the men were looking for was not there; the few prospects that did exist, saw as not worth pursuing.

In his classic study of black men on a Washington, DC, street corner, Elliot Liebow (1967) showed how men try to come to terms with the types of work most readily available to them. He argues that the men contemplate whether such employment is fruitful for them, and whether they believe themselves to be efficacious at performing on the job. Similarly, we have looked at how the men of the Near West Side tried to make sense of employment. My analysis has included the additional factor of how these men made sense of the overall structure of work opportunities in their city. This broader consideration of the world of work takes us beyond Liebow, who stopped his investigation at men's responses to specific jobs. Here, we considered the skills and resources that the men of the Near West Side believed they could bring to employment prospects. Rather than ending with normative judgments of their beliefs about work, this chapter has explored the nuances and subtleties embedded in those beliefs.

The men's deprived childhoods and early adulthoods, replete with unemployment, left them with modest aspirations regarding secure employment and support for a stable family. For these men, an improved family situation entailed an environment that was less threatening and turbulent than that with which they were familiar. For some, this meant aspiring to the long-term goal of moving out of the neighborhood. For others, it meant hope for some form of socio-structural change within the community. In either case, while the men may have had a strong commitment to what Elliot Liebow referred to as preoccupation with the present moment in how they handled daily interactions and transactions, they certainly had the capacity to think about the future. In part, their survival of the tumultuous adolescent years gave them confidence that they could survive much longer into the future.

The men were clear about what would constitute better futures for them. However, as we have seen, their rudimentary and often unrealistic strategies meant that access to that better future would be problematic. The men's strategies for getting ahead in the work world were out of synch with the demands and operations of modern labor markets. The men hoped to rely solely on hard work and effort as prerequisites for employment. They also believed that because a few others in the community had work, they could find it as well.

My discussions with the men of the Near West Side confirmed that the experience of living without work has enduring implications. Most importantly, chronic unemployment continuously corrodes one's ability to effectively engage the employment sphere, even if one happens to maintain an accurate portrayal of obstacles and impediments to finding good work. These men do not simply lack the requisite skills for success in the white-collar service sector (even for the lower-mobility and lesser-skilled occupations in that sector); they cannot offer coherent understandings of what the essential skills might be for such success. Consequently, problems arise due to the disconnect between the men's ideal visions and the realities of the segment of the labor market accessible to them. Some men were unable to adapt to the sporadic employment options that come their way. Others experienced an absence of employment opportunities altogether. For all of the men, the longer they remained unemployed and in the constant company of others unemployed, the more isolated they became from the skills and resources, networks, and means needed to develop a logic for the acquisition of the "good job." Thus, the absence of stable employment did not solely result in a lack of income, but also in a decreased capacity to make sense of the world of work. This effect, in turn, further undermined their employability.

Clearly, the resolution of this condition necessitates micro- and macro-level changes in the relations between inner-city low-income African Americans and employment sectors. At the macro level, efforts to augment the employment prospects of low-income black men with benefits and remuneration that will allow them to lead productive lives would provide a crucial step forward. Additionally, initiatives that involve both job training *and* education about the changing nature of the urban employment arena would assist these men in developing more accurate readings of the transformations taking place around. This training, in turn, would help the men to adjust to the new circumstances. Actual change, however, will necessitate some larger-scale transformations as well. Not only must low-income black men learn to relate better to a white-collar service sector, but, as research has shown (Kirschenmann and Neckerman 1991, Neckerman and Kirschenmann 1991), that sector must relate better to them.

A fundamental argument in urban poverty research is that employment creates the capacity for individuals to effectively organize daily life, and crystallize a longer-term sense of purpose and direction (Wilson 1996). Consistent employment provides a basis for formulating clear and tangible goals and objectives for the future. Lack of participation in the workforce diminishes one's capacity to set and work toward these goals and objectives. Through the understandings of employment and mobility expressed by men who are on society's margins, this chapter argues that the process of attaining adequate employment is a complex one.[9] To assert that gainful employment will help these men to improve other dimensions of their lives is an obvious, yet overly simple, conclusion. To better locate their orientation toward future prospects, it must be kept in mind that these men had already experienced a half-decade of chronic unemployment. They had no consistent employment experience and few credentials that would certify them for more than semi-skilled labor positions, positions that have been disappearing in inner-city Chicago as well as other American cities (Bluestone and Harrison 1982, Wacquant and Wilson 1989 and 1990, Wilson 1987).

Their dire social condition was the basis for their emphasis on being gainfully employed rather than on obtaining a specific job. Therefore, while the men did discuss specific occupations, their central focus in life was on securing employment that would provide them with a certain quality of life. Most of the men believed that the key resource they possessed to secure such jobs was their physical ability. For them, secure employment status meant a job that provided adequate pay and that had benefits. For these men, there was no great preoccupation with far-reaching ideal states in their portraits of a stable life. In the broader quality of life context, stability meant a domicile in a safe community,[10] and maintaining a family with at least the basic resources for sustenance and for ensuring some mobility for their children.

Chapter Eight

Recasting the Crisis of Poor Black Men

That's retarded to think that [black men do not know how to take control of their lives]. People actually think like that? I mean, people with Ph.D.'s and shit.

Vance Smith spoke these words one afternoon when I was in the Western Avenue community office of the 28th Ward. Nothing else that Vance had to say during my time there appears in this book because, as a man in his mid-forties, he is far above the age ceiling for this study. His life on the Near West Side has been filled with a much broader array of opportunities and encounters. Since his adolescent days in the 1960s, Vance has been a gang member and cofounder of a faction of the Vice Lord Nation, an associate of the Chicago chapter of the Black Panther Party and a participant in some of their community organizing efforts, a full-time employee for nearly a decade in domestic service for a downtown social club, and, since the mid-1980s, a chronically unemployed black man.

Vance came to the community office once a week or so to investigate whether there was anything that needed to be done. He grew more interested in my project over time, and would regularly ask me questions and offer opinions about the contemporary struggles of urban black men. For a few months, I was his eye on how the rest of the world looked at people like him. At one point in a conversation Vance specifically asked about what my colleagues and associates at the University of Chicago thought about the research that I was doing in his neighborhood, and what "educated white people" more generally thought about poor young black men. I talked about the emergence of the underclass debate in academia and public policy circles, and how the myriad uses, assertions, and reactions to notions of the underclass and related concepts had much to do with public perceptions of the black urban poor. My comments induced the reply from Vance cited at the outset of this conclusion. If anything, writing this book was an effort to diminish the likelihood that privileged people would continue thinking about poor black men in the way Vance describes.

The most cynical might surmise that the situations of the twenty-six men presented in the foregoing pages represent dead-end scenarios. Yet, as we have seen, a careful consideration of how they thought about their life chances reveals that they possessed much more than dead-end thoughts. Even the men who were the most pessimistic about their chances to move up still held hopes for the future. After thinking about how far away these men are from a decent life, much less the good life, what should we make of their thoughts about getting ahead? If their current conditions and circumstances are as dire as they appear, than what is the point of looking at their thoughts about the social world and their sense of how they could best participate in it?

The simple response is that there is much to say on this matter. Drawing attention to the connections between poor black men's personal histories, their social experiences, and their mental worlds has relevance for developing an agenda for the advancement of their lives, and the lives of people like them. It also has relevance for the agenda of researchers who are exploring culture and the urban poor. There is thus much to gain, both pragmatically and intellectually, from our inquiry. In the remainder of this chapter, after synthesizing the content of the minds of these poor black men, we will turn to the ways this study can further these agendas.

What Is in the Minds of Marginalized Black Men and Why

Exploring the relationship of historical and contemporary experience to the capacity to make meaning provides crucial evidence of some particular ways in which the past lives on in the present. What these men understood about how the social world operates, and how they might operate within it, grew out of their patterns of access to the broader world. Family members, schools, peer networks, and casual associations in the neighborhood influenced the cultivation of the ideas about how people advance themselves in society. The extent to which these social institutions or groups created exposure to larger social hierarchies and mobility possibilities dictated the extent to which the men acquired complex understandings of those elements of social life. Intimate exposure to, and interaction with, the mechanisms and loci of power and privilege showed the men how these forces and structures affected society in general, and their own lives more particularly. The men who lacked such exposure offered the least substantive commentary on how stratification and inequality worked in society. They knew that hierarchies existed, but they could not elucidate how they operated. They also did not grasp how such hierarchies affected their own lives. To be sure, a more focused (and a quantitatively designed) analysis of the kinds of networks in which people are embedded could uncover exactly how, why, and with what level of intensity information flows between members of social groups. This book sets the groundwork for such an exploration by illustrating how different pat-

terns of social relations and experience are associated with different degrees of specificity and depth in the content of certain worldviews.

In addition to social contacts and interactions, exposure to public ideas
and information about societal dynamics and social issues allowed the
men to form understandings about the social world. We have seen that
the most socially isolated men were the most likely to draw from the
standard public script of the American Dream, thereby ignoring broader
structural factors such as class and race. If one's daily life affords few, if
any, chances to interact with the broader social world, than one is left with
the values inscribed in the standard American narrative to draw upon for
guidance. Some men were able to challenge that script even in the absence
of personal experience because they had been exposed to alternate ideas,
often through formal education. Those who lacked the necessary capital
to pose challenges, either justified the acceptance of those scripts or simply
surrendered to them.

In similar fashion to their construction of societal-level worldviews, the
men in this study formulated a sense of their personal life chances as a
consequence of their schooling and social experiences. Again, the family
served as an initial source of ideas about how to navigate the social
world. However, families offered these men little more than the resource
of emotional support and general ideas about how to pursue mobility.
More often than not, the men related that family members were supportive and encouraging of their mobility quests. It is often assumed by traditional cultural paradigms that a lack of familial support plays a role in
the negative social outcomes of low-income individuals. Yet, as we have
seen, there was no great absence of support for these men. Instead, there
was an absence of relevant information for helping these men to navigate
their lives.

Each man's strategic planning to attain a desired outcomes depended
on the kinds of social and cultural capital he possessed. Furthermore,
the planning depended on how he identified different forms of capital as
possible resources for his mobility quests. We have seen that the most
socially isolated men with little to no capital were the ones who almost
wholeheartedly adopted the individualistic stance toward achieving personal objectives. Other men spoke at great length about the social forces
and conditions that had to be negotiated in order for them to get ahead.
This latter group of men had more insights regarding the real challenges
involved in getting ahead. Still, even they lacked sufficient capital for initiating upward mobility.

What is in the minds of marginalized black men, then, are ideas, strategies, and worldviews that not only tell us how these men situate themselves, but how much we must re-situate our understanding of their needs

and capabilities so that they might attain future statuses that are better than their past and present ones.

Proposing a New Practical Agenda for Low-Income Black Men

If a better day is to come for poor black men, then researchers and other parties who are sensitive to their plight must commit themselves to a new perspective on these men. In order for their lives to truly improve, increased employment and job-training opportunities need to be brought into their lives. These men certainly would benefit from an expanded and more secure labor market, but, as we have seen, there is much more that must occur for them to improve their lives. As the men's testimonies about work make clear, however, increased employment opportunities alone will not deliver them from socioeconomic disadvantage. Information about municipal labor market opportunities, including the options and possibilities in the modern urban world of work and the means and mechanisms for accessing better employment, are as important as the jobs themselves.

Of course, this is the utopian vision of change. The current public view of these men is perhaps best conveyed by the "three-strikes and you're out" rationale of recent governmental initiatives on crime and delinquency, increased incarceration rates for nonviolent offenders, and other law enforcement initiatives that have resulted in the removal of many low-income black men from the public landscape. This approach goes hand in hand with the public reaction to notions of the underclass, which centers on control and containment of an apparently troubling constituency.

A number of the men in this book have been victims of that very approach. Incarcerations, detainment, and detention may have sharpened their sense of how American society operates, but these experiences cannot offer the men solid footing for developing alternative visions. Rather than moving to increase these men's exposure to these settings, we must bring them closer to the everyday worlds of the upwardly mobile and recognize them as individuals who can function in a similar fashion if given the chance—and the material means—to do so.

The structural conditions of the Near West Side and American society at large create robust obstacles to significant mobility. Thus, any dramatic changes in the men's prospects must begin from the outside. Accordingly, even if these men were suddenly offered a new range of mobility prospects, they would still have to contend with altering their worldviews in order to allow them to take advantage of these prospects. Those men who would be most challenged by this new scenario would be the most socially isolated, who said the least about external barriers and constraint. These men unequivocally endorsed an individualistic perspective, allowing them no mental preparation to maneuver around socially constructed obstacles or barriers. Their perspective would not provide them with the capacity to respond effectively to negative public images of black men held by Chicago employers and personnel managers. Some other men might be better equipped ideologically to respond to this condition, but they would also lack the capital-enhancing experiences that would allow them to mitigate the effects of racism in the employment sphere. If given the opportunity to undertake substantive work in a new milieu, even these men would have trouble adapting to the daily routines. Recall that, due to their chronic unemployment, most of the men had a very vague sense of time and were often hours late for scheduled interviews with me.

It is imperative that those who aim to contribute positively to the advancement of low-income black men consider the full range of critical components that factor into their worldviews. First, we have seen that rationality guides their construction of meaning about the social world. Furthermore, those constructs emerge as products of personal histories. Most importantly, life experiences embed thoughts in an individual's mind to the extent that, even when changes in the social circumstances occur, they may take time to impact upon individual-level thinking and orientations to action. This caveat should not be taken as a disincentive for initiating change for these men, but rather as a caution that such change needs to be effected and implemented in culturally appropriate ways.

Furthering the New Agenda for Cultural Inquiry on Low-Income Black Men

The portrait outlined here of what these men have to say about mobility and opportunity and how they make sense of their life chances, irrespective of the behaviors they might have engaged in, underscores the need to forge a new cultural framing of them. This new frame must acknowledge that these men are complex meaning-making actors who function as they do because their social world has mandated that they do so or has left them with few if any options for alternative modes of functioning. As meaning-making actors, they function much like the rest of us; they simply do so from significantly less privileged positions. Accordingly, the foregoing discussion of the worldviews of the men of the Near West Side has important theoretical implications that extend beyond the case of low-income African American men. In fact, these insights pertain to any social category of people trying to move up the social ladder and improve their life situation. The most important finding reveals that the imagination (meaning, in this case, the arena of individual being that concerns meaning-making about the future), is a highly relevant area of sociological inquiry. The imagination situates actors for potential action. Exploring the imagination makes it possible to capture how structural conditions affect, but do not determine, the types of action that can emerge (or at least be conceived of) by individuals who experience similar conditions of life. While certain actors share the same public space, the types and sequence of their daily experiences can result in diverse readings of the social world and assessments of their place within it.

As for low-income people more specifically, phenomenological inquiry brings forth a greater understanding of how they contextualize and classify their experiences. This perspective reveals a more complete sense of the meaning that they attach to their experiences. This type of inquiry also provides insight into how social structure is incorporated into the everyday understandings of actors as a consequence of social experience. For these men, the creation of meaning about social life (and the social experiences that are relevant to that process) involves a cultural process similar to that experienced by other actors in society. The difference lies in their context of extreme social isolation, lacking crucial resources for upward mobility.

Social isolation is not simply a conceptual device for interpreting contrasts in norms or values between individuals who live in sequestered and impoverished social environments. More profoundly, social isolation stands as a significant factor determining how meanings about social reality are construed out of social experience. Indeed, this focus on the relevant social experiences for the construction of meanings about social reality is a testimony to the inadequacies of moving directly from an analysis of an individual's social context to that of the norms and values that he or she maintains. As Clifford Geertz (1973) has argued, the construction of meaning is a process that naturally intercedes between and interconnects those two components of social reality.

Since Geertz's pivotal writing, the field of the sociology of culture has been the site of much work aimed at giving more specific attention to the social contexts of meaning-making (Bourdieu 1977a, Giddens 1984, Goffman 1974, Griswold 1987, Sewell 1992, Swidler 1986, Wuthnow 1987, Zerubavel 1997). Much of this debate about meaning concerns appropriate definitions for the term, valid mechanisms for measuring it, and epistemological claims about the capacity to interpret it. We have not had the space in this study to give full due to the complexities of this debate. Yet, by focusing on the content of worldviews, our study does contribute to this debate in a highly specific way, by crafting a new approach to the study of low-income people. My goal was to explore the social and sociological significance of differences and distinctions. This approach does not, in and of itself, resolve any of the issues raised by cultural sociologists regarding sociological pursuits of meaning-making. It does, however, further expand the sociologically relevant terrain for exploring meaning-making in ways that have direct bearing on social policy formation and the provision of remedial social services.

The fruits of exploring the variation in the worldviews of poor black men are twofold. First, the content of the men's worldviews, problematic as some of them might be for the mobility prospects of these men, can been seen as logical after taking into account the social environment within which the men were reared. Second, bringing their thoughts to light provides a step toward building linkages between socio-structural contexts, individual-level conceptions, and the capacity for action. The ultimate aim is to gain a better understanding of the place of meaning-making in the unfolding of individual and collective agency. The portrait of the men outlined in this book, more than anything else, substantiates the claim that the ability to effectively interpret the world around oneself is a prerequisite for taking appropriate and beneficial action within it. The story of their lives also gives cultural inquiry a broader conceptual basis for investigation of life experiences that, in the final instance, should not be exclusively attributed to the normative and value-based orientations of actors.

Appendix _____

THE TESTIMONIES of these twenty-six men were collected through interviews that took place between December 1993 and December 1995. The interviews were loosely structured, combining predominantly open-ended discussion with a few rank-order questions. This age category of twenty through twenty-five was chosen because twenty-five is the upper boundary of the age bracket invoked in public and academic discussion of the crisis of African American men; by age 20, the men are individuals who, although still young, have come into full adulthood while experiencing socioeconomic disadvantage. As adults they have now become their own primary agents for changing their situation, while younger males may still rely on parents or guardians. Having been unable to improve their situation thus far, they are now firmly sedimented into deprivation.

While in the Near West Side, I interviewed another dozen or so more men in this age group. A few of them were as disadvantaged as the men in this book. These other men did not finish enough of their interviews to make them comparable with the twenty-six cases. The rest of the additional men, along with another fifteen or so from similar communities in Chicago, are doing much better than the cases discussed here. They have jobs or are in school: either way, they look like they will leave poverty behind them. Consequently, much more of their lives have taken place outside of the Near West Side. Their stories involve a different kind of complexity that merits its own exploratory space.[1] The voices of a few of these men were brought into this account whenever their statements added some depth or clarity to the points raised.

With the exception of a few phone calls for follow-up information, all of the conversations with the twenty-six men took place in their community. They were asked questions about their schooling, neighborhood life, and family histories, and any other institutional, social, or organizational experiences that comprised their life histories. Specific attention was given to what they believed they learned about getting ahead from these encounters or experiences. The rest of the questions, and the bulk of the formal interview, had to do with whether American society was stratified, and if so, what forces or factors contributed to and maintained the stratification; how they thought that other Americans got ahead in life (and what resources, tools, or kinds of knowledge mattered for getting ahead); and whether and how they took anything from their visions of the social world to build arguments about what getting ahead meant to them.

The men came into this study by way of a modified snowball sampling approach. The project began in 1993, when I started making use of ties that I had established with social service providers mentioned in the preface. Within a month following my first meeting with each of these providers, they grew so committed to my project that they made office space available to me in each of their facilities so that I could hold interviews there. Each introduced me to the first wave of men that I met who fit the desired age category. Other men began approaching me after learning about the project. That knowledge came to them from men who had already been interviewed, from neighborhood associates who informed them of my work, or after some cursory observation of my research activities in the community.

Although I regularly engaged in large group interaction with the men in and near the facilities where these offices were located, I interviewed the respondents in a one-on-one interactive format. Each interview had three components, which took anywhere from a few days to a few months to complete. The first was an initial encounter that allowed me to develop some comfort and familiarity with each man. A formal interview, or set of interviews, then followed. This activity lasted from one to four hours, with two hours being the norm. The third component was an opportunity for follow-up discussion in order to clarify or revisit some issues raised in the formal exchange. These final discussions lasted from thirty minutes to a few hours, and they usually took place over a few days. Even if the formal interview was completed within a day's time, the pre-interview and follow-up discussions took place over a series of days. Each of the men was paid twenty-five dollars for the completion of a formal interview.

I believe that my encounters in the field offered something to a debate that had been building up for a few decades in sociology and anthropology about how researchers relate to the people that they study. The literature on how researchers build relationships in the field is quite lengthy (much of it is cited in various contributions to Denzin and Lincoln 1994). Much of this debate has been about gaining access to people such that they feel comfortable with the researchers and that a rapport is developed that enhances communication throughout the research endeavor. This debate is important, especially as I take account of the power differentials between researchers and low-income residents of American cities. Although I was thrilled that men sought me out to talk, I would continually reflect upon what it meant for these men to share parts of their lives that I would never think of doing for twenty-five dollars and a potentially useful social contact. I knew that my situation (economically, professionally, etc.) was the reason for my feeling this way. However, the debate seems to have encouraged researchers to focus on enhancing proximity, accessibility, and rapport; to reflect upon, in the effort to overcome or make sense as best as one could, the effects of being different from those whom one was studying (by virtue of gender, race, class status, or other characteristics). There has not been as much reflection on how shared personal characteristics matter for the ensuing conversation. My experience on the Near West Side led me to believe that similarities can inhibit or alter discussion as much as it can enhance it.[2] My lesson concerning such relations constitutes my lingering thoughts after the field experience.

In talking to these men both prior to and after formal interviews, I tried to determine how much my being near their age and of the same race and gender might help them deal with the fact that I was from a different class altogether. From their end, the men looked for information on how to relate to me through questions about why I came to Chicago, whether I liked sports (incidentally, being a Knicks fan in the 1990s was especially difficult in the city of Chicago), and how I felt about the situation of black men in America (a topic I addressed in very roundabout ways until I finished my fieldwork).

I thought that the men felt that I connected with them on many levels, but that I was still very different. I had a real job (or what seemed like one to them) and they did not. I also lived in a part of town that was far from where they resided. The result of this is that I often felt like a distant cousin, someone that the men knew and was familiar with, but not in an up-close kind of way. All in all, I do not think that my experience was anything like that of Song and Parker (1995) (in part because my research was not about identity). What I did find more than anything else, however, was that the men would assume that I knew the answers to some of their questions before they spoke because I also was from a large city.

Statements like "I know you know what I'm talking about" would be uttered by the more articulate men when talking about how racism operated, or how urban poverty was experienced by poor people. Some of these men would speak as if New York City was worse than Chicago ever could be in terms of poverty, and attempt to wrap up their views by saying that I already knew about what they were saying. I wonder what else (either more or less) they might have said if I were a white woman asking them these questions. Would there have been more explanation of certain things? Would they have tried harder to prove certain points to me that they instead took for granted that I understood (whether I actually did or not)? I can only wonder about these questions. I do think that all of this demands that more conversation take place with low-income African American men, and poor people in general, so that their perspectives on these and other matters are disseminated farther than they currently are. I caution that what must be extended is the effort to talk *with* these men. The common practice of talking *at* them leads to a societal mis-recognition of who these people are, and what their capacities might be.

For almost all of the men, my interviews were periods of disruption of a daily pattern of idleness and street corner association, interspersed with mostly futile attempts to find work. This was partly what made them so willing to talk. Another reason, as many of them told me at the end of our conversations, was that the interviews did not put them on the defensive about bad things that they did, or that happened to them. It seemed ironic to me at first, but now obvious, that some of the ease in talking about some of the bad things in their lives was due to the fact that bad things were not the focus of the conversations. Another, more instrumental, set of reasons had to do with why they spoke with me in the first place.

Soon after entering the field, I came to regard the men that appear in this book as the "down but not out" because they were willing to interact with me for both monetary and informational rewards. Aside from the eagerness to earn money (for some of the men this was their only source of earned wages in many months), the men expressed an interest in talking to me as they thought that I might lead them to job opportunities or, as it was for a few cases, so that I might instruct them on how to conduct themselves during job interviews. In the latter regard, they inquired about the ways in which the research interview may have paralleled the job interview setting. This implied that they remained willing to take advantage of opportunities that might benefit them, even if only in some small way. Accordingly, their testimonies must be read with the understanding that they are a group of low-income black men who have not altogether given up hope in the possibilities of at least some minimal transformation of their life situations.

Notes

Preface

1. A rich, though sometimes unnecessarily pejorative sense of the specific cultural milieu of urban poverty in East Harlem is conveyed by anthropologist Philippe Bourgois in his book, *In Search of Respect: Selling Crack in El Barrio* (1995).

2. I also knew some members of the small but visible pockets of Italian Americans and Asian Americans who lived on particular streets in the community as well. The Italian Americans were holding onto what was a vastly diminishing presence in the community, and the Asian Americans were apparently maintaining an extremely small but stable presence since immigrating to the neighborhood in the early 1960s.

3. In the early and mid-1980s escalating drug distribution activity in communities like East Harlem led to the implementation of SWAT-like teams of police officers that poured into a neighborhood to make mass arrests of drug dealers. The turbulence created by such actions was a topic of street corner conversation for a good part of that decade.

4. As the sociologist Erving Goffman (1974) has suggested, frames are schemas of interpretation that allow individuals to make sense of the events, encounters, and circumstances in their lives. Frames consist of scripts that provide coherent interpretations of scenarios or phenomena. The development and employment of frames enables individuals to assess and respond better to similar encounters in the future. Thus, frames create the means for personal interpretation or understandings of the people, objects, and ideas that individuals come into contact with in their everyday experiences.

Framing has become a major concept in the last ten years of cultural analysis. It has been used to describe how people come to determine personal or social problems, and how they map out plans of action to respond to the initial occurrences (Gamson 1992). In recent studies of social movements, framing has been used to help better understand how people decide to take action, as well as why they do not take action, especially in circumstances that others may deem worthy of some kind of response (Snow and Benford 1988, 1992; Snow, Rochford, Worden, and Benford 1986; Tarrow 1992).

5. More specifically, my objective here was to elucidate the men's understanding of social structure in American society. The term *social structure* can refer to a broad array of societal arrangements, essentially any kind of formal or informal arrangement of people in space and time. The men here were asked to talk about social structure in two distinct ways. One had to do with the arrangement of social positions. Their views on this topic were articulated through comments on the world of work and job opportunities. Specifically, they discussed the kinds of meaningful work they felt existed, the differences between good jobs and bad ones, and how people access different kinds of work opportunities. The other

reference to social structure concerned differences in individual and group accumulation of societal resources. This aspect of the discussion brought forth their
notions of the nature and forms of social hierarchies in American life, and whether
and how such hierarchies are based on wealth, privilege, or some other factor.
Specific attention was given to whether and how the men spoke of obstacles and
barriers, and, if so, whether they ultimately located them in the external social
world (e.g., racism, sexism, or classism), or within the individual (e.g., laziness or
lack of appropriate skill). The separation of these closely interrelated components
of the mobility scheme in American life may seem picayune. However, the testimonies that follow show that this is far from the case. Paying attention to these
distinctions discloses the varied kinds of information the men drew from the social
world in order to concretize their arguments and assertions.

6. A structural element or structuring device is a mental image used to construct a frame of understanding about reality. It is a tool in the framing process.
My use of the term "structuring device" was informed by the work of sociologist
Anthony Giddens (1979, 1984), who introduced the concept of *structuration*.
Giddens argued that there exists a duality of structure in social life. In his words,
"structure [is] the medium and outcome of the conduct it recursively organizes;
the structural properties of social systems do not exist outside of action but are
chronologically implicated in its production and reproduction" (1984, p. 374).
Put more simply, the order of the social world—rich and poor, black and white,
male and female—does not exist outside of people's own capacity to continuously
re-create or maintain these categories. Thus, people are affected by whatever position or place that they have in the social world, and their subsequent action often
reinforces their status (for example, teachers are in authoritative positions vis-à-
vis students, and members of both groups usually behave in ways that maintain
that authority relation). Social structures, then, are meaningful not only as arrangements of categories that classify people but as outcomes of social action.
The two processes operate simultaneously, and are mutually reinforcing.

The notion of a structuring device is a step away from Giddens's actual definition of structuration, but there is a clear relationship. Structuration has to do with
the social organization of daily life. This is a central issue of concern for Giddens,
and the analytical point of concern for most urban ethnographic research. A structuring device, however, is that element of a frame that explains how characteristics
of the social world, or of the people in it, affect individual and collective action.
It is a tool or a construct that individuals use to organize visions of social reality.
These visions in some sense become the social reality within which people live. It
constitutes their subjective orientation to life. If that orientation is shared by other
people who live in similar circumstances and who communicate with each other,
then an intersubjectivity comes into being.

Meaning-making, then, can be thought of as the adoption and articulation of
frames. The goal of this investigation is to discern whether and how frames about
mobility, opportunity, and life chances include attention to the structuring devices
discussed earlier. Whatever these men include in their frames is affected by the
historical and social contexts that circumscribe their lives. In other words, the
capacity of people to identify and interpret particular aspects of the social world
has a great deal to do with their social locations, and their history of social interac-

tion and social exposure. The work in a number of related subfields in sociology— the sociology of knowledge, symbolic interaction, and existential sociology—has sustained this understanding (Blumer 1969; P. Berger and Luckmann 1967; Cicourel 1974; Douglas 1970; Goffman 1974; Psathas 1973; Schutz 1962, 1964, 1967, 1970; Schutz and Luckmann 1973).

Symbolic interaction, especially as introduced by Herbert Blumer, focuses more on how objects, situations, and events are given meaning. The meaning-making process here involves an actor's registering a sense of how any of these are responded to by other actors. The readings of those responses allows the individual to ascribe whatever meanings he or she does. For example, the object popularly known as a chair gets its name and meaning not by some inherent characteristic of the object, but by the repetitious act of people using the object in the same way, which is to rest themselves. Repetitive enactment of this behavior—as well as others' observation of this—reinforces a shared meaning about what the object is and how it is to be used.

Existential sociology (various strands of which having been pursued by some of the sociologists mentioned above) is more concerned with how lived experience results in the sedimentation of larger-scale belief systems and patterns of meaning. Consequently, those scholars deal more with how ideas and ideologies, which are broader arenas of thought than the formation of meaning about specific material objects, get formed and maintained. Clearly, this book is in conversation with the effort to explore the formation of large-scale systems and patterns.

Introduction
Making New Sense of Poor Black Men in Crisis

1. The names used throughout this book are pseudonyms.

2. All temporal references in this work pertain to the years 1993–95, when the bulk of the fieldwork for this project was conducted.

3. Although the term was formally introduced into public and scholarly considerations of poverty over twenty years ago (Auletta 1982), it is largely associated with urban poverty scholar William Julius Wilson, who included it into his seminal study *The Truly Disadvantaged* (1987). Wilson himself dispensed with the term, given the connotations of extreme profligacy associated with it (Wilson 1991). Over the past two decades, it has taken on a life of its own as a colloquial way of referring to low-income African Americans in urban communities. This has occurred despite Wilson's rejection of it, and the litany of claims about its analytical inadequacies and pernicious implications as a mechanism for describing low-income constituencies (Gans 1995).

4. "Worldview" refers to beliefs that individuals maintain about particular aspects of the social world or their experiences within it. A worldview is not simply an attitude or feeling about some aspect of society, but an articulation of how some aspect of the world or its inhabitants operate. It is a composite of frames. Thus, individuals can *feel* bad about not having a job (which partly constitutes their attitude about their employment status), but they can also *believe* that they do not hold a job because employment opportunities in factory work, an area in which they may *feel* they may have expertise, has declined in their community. In

this case, their beliefs about the situation of factory work in part constitutes their worldview about employment opportunities.

5. Denise is the only staff member at either of the main sites who wanted to keep her actual name out of anything written about this study. "Denise" is a pseudonym.

6. Another indicator of the neighborhood parochialism easily found in Chicago is that although I was less than a half-mile away from the Rockwell Gardens Houses, I met no young men from that development. My contact, Diane, a resident of Horner, never expressed to me the possibility of extending my sample to that area. While Rockwell Gardens was a part of the Near West Side, and consequently within the boundaries of the alderman's office, it was almost as if that development was in another city. Diane felt that she only knew Horner, and that is why this portion of my men came from Horner or a block or two away.

7. See the appendix for a detailed description of how I got in contact with the men and an explanation of how the interviews unfolded.

Chapter One
The Past and Future of the Cultural Analysis of Black Men

1. They include: Darity et al. 1994; T. Davis 1994; Duncan 1994; Farley and Allen 1987; Hawkins 1996; Holzer 1986; Mincy 1994a; Moss and Tilly 1996; Myers 1996; Petterson 1997; Rolison 1993; Sampson 1987. Ethnographic and interview-based studies include: Anderson 1978, Billson 1996, Hannerz 1969, 1972, Hunter and Davis 1994, Kornblum and Williams 1985, Laseter 1997, Liebow 1967, MacLeod 1995, Majors and Billson 1992, Rainwater 1970, Sullivan 1989, Tolleson 1997, Venkatesh 1994, and Young 1997. Finally, analytical and other scholarly commentaries include: Blake and Darling 1994, Dyson 1989; Madhubuti 1990, Monroe 1995, Oliver 1994, Staples 1982, and Wilson 1992.

2. The following works provide overviews of different structural features: Bluestone and Harrison 1982, Kasarda 1995, Massey and Denton 1993, and Wilson 1996. These authors discuss the demise of urban manufacturing employment sectors and the resulting contribution to massive urban joblessness in the past two decades for those individuals who have little access to the service-based employment sector. Massey and Denton highlight the role of race-based residential segregation in cementing African Americans in residential communities that lack the resources and capabilities for promoting socioeconomic advancement. In their view, the effects of the structural transformation of urban economies are heightened by the maintenance of rigid patterns of residential segregation to keep many urban-based African Americans away from good job prospects.

3. One of the most prominent examples of this dual consideration is the work of William Julius Wilson (1996), who foregrounds the structural dimensions of urban life for African Americans, but also pays increasingly more attention to their value systems (which, he asserts, generally reflect those held by middle-income Americans). Another balanced depiction of structure and culture, written without much formal academic jargon or extensive use of field data, is Cornel West's *Race Matters* (1993).

4. Much of this emphasis can be attributed to American sociology's early-twentieth-century preoccupation with the cultural and social assimilation of African

Americans into American society (see McKee 1993). For reasons that will be explained later, that emphasis was steeped in assessments of values, norms, and practices. By the middle of the century, beliefs and meaning-making were placed far off of the sociological research agenda due to the ascendency of Talcott Parsons's AGIL scheme as a paradigm for social analysis (Parsons and Smelser 1956). This framework was the epitome of Parsons's effort to explain how social action, and social life more generally, was based on voluntaristic action within a set of external constraints and boundaries. It was his most explicit expression of his structural-functionalist interpretation of social action (the guiding approach taken in mid-twentieth-century sociology, which he largely initiated). That logic allowed for constraint (structure) and action (function) to come together in explaining social life.

The framework explains how action unfolds in social systems, irrespective of how large or small they are. The operations of a nation-state (like the United States) or a small group (such as a little league baseball team) can be assessed with the AGIL scheme. It consists of four domains. The adaptive domain (A) concerns the material conditions (e.g., economic resources) that shape social life. The goal attainment domain (G) is that which moves people toward desired ends or outcomes (e.g., the political sphere) by managing the impact of external forces. The integration domain (I) is where solidarity and cohesiveness are enforced. Finally, the pattern maintenance, or latent, domain (L) concerns values, or the subjective arena that compels or encourages people to respect, uphold, and work within systemic arrangements. The domains concerning integration and pattern maintenance give explicit places for norms and values. This paradigm was the most influential design for American sociology in the mid-twentieth-century. Its importance in shaping the mid-twentieth-century cultural analysis of black Americans did not lie in its application in social analysis; rather, it gave legitimacy to norms and values as the central cultural traits in social analysis, thereby affecting the underlying logic guiding cultural analysis at that time (Alexander 1987, Martindale 1981).

5. The antecedent of this work was the evolutionary framework for studying social and cultural development. This paradigm, introduced by Robert Park (1950), was a major part of the early Chicago School of Sociology and was used to explain and forecast social outcomes for black Americans in the United States' rapidly advancing industrial social order (for more discussion of the emergence of this line of thinking in American sociology, also see Lyman 1972, McKee 1993, Persons 1987). The framework introduced by anthropologist W. Lloyd Warner, which foregrounded cultural factors such as public behavior, lifestyle orientation, and micro-level social interaction, received less intellectual renown for studies of African Americans than did the evolutionary paradigm introduced by Park. However, both were influential theoretical camps for the work of this generation of African American scholars. In particular, both of the early traditions shaped the work of scholars on the black lower classes (indeed, as students of Park and Warner, respectively, Drake and Cayton included elements of both perspectives in *Black Metropolis*).

Robert Park and the evolutionary paradigm provided formal sociological concepts and ways of thinking about where poor black Americans stood in comparison to the rest of society, and what needed to be done for their cultural progress.

This was best exemplified by his notion of the race relations cycle, a schema that depicted the outcomes of group contact, contestation, and eventual integration within a geographic region. Warner's work solidified the notion that public space was the key platform for observing and assessing cultural practices. His work foreshadowed the emphasis on public behavior in cultural studies of the black American urban poor in later years.

6. A rich account of how much the early literature on the African American urban poor viewed them as culturally underdeveloped is provided in Alice O'Connor's (2001) study *Poverty Knowledge: Social Science, Social Policy, and the Poor in Twentieth-Century U.S. History.*

7. Some later writers argued that the basis of contemporary underclass culture could be found in the African American migration in the first half of the twentieth century (Lemann 1986, 1991). During that migration, so went the argument, southern, rural mores were transmitted to the urban arena. That view was challenged by William Julius Wilson and other researchers (Grossman 1989; Hirsch 1983; Marks 1989; Wilson 1987, 1996). They documented the socioeconomic stability and success of the earlier generations of African American migrants from the South. Wilson further argued that the changing fortune of African American urban residents of lower socioeconomic status was due to labor market transformations following World War II rather than to their adherence to a flawed cultural system.

Surely, there were poor black Americans who migrated North along with those who were somewhat more financially secure. It was the situation of northern urban living, however, rather than some shared cultural system cultivated in the South, that mattered most in understanding the case of the black urban poor. The findings of Wilson and others add some important perspective on the research of the earlier generation of scholars. Writing at the time they did, these scholars were not in a position to assess what became a pernicious process of urban socioeconomic transformation, particularly for the black American lower classes. As Wilson, Grossman, and others argued, in the first half of the twentieth century the city was considered by African Americans to be the site for new and better opportunities. Consequently, throughout that period researchers focused upon whatever might interfere with or hinder the achievement of better lives in the urban sphere. The cultural attributes of the low-income segments of the black American community were a major point of consideration in investigations of barriers and obstacles for social advancement. Aside from combating racism, cultural transformation became the main item on the early-twentieth-century scholarly agenda. To pursue that agenda, the early scholars participated in a debate on culture that was steeped in discussions of behavior, norms, and values, and how low-income African Americans could improve upon each.

8. In fact, a legacy of the interpretation of the values and norms of poor people as "inappropriate" by the more privileged, is the labeling of low-income people as the undeserving poor (Katz 1989b).

9. This argument employed a different logic to make claims about the cultural repertoire of black America than that used during the late nineteenth century. The earlier period couched such cultural notions in beliefs in innate inferior traits (Frederickson 1987, Hofstadter 1945). In contrast, the 1960s orientation sometimes veered toward celebrating the exotic.

10. Lewis presented a number of tenets in explaining the culture of poverty. First, despair and hopelessness were argued to develop from the realization of one's inability to get ahead in life (or to achieve the values and goals maintained in the larger society). Apathy, hostility, and suspicion comprised the general state of psychological being for those immersed in the culture of poverty. Children were explained as psychologically unprepared to take advantage of changing conditions or increased opportunities if any were to come their way. Adults in the culture of poverty were seen as lacking the ability to effectively participate and integrate into mainstream institutions. They also were perceived as incapable of organizing on their own behalf. Finally, adults also were viewed as being minimally engaged with their children due to their preoccupation with the problems of being poor. The result was that children learned to accept adult roles earlier in life because they essentially had to raise themselves (and despite their being unprepared to take advantage of new opportunities).

11. In *The Other America: Poverty in the United States* (1962), socialist intellectual Michael Harrington argued that the language, psychology, and worldviews of the poor necessitated that they would need help to overcome their situation. As a left-of-center contribution that aimed to promote thinking about the need for large-scale social transformation, Harrington's work had a much more progressive tone than that which is most closely aligned with the culture of poverty thesis. However, his argument resembled that thesis in its dismissal of any acknowledgment of the agency of the poor to improve their prospects. A more moderate political tone was struck by Frank Riessman in *The Culturally Deprived Child* (1962). He argued that deprivation from access to middle-class culture was the central issue in the lives of the American poor. Hence, institutions such as schools and service organizations must better adapt to the orientation of the poor if they are going to be effective bases of support. While the social agenda was not problematic, the label "culturally deprived" marked the poor in no uncertain terms. Whatever culturally sophisticated attributes they might have possessed were disregarded if not altogether disavowed under this label, which became a common signifier in discussions of the culture of the urban poor in many liberal-minded scholarly and civic arenas.

Perhaps the most prominent study tied to the culture of poverty concept was Daniel Patrick Moynihan's *The Negro Family: The Case for National Action* (1965). He argued that social disorganization and the disappearance of male leadership was the root cause of the problems in the African American low-income family. Moynihan said much about socioeconomic factors being the most important source of the plight of low-income African American families. However, this study inflamed many social activists, scholars, and civic leaders in the African American community, who paid special attention to Moynihan's argument that "aberrant" social behavior furthered the cycle of poverty (Rainwater and Yancey 1967).

Moynihan's politics were decidedly 1960s-style liberal. He argued that the poor should be helped out of their situation by civic and social intervention. This differed from extreme conservative views that were less encouraging of state intervention, and more assertive about the need to apply punitive measures in response to any profligate behaviors from those in lower-income circumstances. However, Moynihan's alignment with the poverty of culture thesis was exemplified by his view that cultural transformation was essential, this view being based on the normative vision of the poor as culturally deficient.

At the other side of the political divide was one of the major conservative contributions to the culture of poverty framework, Edward Banfield's *The Unheavenly City* (1970). In that work Banfield argued that improper attitudes, values, and modes of behavior were the principal causes of and reinforcing factors for poverty. He asserted that moment-to-moment orientation toward life, impulsiveness, and action-oriented responses were common behavioral traits of the urban poor, rather than careful, future-oriented planning. Banfield was much less hopeful or interested in remedial action than Moynihan. As far as he was concerned, the city essentially was damned by the proliferation of poor people within its terrain.

12. The past decade in particular has seen an emergence of some critical assessments of the 1960s era ethnography (Kelley 1997, D. Scott 1997). This new effort has posed a robust challenge to some scholars' quest for a durable, comprehensive conception of African American urban or low-income subculture. Historian Robin Kelley argues that the implications of the behavior of poor black Americans, and the psychological ramifications of their social functioning, have been overstated. He has criticized the strong cultural frameworks placed around the practices and orientations of poor blacks. As he put it, the verbal banter that black men engage in with one another on a street corner does not always reflect deep-seated hostility or discomfort with their social predicament, but may just be about a desire to get a good laugh (p. 34). Similarly, historian Daryl Michael Scott suggests that notions of a damaged black psyche have been fostered in American social science throughout the twentieth century at the expense of more careful studies of how black Americans have adjusted to urban living. These contributions resemble those of anthropologist Charles Valentine, whose position about the faulty foundations of the cultural theory in some of this work was already discussed.

13. In one case, this was done by arguing that people who face the same kinds of economic constraint over time will most likely respond to it in the same ways, thus positioning structure as the primary causal force rather than culture (Liebow 1967). A more elaborate account of the power of structural factors was provided by Lee Rainwater in his classic study, *Behind Ghetto Walls: Black Family Life in a Federal Slum* (1970). Included in this work, a study of residents in the Pruitt-Igoe public housing development in St. Louis, was a diagram of the links between various factors such as racism, economic deprivation, and the absence of institutional resources, and the behavioral outcomes that emerged for these residents.

14. Some attention was given to beliefs in the classic 1960s era ethnographies. For instance, in the second chapter of *Tally's Corner: A Study of Negro Streetcorner Men* (1967), Elliot Liebow stressed that beliefs about the poor quality of jobs factor into how and why men who associate on a Washington, D.C. street corner decide not to take employment opportunities. Liebow argued that employers bring pathetically few job opportunities to these men, and the men know that such work will not allow them to garner meaningful wages. Employers think that the men will not take the work seriously, and might steal and cheat on the job in order to get as much as they can from work. In response, the men often do not take the work seriously, and sometimes go without it because other problems had to be handled that day or physical incapacities make that work option untenable.

Here Liebow showed how different understandings about the legitimacy of certain work opportunities led to little or no work for the men, and depictions of them by employers as lazy or irresponsible.

A more extensive account of the role of beliefs is found in Lee Rainwater's *Behind Ghetto Walls: Black Family Life in a Federal Slum* (1970). Essentially, two contrasting formulations illustrate how beliefs matter for Rainwater, the "is" and the "ought to be." He stressed that poor black Americans are like everybody else in that Americans share the same notion of what ought to be a happy, wholesome life situation. That is reflected in their notion of the "ought to be" perspective on life. The "is" comprises beliefs and worldviews about everyday reality, which severely contrast with the "ought to be." Those beliefs, according to Rainwater, emerge from daily encounters with the "anomic" street culture, scarce access to opportunities for socioeconomic advancement, and the racial discrimination that poor blacks have to face. Those conditions pull poor black Americans into ways of living that necessitate suspending their notions of an "ought to be" lifestyle so that they can get on with dealing with what are the often horrific realities of their lives.

As two of the most highly regarded ethnographies of the 1960s, these works did an important job by clearly situating beliefs in the analytical picture. However, they also contributed to the underdeveloped framework in critical ways due to their analytical shortsightedness. Liebow did explore in great depth how men form certain meanings about work opportunity and what troubles come to them when they choose not to take what they feel are inadequate or problematic work options. However, most of the rest of *Tally's Corner* relies upon norms and values as the vocabulary for his cultural analysis. Consequently, his major statement about culture is that the values of poor black men resemble those of the rest of American society, and their norms differ only to the extent that their experience in poverty necessitates that they interact and make use of public space in particular ways such that their moral worth can be promoted.

The relative brevity of his attention to beliefs and meaning-making is not all there is to be concerned about in *Tally's Corner* and its relationship to the culture of poverty thesis. Although Liebow provides empirically informed criticism of the argument that improper norms and values are what hinder poor black men from taking advantage of prospects, at other moments he actually shows support for that argument. For instance, Liebow spends a considerable amount of time exploring what he calls their shadow system of values (p. 213). He argues that this system allows them to manage certain stresses and strains in their lives, mostly concerning family and social relationships. In Liebow's thinking, the shadow system is a cultural configuration that is altogether independent from mainstream values. He regards this shadow system as a complete alternative to mainstream values, which makes it unlike Hyman Rodman's (1963) value-stretch argument. According to Liebow, the shadow culture is a property of the low-income street corner life, and is employed during moments of great tension. Rodman, on the other hand, sees the values of the poor as related to those in mainstream culture. It is only that they are stretched so that the poor can uphold them, given that they lack the resources to uphold the mainstream pattern. Liebow's shadow system of values is exemplified by violence and aggression, which, according to Liebow, are regarded by poor black men as a legitimate form of expression on the street corner.

Lee Rainwater's shortsightedness appears in his restricting belief systems, or the "is" dimension of the lives of Pruitt-Igoe residents, to their views of life in that housing development. There is no detailed exploration of beliefs and worldviews about the broader society that established the contexts for everyday life in the housing project. Hence, he offers only a very narrow field of beliefs in his study.

15. Liebow's *Tally's Corner* was the first of the classic 1960s urban ethnographies to render images of the public persona of low-income black men coping with defeat and deficiencies. Liebow shows how these facets of everyday life are managed on the street corner as the men do things to elevate their public image among their peers (e.g., animated interaction with their children, for whom they otherwise cannot provide much material support) and reduce the emotional turmoil in their lives. He argues that much of what these men did on the street corner helped them to present a positive public persona as compensation for the personal and family-based problems they encountered.

16. Indeed, in *Soulside*, Ulf Hannerz was so intensely preoccupied with public expression that he devoted a portion of his book to a discussion of "soul," a common term used in the 1960s and 1970s to refer to general attitudes and styles of expression by black Americans (pp. 144–58). He aspired to understand the meaning and utility of "Soul" for black Americans, and investigated its potential implications for affirming a coherent definition of urban-based African American subculture. Hannerz seemed unsure about what to make of the term as a referent for some definitive quality or aspect of African American urban life. He is as unsettled in his analysis here as was Liebow in his discussion of shadow culture. In the end, Hannerz stuck to his claim that culture is a public property, available for possession by anyone who desires to make use of a cultural tool or artifact. However (and despite Hannerz's attention to meaning-making), his emphasis on soul and other expressive dimensions of low-income life make his work, like the other classic urban ethnographies of the 1960s, principally a statement about the public aspects of the lives of urban-based black Americans.

17. This term was first introduced in social science literature by the Swedish economist Gunnar Myrdal in a short book entitled *Challenge to Affluence* (1963). Myrdal used the term as a descriptive device to discuss who he believed would be the greatest victims of deindustrialization in modern societies. In his work, "underclass" implies a strictly economic category; its behavioral and racial implications developed in the 1970s and were established by the mid-1980s. The proliferation of the term was due in no small part to the publication of journalist Ken Auletta's book *The Underclass* (1982), which was written for a popular audience and was widely distributed. Sociologists Herbert Gans (1995) and Robert Aponte (1990) and historian Michael B. Katz (1989a, 1989b) provide detailed historical accounts of how the term was introduced and eventually applied to low-income, urban-based racial groups, especially African Americans, by researchers and in the media.

18. It must be said in all fairness that a depiction of the differences in the content of images of social reality is not in the purview of ethnography. A prime example of the point is found in an earlier work by Elijah Anderson, *Streetwise: Race, Class, and Change in an Urban Community* (1990). Anderson's major point of emphasis in that work is on public interaction across community boundaries. Consequently, he is not overtly concerned with how black men construct images

of reality about the social world beyond their own community and the neighboring one. However, his study does provide some insight into how low-income black men may construct some images of reality, especially as they concern their own neighborhood (a space that Anderson calls Northton), their neighbors' and those of the next community (called the Village). The visions of reality that the low-income inhabitants form of themselves include a sense that they are less well off than are the residents of the Village, but more free and able to take command of the (public space that connects the neighborhoods). What they believe themselves to lack in terms of personal agency for socioeconomic advancement is matched by increased efficacy at managing the immediate public space.

Not much else is said in this work that concerns meaning-making because Anderson aims to tell a story about public interaction, community organization and structure, and boundary development. He cannot be faulted for not fulfilling an agenda that he did not set out to fulfill. Hence, critical readers must not mistake work like Anderson's as representing all or even most of what can be explored about meaning-making by low-income urban dwellers.

19. As will be explained more fully later on, personal understandings of the social world do not always lead to the adoption of norms and values in a clear-cut or direct way. Additionally, sometimes people cannot definitively account for why they see the world in certain ways. Social experience consistently informs people about the world in ways that are not always easily detectable or knowable. As successful as anthropologist Clifford Geertz's (1973) effort was to place meaning more at the center of social-scientific attention, even he could not overcome the difficulty of defining what constitutes the webs of significance for any group of people (see Wuthnow 1987 for a controversial but more elaborate account of the difficulty in ascertaining subjective orientations to meaning-making). That is why the present work only aims to explore patterns of meaning on a specific set of issues, assess where differences in such patterns emerge, and explore how they relate to personal experience.

20. MacLeod explained that his men were products of the post–civil rights era. They came into adulthood in the early 1980s. This information not only provided important historical context for his study, but allowed him to argue that their readings of the relevance of race and other factors concerning mobility were tied to larger social framings of how important these factors were in American life. His African American men were less inclined to talked about external constraints of discrimination and upward mobility because they believed that the civil rights movement had eradicated much of the problem. The white men were much more comfortable placing the blame for *their* lack of mobility on government assistance programs and systemic processes that benefited members of other racial groups.

Chapter Two
Time, Space, and Everyday Living

1. I rarely held formal interviews outside of the two offices. In a few cases, however, short meetings took place at a McDonald's restaurant (each site was within three blocks of one) or in the street, usually someplace around the corner from one of the restaurants.

2. I took one bus downtown, and then the Madison Avenue bus west to Henry Horner or the Roosevelt Road bus west to ABLA. On occasion I took the Chicago Avenue bus home from Henry Horner if someone told me that Madison Avenue might be "busy" that night (some kind of potentially dangerous activity was going to unfold). Taking Chicago Avenue home meant an additional bus ride, but the inconvenience was more than balanced by the gratitude that I felt for the men who chose to look out for me. I only know for sure of one violent outbreak on a night when I rode the Chicago Avenue bus: a shootout near Madison within an hour of my departure from the alderman's office. There was also a shooting near Roosevelt Road one morning about a half-hour before I arrived at the ABLA facility. I never received details about these two events, nor did I spend much time trying to seek them out. People in the community expressed no surprise or consternation about these occurrences, and it seemed best not to dwell on them too much.

3. Ken's finding a job a few months before our meeting left him outside of the formal group of twenty-six men that I include in this account. Had I met him six months earlier he would have fit easily into the group. Some of his experiences resemble those of the men in this study, so at times his views are included to add clarity to certain parts of my argument.

4. Another circumstance helped to cement this event into my memory. When I got home that evening my fiancée rushed to the front door of our apartment to tell me that I picked one heck of a day to come home late. Apparently, in response to the intense public scrutiny and pressure over his being implicated in the murder of his ex-wife, former professional football star O.J. Simpson was riding around a southern California freeway in a white Ford Bronco while holding a gun to his head. Coverage of this event was interrupting regularly scheduled broadcasts on every major television network, including the National Basketball Association final round game that I had hoped to see that evening. While the larger public had already been exposed to the story of the day, I remained slightly more immersed in my much more personal one.

5. Pierre Bourdieu's study, *The Algerians* (1962), was the first major work in his long line of publications. It garners much less attention than his more recent richly theoretical work that attends to the differences in how people function along positions in social hierarchies (see Bourdieu 1977a, 1990, and especially Bourdieu and Wacquant 1992 for an overview of other contributions).

6. Of course, poor people who have to schedule a lot (especially if they are caring for children or a household that has many people) and have few resources to manage such commitments may also be too late, too early, or absent altogether given the demands upon their time. Anthropologist Carol Stack explores this while looking at low-income black women and their families in her study *All Our Kin: Strategies for Survival in a Black Community* (1974).

7. Toward the end of his life Bourdieu had much in common with British sociologist Anthony Giddens, who is also interested in how action simultaneously shapes and is shaped by social structure. Giddens (1979, 1984) forwards the concept of structuration as his central term for defining how this process unfolds. Structuration implies that any human action is an effort to abide by some previously understood set of social rules for behavior (i.e., norms) but that the very

enacting of behavior either can reinforce the rules (which for Giddens is the usual order of things) or provide new models of behavior that lead to changing expectations for the future (i.e., new norms). Giddens proposes, then, that nothing about social life is static. Action reinforces cultural patterns or promotes social and cultural change, sometimes doing a bit of both at the same time. A core difference between the approaches of Bourdieu and Giddens toward understanding how action relates to external factors is that Bourdieu's notion of habitus includes explicit attention to the unconscious. Bourdieu asserted that much of any individual's action is based upon such a strongly endorsed set of rules that the behavior is not consciously planned or thought about, but simply unfolds within the individual's accustomed social contexts. Think of people applauding during performances: the action is not often thought about just before it happens, but occurs at especially titillating moments and precisely at the beginning and conclusion of the performance. Social custom has established at least some of the times when applause occurs, and people simply follow the program without putting much mental energy into what they are doing. Anthony Giddens is much more interested in exploring what he calls the discursively accessible dimensions of consciousness, or those aspects reflected by what people say about themselves and the social world. Consequently, he does little with the unconscious dimensions of action save for placing them beyond the parameters of formal sociological analysis.

Habitus, then, is a term that captures entire ways of living and thinking, whereas structuration refers to an explicit process in social life. Habitus reflects the conscious and unconscious ways of living and thinking that are fostered by groups of people on the basis of where they stand along social hierarchies. It is what makes modes of behavior seem common-sensical to certain people, while those same modes may be unthinkable to another group. Any group's notion of common sense includes conscious and unconscious elements (like why people applaud at certain moments without necessarily giving conscious thought as to whether they truly like or appreciate whatever has occurred). Whatever groups of people do over time is informed by what other people in the same grouping or conditions do, and this gets constituted over time as common sense.

8. Those patterns of functioning, including verbal and physical behavior, and the subsequent ways in which people account for or come to understand their styles, are a part of a group's *doxa*. The doxa is the "uncontested acceptance of the daily lifeworld" (Bourdieu and Wacquant 1992, p. 73). It is, in other words, the common sense of people functioning within their own social groups.

9. Jay MacLeod incorporated habitus in his work to explain how the life experiences of the black and white men in *Ain't No Making It* led to their respective aspirations and expectations. There MacLeod attempted to use race not just as a structuring device or analytic category, but as a divider of people into different kinds of habitus. He went on to show that being white and working class was very different than being black and working class in terms of how lived experience led people to express their aspirations and expectations. This took Bourdieu's conceptual scheme in a new direction. While implying that race and other factors may designate different patterns of habitus, Pierre Bourdieu tended to focus on class differences in his work (1977a, 1984, 1986, 1988, 1990).

10. In social research, the concept of habitus allows for an understanding of the relationship between an actor and the external world in the processes of interpreting reality and creating rules and options for human action. The distinction between the actor and the set of rules or standards that regulate action is at the core of scholarly debates concerning the subject-object duality in social analysis. Rather than maintaining a rigid separation between the individual and the elements (rules, patterns of organization, etc.) that comprise the social world, Bourdieu maintains that there exists an "ontological complicity" between the subject and the object. By this he means that the production of individual-level perceptions and apprehensions of the world (both its material and ideational content) is interwoven with the external conditions and forces in the world that allow people to make such perceptions and apprehensions.

11. For reasons that are obvious to urban field researchers (and can be surmised by others), there was never any direct inquiry on my part into whether they were ever involved in a gang. This kind of invasion into their privacy could have disrupted the completion of an interview, or created anger or hostility (the consequences of which could be more problematic than a simple termination of the interview). The knowledge I acquired about gang activity was submitted by the men on their own initiative. Some men said nothing about their own status with regard to this matter. A few went as far as to state that they knew of no gang members in their community, but would talk about the presence of gangs as if they were an ordinary part of the social life of the community. However, a few things can be said about the dialogue concerning gangs. First, those men who were apt to admit their membership were also quite heavily involved; I imagine that they felt I could find out about their membership if they did not want to talk about it, so talking was no major issue. Second, people either said that the knew plenty of gang members because large numbers of men in the community were associated, or they said that they knew of none personally because they dared not identify themselves as associated with such men. Third, when talking about gangs without having to address any personal connection to them, everyone had a lot to say on the topic.

12. Travis, Devin, and Barry spoke at length about the significant sums of money that they made at times while selling drugs. In each case, though, they also said that their money went as fast at it came.

13. In both general conversations and formal interviews, many of the men reported to me that media figures and politicians too quickly asserted that each violent act in their neighborhoods was gang-related. In their view, the hyperutilization of the term "gang-related violence" oversimplified the complexity of community-level criminal activity, thus making authorities less inclined to seriously investigate particular crimes or violent encounters. They also made it clear that they felt that the concept reinforced the notion of black men as a public threat by denying that many criminal acts result from personal conflicts. In offering this viewpoint I do not intend to deny the role of gangs in perpetuating community-level violence. I only seek to emphasize the greater complexity inherent in a matter that sometimes is regarded too simplistically, even by those who are intimately involved in the affairs of low-income communities or sympathetic to the plight of their inhabitants.

14. Wacquant and Wilson, 1989. Poverty areas are those in which 20% or more of the population is poor. Extreme poverty areas are those in which 40% or more of the population is poor. These measures, used to assess poverty rates in census tracts, have been used to plot trends and patterns in Chicago community areas, which are comprised of a series of census tracts.

15. More than a few of the men could not fully understand that I was "at work" just interviewing them about their lives and opinions on social issues. They thought that if I found such work meaningful, then they could perhaps help me in doing it, and thereby help themselves. None who asked about working for me had any initial idea about what exactly they would do. Aside from simply wanting to go to work, they seemed intrigued by a form of work that they had little exposure to, and curious about what might become of all of this interviewing. A part of what made this intriguing to them was that unlike reporters, whom many of the men had talked to or at least seen in the neighborhood, I did not center my interviews on some violent occurrence, but on their everyday views.

16. The discussion of relatives was restricted to those with whom they interacted at least on a monthly basis (which usually meant relatives that also lived in Chicago, if not in the same community). They were left to their own devices in accounting for friends. Acquaintances were defined as people they regularly saw in the street or other public settings but whom they would not identify as friends.

17. I am referring here to Mark Granovetter's (1978, 1983) notion of weak ties, which are those associations that people have outside of durable, regular, or intimate relations with others. He argues that weak ties provide the researcher a broader array of information and other resources than do strong ties to a close-knit group of people.

18. This resembles the argument that Ulf Hannerz made in *Soulside: Inquiries into Ghetto Culture and Community* about the functions of male friendship ties in a low-income community. Recall my discussion in chapter 1 of his claim that such ties help each participant reconcile his constructions of reality and evaluate them against the views of other men.

19. A rather lengthy debate has ensued over the concept of capital since its introduction into social science research (Bourdieu 1986; Bourdieu and Wacquant 1992; Calhoun, LiPuma, and Postone 1993; DiMaggio 1979, 1982; DiMaggio and Mohr 1984; Lamont and Lareau 1988; Robbins 1991; Swartz 1997; Young 1999). In a critique that has particular relevance to this work, sociologist Craig Calhoun (1993) argues that Pierre Bourdieu does not show precisely how any of his varied forms of capital have acquired the value that he claims is attached to them, that he does not offer a theoretically informed account of why particular objects acquire the value that they do in particular societies, or address how that value may be transformed over time (pp. 66–69). The process of achieving (or losing) value is social, meaning that some people somewhere in time determined that something has (or hasn't) value. The fact that they did so at some point in time means that there is an important historical dimension to the determination of value. I do not address all of Calhoun's concerns in this work. Selective attention is paid to how certain entities or ideas got constituted as capital. Most attention is given to those that are capital in the Near West Side rather than those that are capital in wider American social contexts. The latter (such as a good job, a nice

home, and a stable family) are taken as a given here. However, I do take very seriously the fact that action or events that produce capital in one context contribute to its demise in other contexts. Therefore, capital is never of pure and insistent value. Moreover, particular forms of capital can be simultaneously advantageous in certain spheres of life and destructive in others. An example of this is the nature of friendship as it is analyzed at the end of this chapter.

20. These definitions are adapted from the work of Browning and Rodriguez (1985).

21. The acquisition of educational credentials that may have little to do with the specific skills needed for a task also may be regarded as human capital because they certify a general level of competency to complete tasks or duties. For example, one may think of the social utility that a law degree holds in the minds of many people. The study of law involves exposure to specific styles of writing, types of literature, and ways of thinking about that literature. However, possession of a law degree also implies for many people some general level of competence or ability, so that acquisition of one is thought to open up various fields of opportunity.

22. The latter definition of social capital reflects the meaning attributed to it by sociologist James Coleman (1988). Coleman argued that social capital is a byproduct of relations between people that produce trust, comfort, security, and other expectations that can facilitate mutually desirable outcomes (pp. 98–100). In his view, social capital is not a property of individual actors, nor is it produced by individual effort. Instead, social capital emerges from adherence to norms of behavior by a group of people in specific contexts (e.g., an institution or an organization) such that everyone benefits from the mutual practice.

Chapter Three
Coming Up Poor

1. In his social history of the Robert Taylor Houses, perhaps the most infamous of public housing developments in Chicago, Sudhir Venkatesh (2000) discusses various social and entrepreneurial activities that occur in the apartments of that development, all of which take place precisely because there exists no formal scrutiny or official supervision of the premises.

2. By no means does this excursion into the past intend to capture the complete and complex life histories of these men. Instead it focuses solely on how they talked about their pasts. It gives some indication of how they came to their present situation of chronic unemployment and their crippled prospects for upward mobility. More specifically, it helps detect how prior social experiences and institutional attachments have shaped their capacity to imagine how people plan and go about attaining desires for the future, and within that vision, how they come to account for their own future prospects.

3. In its true form, first-person life historical inquiry offers no more than a person's own account of his or her past, from which one must draw inferences (Linde 1993). While there clearly are some weaknesses to this approach for making sense of a person's past experiences, there also are some strengths, particularly for the kind of undertaking at hand. First-person accounts provide a more vivid

sense than can any other form of inquiry of what matters most to an individual. The person is given a platform in order to present whatever he has conscientiously held onto in making sense of his past. The analyst is charged with paying attention to what is said for multiple purposes. One is to ascertain the discursive patterns in a style of expression. This is what formal narrative analysis aims to do (C. Riessman 1993). This approach, for example, can be used to address the issue of whether a person tends to place himself in the position of causal agent for the events occurring around him, or to talk about himself as a passive presence in a dynamic and often capricious social milieu. Another approach, which is the one taken here, is to attend to what has been said in order to assess it with respect to the remarks of other people who have encountered seemingly similar experiences or situations. Both approaches are intended to detect the factors in the individual's life experience that lead him to respond as he does to his past. However, the option chosen here aims to depict not the complexity of a single life history, but the subtle and not so subtle distinctions between people who seem to have encountered the past in similar ways. Consequently, this approach recognizes the greater complexity of a group of people—low-income black men   more than that of any particular individual.

4. The study of causal relationships is a much valued approach in urban poverty research (see these collections of essays for prime examples: Ellwood and Cottingham 1989; Danziger, Sandufer, and Weinberg 1994; Freeman and Holzer 1986; Jencks and Peterson 1991; McFate, Lawson, and Wilson 1995; Peterson and Harrell 1993; Sawhill 1995; Wilson 1993). My comments do not aim to deny the importance of this mode of inquiry, as it has established an understanding of important relationships between actions or states of being and measure of poverty. I only aim to show that the larger picture of how individuals remain immersed in the social conditions associated with urban poverty is grounded in a set of multiple and reinforcing factors that do not necessarily fit together in linear patterns.

5. Each of these fathers also worked constantly at some kind of job. Jason's father was a minister of a storefront church in Arkansas. He sent Jason to live with relatives in Chicago early in Jason's childhood. Lester's father was a distributor of contraband who was incarcerated during Lester's early adolescence. Ted's father was the owner of a small bar that went out of business during his childhood. Roy's father was a part-time security guard (Roy did not know exactly where) and part-time laborer for the Chicago Housing Authority. Finally, Larry's father was a factory laborer.

6. See the following for varied perspectives on the matter: Biller 1993; Berman and Pedersen 1987; Boyd-Franklin 1989; Bronstein and Cowan 1988; Cosby 1986; Furstenberg and Harris 1992, 1993; Gerson 1993; R. Griswold 1993; Hood 1986; Ladner 1971; Lamb and Sagi 1983; Lerman, 1993; Levant and Kelly 1989; C. Lewis and O'Brien 1987; Parke 1981; Taylor and Johnson 1997; Willis 1996.

7. More evidence of the perspective of black Americans in Chicago on the social institutions there as compared to the South can be found in studies of the African American northern/urban migration in the early and mid-twentieth century (see Drake and Cayton 1945, Grossman 1989, Hirsch 1983, Lemann 1991, and Marks 1989).

8. For examples, see Aschenbrenner 1975, Clark 1983, Jarrett 1994 and 1995, Rainwater 1970, and Stack 1974.

9. Earl's father, a graduate of a segregated high school in Mississippi, died well before he reached his teens, thus leaving him in a single-parent household. (His mother also graduated from a segregated Mississippi high school; she worked as a laborer in a Chicago hospital after his father's death.)

10. Discussions between teachers and parents were restricted to disciplinary matters. The work of Annette Lareau (1989, 1999) provides a complex portrayal of how social class demarcates the approaches that parents take toward involvement in the schooling of their children. Her description of the approach taken by lower-income parents is more thorough than what has been presented here.

11. The documentary entitled "Hoop Dreams" (Marx, James, and Gilbert 1995), an account of the adolescent years of two African American youths who showed early signs of being standout basketball players with the potential of making it to the National Basketball Association, illustrates vividly the tension involved in parents of west Chicago youth attempting to approach and interact with institutional figures in school. Early in the documentary, the parents of Arthur Agee go to collect their son's academic records from St. Joseph's High School, a private, suburban institution west of Chicago where Arthur first began playing high school basketball. In a poignant exchange, the parents hug Arthur's high school counselor and thank him for his help after conversing with him about Arthur's poor performance in school. This occurs after the counselor has explicitly denied the parents access to Arthur's records, access which the documentary implies they were entitled.

12. The significance of the military as a site for establishing stability, if not upward mobility, for low-income African Americans is discussed in Charles Moskos and John Sibley Bulter's *All That We Can Be: Black Leadership and Racial Integration the Army Way* (1996).

13. The role of extended family members is a rich part of African American family history (see Billingsley 1992, Bowman 1993, Furstenberg 1988, Jarrett 1994 and 1995, Ladner 1971, Liebow 1967, Moynihan 1965). Thus, it should not be surprising that these men experienced a great deal of intimate involvement with these figures.

14. Roy and Kurt attended Catholic school for a large part of their elementary school education (Earl for just a few years). Kurt could not continue as family finances became depleted, and Roy was expelled for disciplinary reasons and subsequently entered and remained in public school from junior high through high school.

15. All of the following data reported on these schools come from an annual report published by the Chicago Panel on Public School Policy and Finance entitled *Chicago Public Schools Data book* (1986–92).

16. Detailed descriptions of the experiences of low-income students in the public schools of Chicago, and the Near West Side in particular, at about the time that these men attended them are found respectively in Kozol (1991) and Kotlowitz (1991). Both works claim that Near West Side schools were staffed with many teachers and administrators who were concerned and cared about the children under their charge. Moreover, a range of forces and conditions in the commu-

nity, coupled with the lack of appropriate financial resources and adequate staff, leave the schools unable to provide an education that meets the social, cultural, and intrapersonal needs of low-income African American youth.

17. Such rules of street life in low-income communities are documented Elijah Anderson's *The Code of the Streets* (1999).

18. Pierre Bourdieu reminds us that individuals are products of history, and thus accumulate experiences that lead to regularities in their responses to similar experiences. These include physical as well as cognitive responses (Bourdieu and Wacquant 1992, p. 136). In further discussion of habitus, Bourdieu argues that "a homogeneity of conditions of existence, which enables practices to be objectively harmonized without calculation or conscious reference to norms, nor mutually adjusted in the absence of direct intervention or explicit coordination," results in the formation of a class-habitus (1990, p. 58). By this Bourdieu means that individuals who regularly share a social space that exposes them to similar experiences, and equips them with similar resources to navigate those experiences, adopt similar modes functioning. This functioning includes actual behavior within, apprehension of, and ideological orientations toward that environment. The homogeneity of conditions of existence for the men who comprise this study have been illustrated in this analysis. Hence, Bourdieu's ideas enhance an understanding of how the men in this study experienced many of the same types of social institutions and socializing processes. However, the fact that the men acquired both similar and contrasting understandings about their future prospects as a consequence of those experiences, indicates that habitus is not deterministic.

19. However, the men still had very little consistent or long-term employment experience, and no clear sense of any that would be forthcoming. Thus, this was a crucial phase of their lives, during which they began to feel almost certain about some things, like a longer life, yet virtually unsure about other things that are crucial to a good life, like a job. The tension between these two facets exemplifies a lot of what living in poverty as adults meant to them.

20. Butch lived with the mother of his two children, in walking distance of his mother's residence. Devin lived in his own Henry Horner apartment with the mother of his child and her three other children. Ted lived with his two sons in his parents' household.

21. This study did not involve contact with any of the mothers of their children. Thus, as with other aspects of this inquiry, only the men's perspectives are included.

22. This point contrasts with the findings of Maureen Waller (2002) regarding how adult identity was located with respect to parenthood for working class and low-income men in a New Jersey urban community. The men in her study argued that their assuming an adult identity had little do to with becoming parents.

23. Much of this is consistent with the findings of research of low-income distal African American fathers (Anderson, 1989; Bowman, 1989, 1992, 1993, 1995; Bowman and Forman 1997; Evans and Whitfield 1988; Gordon, Gordon, and Nembhard 1994; Hood 1986; McAdoo, 1981, 1986, 1988a, 1988b, 1993; McAdoo and McAdoo 1994; Mincy, 1994a, 1994b; Price-Bonham and Skeen 1979; R. J. Taylor, Leashare, and Toliver 1988). This research highlights the stress placed by these men on the role of financial provider (and the distress associated

with the inability to fulfill that role). However, the literature also points out the near exclusion of other types of roles and provisions that the men could adopt (emotional nurturing, socio-developmental nurturing, home caretaking such that overall child care is set within a healthy home environment, etc.). Other research has shown that economic hardship is linked to stress-related illness, violence, and drug abuse, and at various points in the life cycle, all of which has some bearing on how provider or expressive roles are performed by fathers (Bowman 1989; R. Cohn, 1978; Gary 1981; Gary and Leashore, 1982; Heckler, 1985; Pearlin et al. 1981; Sampson 1987; Staples, 1982; Wilson, 1987, 1996).

24. Note that this study did not call for elaborate discussions of the men's relations with their children. Therefore, things that were not said cannot be taken as things that the men did not care about or do. We can only acknowledge that what was said was indicative of some of the more important things on the minds of these men, and raise questions about why certain things were given greater attention than others.

25. The types of jobs held by the men when they did work included serving and preparing in fast food establishments, functioning as couriers, or working in manual labor positions. The men left their jobs voluntarily, by virtue of completing the assignment, or by being fired or forced out of work (e.g., bosses giving standing jobs to other people). It is not possible to generalize about how jobs came and went.

26. For further discussion of the importance that black men place on receiving respect in the workplace (and the consequences of their feeling disrespected), see Liebow (1967) and Taub (1991). An analogous argument about Hispanics can be found in Bourgois (1995).

27. Further evidence of the vitality of these communities can be found in the community area descriptions provided in the Local Community Fact Book by the Chicago Fact Book Consortium (1995).

28. When discussing violent crimes, the men were extremely careful about what they said. It was rare that a man gave specific information about his role in a violent encounter (unless, like Earl, it was one that he had been convicted for and served time). Instead, the men would imply their involvement or association in such an event or circumstance. They did so in ways that made it seem as though they were causal agents or major participants, yet they never provided clear evidence of precisely what they did. Thus they tended to use language like Ken's when he said, "My gun went off in the locker room in school," rather than state that they were involved in a shootout in the high school's locker room. I suspect that this was because the men knew full well what the presence of a tape recorder could mean.

29. Some of the men had difficulty in recalling the exact length of their stay outside of Chicago.

Chapter Four
Framing Social Reality: Stratification and Inequality

1. Sudhir Venkatesh (2000) provides a detailed discussion of how organized gangs in the Robert Taylor Homes (located in the south side of Chicago) assumed control of the illicit and informal ventures of many residents once the gangs had

solidified their drug distribution system. Many of those who were not put out of business simply paid a "tax" or provided some in-kind services to the gangs in order to remain active in their affairs.

2. Here I was attempting to follow some basic rules of the trade in qualitative research. Some scholars argue that a principal logic of the qualitative method is to separate—at least analytically if not existentially—the data collection phase from the data analysis phase so that the researcher does not construct "blinders" before having access to the full range of data (Bertaux and Kohli 1984, Denzin 1978, Glaser and Strauss 1967, Miles and Huberman 1994). Existentially, these two tasks are not always kept separate because time is of the essence (especially when research funding is closely tied to a time line for a project), and one must often start analyzing notes and transcripts before the collection phase is complete. Fortunately, this was not a circumstance that I had to face. My time lines were fully internally derived. The analytical merit in keeping the two separate is that data sometimes begins to make much better sense only after one has stepped out of the field site and experienced some emotional and cognitive distance from the setting.

3. This revelation only became clear to me weeks after leaving the Near West Side, once I began listening repeatedly to the audio-taped voices of the men and rereading the interview transcripts. Indeed, this was not a solitary endeavor. Early on, my partner (and, soon thereafter, wife) and I shortchanged ourselves of some good meals as we used our usual dinner time to discuss and plot out what the men were saying and, more crucially, which men were not saying much at all on certain topics. As I tried to determine how to make these men say more, my partner steadfastly and repeatedly informed me that their lack of commentary was as much of a finding as was the commentary of other men. It was essential, she instructed, that I try to discern why they may have had less to say (or at least, what kinds of men had less to say). The fact that this discussion is a part of this chapter is evidence that I eventually got her point.

4. Silence has emerged in the past decade as an important topic of concern in social research (Denzin 1997, Hertz 1997, Kvale 1996, Poland and Pederson 1998). Much of the emphasis has been on its significance in one of three situations: (1) as intentionally employed by people to protect themselves by not revealing too much to an investigator; (2) as a result of cultural differences between the investigator and the people that he or she is investigating (e.g., the absence of lengthy discussion on a topic because the respondent does not understand how or why the investigator has framed an inquiry); and (3) closely related to (2), the appearance of silence as a result of being asked about a common, regular, nondescript aspect of one's life such that the respondent has difficulty providing an extended commentary on the matter (e.g., why someone starts eating a meal with the vegetables rather than the meat, or why a particular white shirt or pair of socks was worn on a given day). The form of silence relevant to this project, and one that has received less attention from research methodologists, is categorical silence, which occurs when the person interviewed lacks the requisite understanding or insight by which to frame an elaborate response or commentary (Poland and Pederson 1998). A researcher's awareness of this form of silence comes from knowledge of possible alternative articulations or, as in this study, the existence

of other actors who, by virtue of certain circumstances or conditions, are able to provide more elaborate commentary.

5. In her analysis of the contemporary situation of African American women, Patricia Hill Collins (1998) offers a highly provocative investigation of the idea that the most powerful forms of oppression are those that are not consciously recognized by the oppressed.

6. One might imagine that television, radio, and other forms of mass media would have introduced new paradigms to the men. Indeed, I began my study with the premise that elements of what sociologist C. Wright Mills (1963) called the "cultural apparatus" of American society (radio, television, popular literature, and other modes of transmitting ideas) would form a source of information about society akin to personal interactive experience. Three decades ago, anthropologist Ulf Hannerz (1969, pp. 70–71) provided a succinct overview of the 1960s debate on how television and other media influence the values of lower-income African Americans. Hannerz's work explored in particular the images of appropriate family structure relayed by these media. Presumably, then, one might extend Hannerz's analysis to include an examination of messages about social processes and upward mobility. I asked a number of questions about what they watched on television. I also posed questions about the print media and the radio. I asked them to talk about what they had learned about social mobility and opportunity through these resources. In presenting their arguments most of these men made reference to aspects of the cultural apparatus as a *supplement* to what personal experience had shown them. Thus, while radio, television, and print media provided these men access to a public vocabulary as well as a mosaic of images to substantiate their claims about the social world, the source of those claims was their personal experience. What they felt they knew about American society, and could talk about with confidence and depth, came from direct experience. Conversely, when the men lacked direct experience with certain issues, they spoke with great uncertainty or not at all (recall here Barry's statement about his knowing no white people, so that he could not talk about the intricacies of race relations or racism).

A number of the men talked about serial killer Jeffrey Dahmer in the course of discussing the views that Americans have of young black men. Dahmer received national attention when he was discovered in the early 1990s to be the murderer of seventeen young men, mostly African American and Latino residents of Milwaukee, and to have allegedly eaten some of the body parts of his victims. The men expressed great anger over the notion that the public wanted to study this man's brain in order to discover why he functioned as he did. They believed that if he had been African American, the police or corrections personnel would have killed him instantly. They also believed that the public, rather than expressing wonder and astonishment about the situation, would have been unremitting in calling for his death. The men learned about the Dahmer matter through the media. Their reaction to it, however, reflected how much more emphatic they were about their own interactions with the police and legal authorities, and their sense of what the public thought about them as poor urban-based young black men. This was the most notable of a number of scenarios whereby the men referred to an event or circumstance that they learned about through the media, but accounted for the matter by drawing upon personal or local experiences to make sense of it.

7. A cautionary note must be offered about the claims made here concerning the cultural apparatus. Some may argue that this apparatus primarily serves to produce effects at the subconscious, or perhaps unconscious, level. This study cannot inform about how the cultural apparatus relates to either the subconscious or the unconscious. Whatever may have taken place subliminally for these men simply cannot be apprehended by a series of interviews (at least those conducted for purposes other than psychiatric or psychological assessment). Instead, the claim made here is that any regard that the men had for the role of the cultural apparatus in shaping their worldviews and interpretations was secondary to the role that personal experience played for them. Accordingly, research of the sort conducted for this study provides for a consideration of the extent to which people attribute their worldviews to personal experience, vicarious experience, or information garnered from the cultural apparatus. As these men overwhelmingly underscored their personal experiences more than anything else, the tentative conclusion drawn here, at least as far as meaning-making about social mobility and opportunity is concerned, is that the cultural apparatus can provide information that either extends or limits the capacity of people to construct worldviews about these issues.

8. Few of the men spoke of gender as a crucial stratifying mechanism. It was almost never mentioned in general discussions of social stratification and inequality, and only a few men said it was relevant when asked directly about the importance of gender in getting ahead in life. Some of the men in the study felt that women could sometimes get jobs more easily than men because employers might desire to have the presence of women in the workplace. The only appearance of gender as a consistently important concept was in discussions of the status of black Americans. This portion of the discussion also included direct questioning of the situation of black men and of black women in American society. The men's comments almost strictly focused on women of low-income status, precisely the type who resided in the men's communities. The men had little contact with black women of other class statuses, and thus had nothing to say about how they factored in the issues that we discussed.

9. Those that accept the standard understanding of what poor black men are inclined to do when hanging around the street might wonder whether Lester provided a truthful account of his involvement in the looting. I provide nothing more than his own words on the matter. However, it is a reality that the Chicago Police Department regularly conducts sweeps in around public housing and picks up virtually whomever they want to in the process. Because of my casual slacks and button-down shirts, I looked like one of the social workers that frequented the community; I also had a university-issued identification card that helped to distinguish me from the type of men who get picked up by the police on the Near West Side. Those men have little capital with which to deflect or dispel the interest of the police. Consequently, when police officers are looking for someone on the Near West Side, these men have little to draw upon to make them seem unlike the typical perpetrator or potential collar. Thus, there may be a great disparity be-

tween what these men were detained for and what they were actually doing at the time they were detained.

10. An intriguing finding, made evident by some of the previous comments, is that approximately one-third of the men referred to sexual orientation as a basis for important social divisions. I am not clear as to why they stressed this distinction as much as they did. The questions were worded such that the men could bring in whatever social groups they desired in order to make their points. However, some of my follow-up questions focused on specific categories such as Caucasian men, Caucasian women, African American men, and African American women. They were not asked about their own sexual orientation, but none of the men in the study identified themselves as anything other than heterosexual. Therefore, I do not know if issues having to do with undisclosed aspects of their personal identity or behavior were relevant factors for their views. Their remarks led me to believe that matters pertaining to sexual orientation may have greater salience for everyday life in low-income communities than is now imagined by researchers (cf. Beam 1986, Harper 1996, Hemphill and Beam 1991). Such an understanding may be suppressed by the preoccupation of scholars with some traditional focal points in low-income communities (poverty, delinquency, etc.).

11. A number of scholars have tried to make sense of the diminished public dialogue about race since the 1960s at the same time that racial conflict and race-based inequalities have become exacerbated in many ways. Sociologists Michael Omi and Howard Winant (1994) argue that public discussion of race has been transformed since the 1960s to make it harder for organizations and groups to foster race-specific arguments for governmental intervention or redress. This point is more fully elucidated by Stephen Steinberg (1995) in his consideration of contemporary American sociopolitical thought concerning race, which centers on the absence of substantive public discussion on the matter. A similar phenomenon is the assertion that Americans are becoming more color-blind in everyday life; such logic is associated with the persistence of racism because color-blindness serves as a shield or mask for everyday racism (see Bobo, Kluegal, and Smith 1991; Bonilla-Silva 1997; Crenshaw 1997; Peshkin 1991; Smith 1995; Wells and Crain 1997).

12. These men included Donald, Anthony, Arthur, Tito, Travis, Dennis, Damon, Roy, Felton, Kurt, Earl, Gus, and Leon.

13. The difficulty of having to endure this radical change in social status and family wealth was worn on Peter's face. He would visit me at the community office on Western Avenue more often than any of the other men who participated in this study (at one point being told by one of the staff at the office that he was coming around too often). Peter never explained why he wanted to talk so much to me (and most of our conversations ventured far from the topics concerning this study), but it seemed to me that I was something of a link to his past life—perhaps a portrait of what he might have become if things had continued as they started out for him. His comments, as exemplified throughout this book, comprise a stark blend of pain and anger. In many ways they are unlike those of any other man in this account because he spoke of a life that he once had, rather than, like the other men, one that could only be imagined.

14. Devin is a Vice Lord. You may recall in earlier discussion of the history of inner-city Chicago gang activity that the Disciples (colloquially known as the

Folks) are an association of gangs that maintain a rivalry with the association of gangs identified as Vice Lords (colloquially known as the People).

15. In the course of my fieldwork I found that many black Americans in Chicago consistently identified Latinos as white. I believe this pattern of racial labeling to be geographically specific. In New York where I was born and raised, the common practice was to associate Latinos with African Americans in discussions of sociopolitical issues, alliance-building, and life situations. In the case of Chicago (at least on the Near West Side), many of the men seemed to cast racial labels upon groups in ways that reflect the specific history of power relations in the city. For instance, Roy extracted Polish Americans out of the category of Whites, explaining that Whites were second to Polish Americans in social influence in Chicago. His evidence for this was that many of Chicago's political leaders of the past and present had Polish-sounding names.

16. The "fifth," the "sixth," and "ride up" refer to gang terminology. The emblem of affiliates of the People is a five-pointed star, while that of the Folks is a six-pointed star. There are various other actions, attributes, and symbols that are employed by each faction as a means of public identification. "Ride up" simply refers to an association with a gang ("What you riding?" means "With which gang are you affiliated?").

17. A number of sociologists (and some psychologists who have chosen to pay greater attention than their colleagues to social contexts) have made contributions to the research area loosely labeled as cognitive sociology (Berger and Luckmann 1967, Bruner 1990, Cicourel 1973, DiMaggio 1997, Luria 1976, Schutz and Luckmann 1973, Zerubavel 1997). In part, this line of inquiry seeks to understand how social locations provide people with the capacity to visualize, label, and interpret aspects of the social world. It pays equal attention to why and when they may lack the capacity to do so.

18. A thought community, therefore, reflects the cognitive elements of habitus. Zerubavel and others do not focus so much on behavior or interaction, but argue only that the social categories that people hold membership in, and the consequent experiences that they have due to such membership, affect their social outlook.

19. Consequently, it was not that every ex–high school athlete, by virtue of competing in different communities, came to regard race or class as an important dimension of the stratification scheme in American life. Rather, men who played sports and who also experienced other forms of consistent cross-class and cross-racial contact tended to promote those views. Here is yet another context in which the application of a simple cause-and-effect logic is faulty. Instead of looking for one type of social experience that led to adherence to a worldview, it is essential to consider patterns of social experience.

Chapter Five
Framing Individual Mobility and Attainment

1. See Hochschild (1995) for a critical overview of mid- to late-twentieth-century studies that affirm Americans' commitment to individual initiative, irrespective of whatever else they think matters for mobility in American life.

2. Rank-order questions were employed to help ascertain the men's views on these topics. The intention here was to discover whether the men maintained any

rank ordering of factors concerning mobility. No clear patterns emerged. In the course of these discussions, the men often said things that were not consistent with the numeric rankings they had given, or that provided more clarity than did the rankings. They also sometimes invoked some of these factors at certain points in during our open-ended discussions as being of critical importance, then later modify, and still later remodify, those remarks. Thus, a cautionary note must be offered about any attempt to measure precisely how committed any man was to a specific order or ranking of attributes for upward mobility.

3. The significance of this cannot be overstated. Any attempt to create a linear explanation of what these men felt most (and least) mattered for mobility would fail given what was said in open-ended discussion around these rankings. The essence of their arguments is better found in their narratives about such factors rather than in their rankings.

4. Another caveat concerning questioning that asks respondents to numerically rank certain factors has to do with the temporal dimension of talk. Clearly, any of these men's utterances about mobility are time-bound. That is, a man may come to a completely different understanding of mobility processes at another point in his life. A narrative account of this understanding may be more durable over time than a straightforward ranking, because the narrative is constructed out of an accumulation of historical experiences and encounters, while a ranking more easily reflects an at-the-moment style of contemplating. Rankings are more susceptible to shifts over time (even over short spans of time). This is the case because of the serendipity and fluidity inherent in social life: an arrangement of variables concerning mobility could become susceptible to shifts as people experience different circumstances. Thus, for a particular person, at one moment social ties may rise in importance over educational credentials because someone recently got a job through a friend. At a point later in time, the same person might encounter people with significantly better educational credentials that experience more mobility at the work site.

5. This line of thinking is associated with work done by Paul Willis (1981), Signithia Fordham (1996), and John Ogbu (1978).

6. The concept of closure has been defined in sociological literature by Frank Parkin (1979) and Raymond Murphy (1988) to be the collective effort to construct and reinforce boundaries such that individuals who do not hold membership in a group may be precluded from doing so. Theoretical and empirical work on closure also focuses on how subordinate or oppressed groups work toward social inclusion by shifting or restructuring boundaries. Indeed, boundary-shifting and boundary-restructuring also serve as two means for formerly subordinate groups to restrict newly discovered or acquired resources such that they can garner social power over groups that formerly were superior to them.

Chapter Six
Looking Up from Below: Framing Personal Reality

1. Almost to a person, the men who talked about business ownership emphasized less the nature of the work that interested them than the status of being business owners. They were preoccupied with the extent to which business owner-

ship would create for them a measure of control over both their daily time and their means of generating income. This analysis resembles what Jay MacLeod (1995) found in his exploration of conceptions of the "good job" for black and white low-income and working-class young men in Boston. Many of MacLeod's respondents spoke of their quest for greater personal freedom and control of time as the principal benefits of self-employment.

2. The talk about business ownership also was consistent with the priority placed by most of the men on being respected by others in the workplace. For those who had very brief spells of employment, this surfaced in their discussions of treatment at the hands of their employers (refer back to chapter 4's investigation of their work experiences).

3. For an excellent summary and analysis of such findings, see Jennifer Hochschild's *Facing Up to the American Dream: Race, Class, and the Soul of the Nation* (1995).

4. Of course, another basketball player with the same level of skill may maintain a set of future orientations that do not converge. For instance, he may *expect* to get drafted and play professional basketball, but his actual *aspiration* may be to become a star in the NBA. Furthermore, his *ideal* state may be to be inducted into the NBA Hall of Fame. For the sake of comparison, let us presume that both of the athletes in our examples have similar levels of skill. The difference lies in the ways that each approaches his future circumstances. The first athlete's sense of what is accessible includes his idea/state, what he aspires to, and what he expects. The second is focused on that which extends beyond the apparently accessible, because his ideal state is a loftier one. Each pattern of future orientations can result in different action plans, reactions to life experiences (e.g., what happens once each begins to play in the NBA), or reevaluations of self and goals.

5. An overview of this simplification in mobility studies can be found in O'Connor and Young n.d. The vocabulary used to explore mobility and ambition is drawn from this more extensive commentary on extant gaps in mobility research. In it, we review the often contradictory and inconsistent use of terms in mobility research such as *expectations* and *aspirations*. We argue that this research would benefit from an extended vocabulary that draws more precise distinctions between an end state (the position or place that a person or group hopes to be in in the future), ways of getting there (strategies or pathways for movement), and material or abstract obstacles, barriers, and facilitators affecting such movement (the material includes money and tangible skills, and the abstract includes social phenomena, such as discrimination, or psychological factors, such as lack of motivation).

Ideal states, aspirations, and expectations are explained in this work as types of end states or positions to occupy in a structure. The "ways to get there" are divided into (1) recognized strategies for getting to those positions and places, which are what we call potentials, and (2) those recognized strategies that individuals or groups feel that they can employ for their own behalf, or what we call *strategies*. In short, individuals or groups extract a strategy from a package of previously identified potentials. For example, a man may think that he will reach a certain end state because he has the social ties to help him out, or because he has the material resources to help him get there. Knowledge of both resources makes them *potential*. The perceived ability to enact either would make it a *strat-*

egy. This distinction is drawn between strategies and potentials because it was determined that some people have insight into how a desired end is achieved, yet feel lacking in the capacity to personally achieve it. This condition differs from (but may resemble in lived experience) the case of the person who desires to be in a place or position, but has no idea of how one gets there (think of a child who wants to be an astronaut, but has no idea about how to pursue that goal, versus one that shares that desire, and knows what kind of training is necessary to achieve that goal, but cannot imagine how she would acquire that training for herself). Lastly, *obstacles* or *facilitators* can take the form of material resources like money or social ties (the absence or presence indicating an obstacle or facilitator), or in a more abstract sense, they can be embodied by one's sense of empowerment or weakness due to identity traits (e.g., feeling that one's gender or race can better equip one for acquiring certain kinds of work, but be a disadvantage for other kinds).

These distinctions are not picayune. In providing greater specification of each of these conceptual categories, we argue that more precise analyses of collective and individual mobility can unfold. Using this extended vocabulary as an instrument for organizing and exploring the material in this chapter is a step in that direction.

6. Perhaps here is a good opportunity to list exactly what the men aspired to in terms of occupational positions:

Jake, Anthony, Jason, Dennis, Travis, Roy, Earl, Peter (construction or skilled labor such as mechanic or machine operator)

Butch, Gus, Leon, Damon (support staff in office setting, such as x-ray or computer technician)

Donald, Larry, Lester (police officer or civil servant)

Felton (physical education teacher)

Casey (politician)

Ted (politician or business owner)

Kurt, Joseph, Arthur (business owner)

Tito, Barry, Jordan, Devin (any available job with benefits and a solid income)

Conrad (unsure at present but wants to go to college before determining)

It should be noted that on the whole the men talked not about particular jobs, but about the kinds of work-related duties that they wanted to have, or the kinds of skills they wanted to employ. This listing simply acknowledges the specific types of jobs that were mentioned in our discussions; it does not give an accurate sense of the complexities involved in how the men regard their future prospects. It is more important to understand the way in which they talked about the importance of the occupational *status* that they desired to secure. While they often did talk about specific occupational interests, they were less emphatic about specifying a type of work than about conveying what they wanted to achieve from gainful employment in terms of a quality of life.

The men's emphasis on specific occupational interests thus must be located within a more expansive discussion of what they sought or desired from the employment sphere and in life more generally, including attention to why they maintained those desires, whether or not they felt it possible to achieve them, and if so, how they planned to do so. Considerations of this issue, and others which follow in this chapter, provide a more comprehensive approach toward exploring how individuals contemplate future desires.

7. Arthur was one of the men who made this argument. His brief association with neighborhood stores brought him exposure to informal employment arrangements, off-the-book payment plans, and other procedures that did not create much job stability or security. Additionally, chapter 4's discussion of the life histories of these men revealed some of their suspicion and anxiety about how bosses and business owners operate. The men's attitudes must be kept in mind in order to understand much of what they said about work.

8. The testimony thus far shows that a more systematic inquiry was needed into what constitutes a decent day's pay for these men. They did indicate what they thought was a decent salary, and this figure ranged from twenty to over fifty thousand dollars in annual income. For a variety of reasons, it was more difficult for them to answer questions about what a decent day's pay would be for specific jobs. The men without any work experiences were the most vague, saying things like, "I have to know exactly what kind of work it is, or what the work situation is all about." The men who professed to have some manual skills (more on this distinction follows in this chapter) were the most insistent on having to see or know more about the work situation before being sure.

Such replies make at least two points about their relationship to the world or work. First and most obviously, without much work in their pasts they knew little about what various kinds of jobs paid in hourly or weekly rates. Second, those who did a little per diem or short-term work were highly suspicious of street corner employment recruiters for day-laboring jobs or others who wanted to give the men as little as possible for as much work as possible. The men said that in any case, such employment opportunities were not very plentiful. Usually one had to be in the right place at the right time—and this never happened more than a couple of times a year. They were extremely frustrated and angered by what they felt was an overall taken-for-grantedness about what they would accept and be willing to do for such work opportunities.

9. While none of the men stated explicitly that they had committed a violent crime (although a few implied their involvements in such activity), many did discuss their involvement in thievery in order to generate income. Others discussed quite candidly their involvement in drug selling. It is interesting to note that absent from any remarks about participation in illicit activity was any effort to make overtly moral claims about the legitimacy of such activity. Instead, they discussed their past and present involvements in matter-of-fact conversational styles. They knew that few people over the long term improved their socioeconomic status through such efforts. They also knew that the odds were not in their favor for doing so. Although at certain points in their lives some of them did attain significant short-term gains through these pursuits, having reached adulthood, the men began to think about living long lives, even if they were not in positions to always act in the best interests of their long-term future.

10. In his study of a low-income housing development, Lee Rainwater discusses what he believes was a heightened regard for physical health by the residents (1970). The commentary of the men in this study resembles much of what

he said about the experience of living in an impoverished community as a basis for a highly conscious preoccupation with one's own physical well-being. Recall that in chapter 3 Ken provided a relevant argument for this issue in discussing the importance of getting out of prison with his physical capabilities in tact.

11. We saw that in chapter 3 most of the men grew up in homes where the head of household (mother, grandmother, or female guardian) worked in such capacities as cashier in a local store, housekeeping and custodial work, kitchen duty in a hospital, or security work. As for the exceptions, Kurt, Felton, Joseph, Anthony, Damon, and Arthur grew up in single-female households where their mothers were on public aid for most of their childhoods. Of those men who lived or interacted consistently with their fathers, Lester's was a factory worker prior to receiving the prison sentence that was mentioned in chapter 2. The fathers of Jason, Larry, Roy, and Dennis worked in factories on the West Side of Chicago or did security work for large firms or businesses. Ted explained that his father worked around the neighborhood "here and there" as a means of earning and income; I suspected that he moved between illicit and legitimate activities throughout the course of Ted's youth.

12. Although the intense preoccupation in social science research with hyper-masculinity was regarded in earlier chapters as a part of a narrow cultural lens through which low-income black men are viewed, much of that research framed black masculinity in the same ways that these men did. Thus, my point was never to dismiss the importance of that focus but simply to include other perspectives. While focusing on men who seemingly stand at an extreme end of the masculinity scale, Loic Waquant's (1992, 1995) work on African American boxers on the South Side of Chicago presents a balanced depiction of the reverence that black men hold for their bodies, and for other masculine traits and characteristics, without defining the totality of their social character as hyper-masculinized beings.

13. The story of how males in working-class and lower categories get oriented to such a labor sector is told by Paul Willis (1981) in his study *Learning to Labor: How Working Class Kids Get Working Class Jobs*. There he argues that working-class youth are predisposed toward such jobs because their cultural orientation to educational opportunities precludes them from desiring and well as acquiring the relevant credentials for higher status employment.

14. See Kirschenmann and Neckerman (1991) and Neckerman and Kirschenmann (1991) for arguments about how Chicago-area employers in particular regard black men as prospective employees.

15. The vocabulary discussed in note 5 above helps delineate the process that allowed them to couple their aspirations with expectations. In short, they acquired knowledge of a potential (formal training and certification) that led toward an end state (in this case, a job in a specific industry). Their ability to appropriate that potential (get financial help in order to get trained and certified) meant that each identified a personal strategy to help him achieve his desired ends.

Framing the situation of these four men in this way calls for the exploration of a much larger project, and one that is far beyond the purview of this book. More investigation is needed as to how one's sense of end states (the ideal, aspiration, or expectation) develops with respect to one's sense of potentials and strategies. In other words, the question remains as to why some people might form a sense of desired end states after taking into account whatever strategies they have at their disposal, whereas others form a sense of end states first, then struggle with determining strategies to get them there. The latter approach causes more problems for people because if an end goal remains in one's thinking without a prior or coinciding adaptation of a strategy, then it may linger as an ideal state and nothing more.

16. The inability to say "I don't know" much about expectations indicates not only how despondent some of these men were, but how constrained they were as well. A lingering question remains as to whether a lack of efficacy is the cause of such constraint (for further discussion of this possibility, see Bandura 1977, 1978, 1982, 1986, 1997), or a lack of knowledge of how to take modest steps is the root cause. Again, such investigation calls for a study beyond the scope of this one.

17. The preceding discussion suggests that values, norms, and behaviors do not exhaust the categories of cultural response. An undue focus on values regarding work, or how men react to its absence, makes for an incomplete cultural analysis of how such men relate to employment opportunities. It is clear that actions regarding work are not determined by values and psychological factors alone. A more complete cultural framing of low-income black men must include attention to beliefs and worldviews about matters such as the employment sphere because those cultural elements are the building blocks for making meaning about—and situating future action within—the social world.

18. The basis for these men's attention to their bodies is much the same as that for their emphasis on manual, skilled labor prospects. Men often positively define themselves as much while referencing their bodies as by the kind of work that they do (Connell 1995, Kimmel and Messner 1992). Hence, both kinds of emphases were consistently made by the men in the study. The body has a heightened sense of importance for some of these men because they have neither work nor a rich repertoire of work-related skills to draw upon. Therefore, discussions of bodily capability substitute for the absence of other skills while reinforcing a sense of moral worth and utility as men.

19. Wacquant's (1992, 1995) work on boxers speaks to how black men without formal credentials or service-sector skills take special regard for what they can do with their bodies.

20. As an example of how potential employees may provide symbolic resources, think of what hiring women or members of underrepresented ethnic groups meant for businesses that sought government contracts in the early history of affirmative action, especially if those firms initially had no particular desire to hire people from those categories. Another case of a return from a symbolic resource is exemplified by a business that hires physically challenged people, women, or members of underrepresented ethnic groups and displays them prominently at work so that customers or clients may develop a greater appreciation for the business. In many cases, the latter effort leads to the type of material outcome sought after in the first scenario (particular if clients or customers respond positively to the initiatives of the business). None of this is to say that every business engages in this sort of practice. Indeed, another symbolic dimension would be represented by a business that simply determines to take a principled stand on

the importance of hiring certain kinds of "nontraditional" employees. In any case, it is not farfetched to imagine that some business leaders employ certain symbolic tactics for the sake of increasing profit, yet profess publicly that their actions were nothing more than the "right thing to do."

21. I had no grounds to actually find out what these men could or could not do in terms of hands-on work. I can only report that they talked about what they could do, and then went on to talk at length about how their lack of certification and of more schooling prevented them from being able to better market their abilities.

22. Other than Jason and Dennis, this claim was made by Butch, Anthony, Jake, Barry, Joseph, Lester, Peter, Travis, Devin, Casey, Ted, Earl, Gus, Roy, Damon, and Tito. One slightly puzzling finding here is that although Kurt reported receiving a certificate from a trade school, he never mentioned any particular mastery of the skills relating to that schooling experience. I could not confirm that this was the case, but I surmised that Kurt was a victim of the type of noncertified "fly-by-night" trade schools that target low-income citizens with the promise of helping them to find employment and a better future after they put forth the necessary tuition dollars. I make this case from Kurt's saying that the school closed down shortly after he completed his training, and he received no further information about why this occurred.

23. Interestingly, those who claimed to possess skills like typing were not especially cognizant of the white-collar service sector as an appropriate site for their skills. The men who mentioned typing did so as if they were simply listing what they knew how to do rather than what they thought would matter for their potential employment.

24. Gus, Earl, Joseph, Devin, Tito, and Jake spoke about having both manual and social skills.

Chapter Seven
Getting There: Navigating Personal Mobility

1. Higher education was the only educational arena that came under regular criticism, and this had to do with its costs and concerns over the utility of studying in areas like liberals arts. Peter's remarks were some of the most direct (probably because he went to college for a term, thus actually experiencing the institution that he was talking about). Many men seemed to have ambiguous attitudes about higher education. They had an idea that possession of a college degree was a valuable thing. Beyond that, there was not much about college that made a great deal of sense to them. The fields of study did not connect to what they saw as relevant work skills. They also could not fathom why college education costs as much as it does for these seemingly irrelevent fields of study. None could state with precision what a year of schooling costs at the University of Chicago or the University of Illinois at Chicago. Instead, they all estimated that a college education costs thousands upon thousands of dollars every year, and they were not at all clear as to why that had to be the case.

2. See Swidler (1986) for a discussion of how cultural tool kits serve as packages of meaning and action plans for people. She argues that these kits are assem-

bled from practices, beliefs, values, and norms that are reinforced or validated in social settings as well as within social groups, and they serve as repositories of cultural resources and guidelines for managing everyday life.

3. One of the men said that he had a brother-in-law in the National Basketball Association, and a few mentioned high school associates or teammates that made it to the professional ranks.

4. As discussed earlier, the saturation of gangs in low-income African American communities in Chicago is such that many men maintain such memberships, yet the depth of commitment varies. The actual activity that one pursues as a gang member can range from illicit activities to little more than casual association with others known to be in a gang. Such variance indicates that not only does gang association differ from actual involvement in illicit activity, but that different levels of involvement relate to different levels of adoption of a gang identity, irrespective of how the police or other authority figures label any particular young man in the neighborhood. Finally, gang membership, while perceived by many outsiders as a impediment for upward mobility, may introduce one to social networks that can facilitate such movement (recall Earl's discussion in chapter 3 of fellow gang associates who did quite well after transforming money earned in illicit activities into capital for the start of legitimate small businesses). Thus, under the right circumstances gang membership can also enhance one's mobility prospects by facilitating access to certain resources that can support one's quest for mobility.

5. This argument extends from a discussion by sociologist Wayne Brekhaus (1998) on marked identities. Brekhaus argued that certain identities are marked in public life such that a host of additional identifications and signifiers are attached to an identity, some (and sometimes all) of which are not necessarily associated with it. For example, in the public discourse of crime and delinquency, urban-based young black men are marked as more likely to engage and/or promote those activities than are white upper-income youth. Thus, when urban-based young black men are seen in large groups in public settings, they often conjure up feelings of threat and insecurity. They also may come to mind more readily when people form images of drug abuse and other profligate activity.

6. See Blauner 1989, Collins 1998, Feagan and Sikes 1994, and Hochschild 1995, for case studies and references to other works that make this point.

7. As pedestrian as the remark about having a family may seem, it underscores an important dimension of Devin's sense of self that is left out in his public depiction as a gang member and ex-convict. While Devin, by his own admission, certainly committed more than his share of heinous acts, he was also a man who strove to preserve and support a family in accordance with his definition of the term. His notion of family included a woman that he had not yet married but always referred to as his wife, her two children by previous involvements, and his own son, with this woman. Indeed, in every question that I asked concerning his outlook on future prospects, he invoked the issue of his family as a crucial concern. His doing so adds an important point of consideration for understanding how individuals conceive of themselves and their interests in ways that are not consistent with their profligate public image. Thus, Devin's public identity as a gangbanger and public menace overshadows that part of him that responds to his social world as a responsible father and household provider. This greater complex-

ity of his character is unrecognized, while it has as much to do with his assessment of mobility prospects as does his life as a gangbanger. Indeed, perhaps other relevant features of his life suffer the same neglect. Recognizing this complexity does not mean excusing any of his delinquent behavior, but it does create the capacity for understanding and ascertaining better how such individuals might be able to alter their lives for their own betterment as well as for others.

I argue that a more complete effort is necessary to make sense of the lives of men like Devin and Casey. When looking at how they define themselves in ways that have little to do with their more prominent public images, researchers come to understand the more profound complexity in how these individuals respond to the social world. That response includes so much more than what is conveyed in labels such as delinquent, indolent, or maladaptive. These alternative understandings do not erase the more visible identities, nor should they. What they do is help round out a sense of the humanity that is a part of these men, and giving some sense of the other dimensions of their lives that matter for any serious attempt at policy or programmatic intervention in the lives of poor black men.

8. As previously noted, I found that these men and others on the Near West Side adhered to a specific process of racial coding that was particular to Chicago (although further research needs to be done to determine if it is exclusive to this city and region). Latinos were often regarded by lower-income black Americans as white. While this may hold for other regions of the country, it is in stark contrast to the social coding that occurs in my hometown of New York City, where African Americans and Latinos tend to reside in the same neighborhoods and are viewed as more socially and culturally cohesive.

I suspect that the Chicago circumstance may be due to the fact that black-Latino residential segregation is as much a fact of life in Chicago as is black-white residential segregation. Therefore, without intimate interaction, there is no convergence between Chicago-based African Americans and Latinos in order to form an urban "subculture," nor is there much basis for African Americans in that city to discern how Latinos constitute a distinct ethnic group other than over language differences. The fact that white ethnics in Chicago speak multiple languages, but still coalesce around whiteness, prevents such a language difference from being important to African Americans in making better sense of the Latino situation.

9. At least one other Chicago-based study has a similar focus (Venkatesh 1994). However, it examines an older category of black men, aged 27–44, and specifically addresses how those men interpret job-specific mobility prospects (what attributes or resources one needs for a good job, and the difficulty the men express in finding work). Unlike the present work, it does not comprehensively address how these men frame an understanding of the structure of work opportunity in Chicago and what specific skills the men feel they can bring to it.

10. This should not be taken to imply that they men necessarily wanted to leave the community where they were currently residing. Certainly, some of the men did, and others said that they would if they knew of specific job prospects elsewhere. However, some of them simply desired greater safety in their own community. The desire was maintained by men who had engaged in violent and turbulent activity as well as those who did not. Most of the men who reported that they engaged in violent activity (e.g., Devin, Tito, Anthony) understood their actions

as potential causal forces for promoting violence in the community. For various reasons, they were not always contrite about their actions, but they were aware of the social effects of those actions on the quality of life in the community.

Appendix

1. The more upwardly mobile men of the Near West Side, together with men from other Chicago neighborhoods who have moved from poverty to some kind of better life, will be explored in a publication tentatively entitled "American Dreams against the American Dilemma: How Upwardly Mobile Black Men Confront Race" (forthcoming).

2. Sociologists Miri Song and David Parker (1995) argue that interviewing members of their own ethnic groups can involve a great deal of pre- (and sometimes post-) interview conversation that functions as time for the research participants to determine the extent to which the researcher shares their ethnic values, ideologies, and worldviews. Rather than taking membership in the same racial or ethnic category as an immediate indication of the researcher's insider status, the participant is thus given the chance to gain some insight into the extent to which the researcher identifies along the same ethnic lines and, consequently, to decide whether the researcher should be regarded as an ethnic insider with whom the participant can talk more freely and openly.

References _____

Abrahams, Roger D. 1964. *Deep Down in the Jungle*. Revised edition. Chicago: Aldine Publishing Company.

Alexander, Jeffrey. 1987. *Twenty Lectures: Sociological Theory since World War II*. New York: Columbia University Press.

Anderson, Elijah. 1978. *A Place on the Corner*. Chicago: University of Chicago Press.

———. 1989. "Sex Codes and Family Life Among Poor Inner-City Youth." *Annals of the Academy of Political and Social Science* 501: 59–78.

———. 1990. *Streetwise: Race, Class, and Change in an Urban Community*. Chicago: University of Chicago Press.

———. 1999. *The Code of the Streets*. New York: W.W. Norton.

Aponte, Robert. 1990. "Definitions of the Underclass: A Critical Analysis." In *Sociology in America*, ed. by Herbert Gans. Newbury Park, CA: Sage.

Aschenbrenner, Joyce. 1975. *Lifelines: Black Families in Chicago*. New York: Holt, Rinehart, and Winston.

Auletta, Ken. 1982. *The Underclass*. New York: Random House.

Bandura, Albert. 1977. "Self-Efficacy: Toward a Unifying Theory of Behavioral Change." *Psychological Review* 84: 191–215.

———. 1978. "Reflections on Self-Efficacy." In *Advances in Behavior Research and Therapy*, vol 1, ed. by S. Rachman. Oxford: Pergman Press.

———. 1982. "Self-Efficacy Mechanism in Human Agency." *American Psychologist* 37: 122–47.

———. 1986. *Social Foundations of Thought and Action: A Social Cognitive Theory*. Englewood Cliffs, NJ: Prentice Hall.

———. 1997. *Self-Efficacy: The Exercise of Control*. New York: Freemen Press.

Banfield, Edward. 1970. *The Unheavenly City*. 2nd ed., Boston: Little, Brown.

Baumann, John F., Norman P. Hummon, and Edward K. Muller. 1991. "Public Housing, Isolation, and the Urban Underclass." *Journal of Urban History* 17: 264–92.

Beam, Joseph (ed). 1986. *In the Life: A Black Gay Anthology*. Boston: Alyson.

Bell, Bernard W., Emily Grosholz, and James B. Stewart (eds.) 1996. *W.E.B. DuBois: On Race and Culture*. New York: Routledge.

Berger, Bennett M. 1960. *Working-Class Suburb: A Study of Auto Workers in Suburbia*. Berkeley, CA: University of California Press.

Berger, Joseph, Bernard P. Cohen, and Morris Zeldich, Jr. 1972. "Status Characteristics and Social Interaction." *American Sociological Review* June: 241–55.

Berger, Peter L., and Thomas Luckmann. 1967. *The Social Construction of Reality*. New York: Anchor Books.

Berman, Phyllis W. and Frank A. Pedersen (eds.). 1987. *Men's Transition to Parenthood*. Hillsdale, NJ: Lawrence Erlbaum.

Bernard, Jessie. 1992. "The Good-Provider Role: Its Rise and Fall." In *Men's Lives* (2nd ed.) ed. by Michael S. Kimmel and Michael A. Messner. New York: Macmillan Publishing Company.

Bertaux, Daniel. 1981. "From the Life-History Approach to the Transformation of Sociological Practice." In *Biography and Society: The Life History Approach in the Social Sciences*, ed. by Daniel Bertaux. Beverly Hills, CA: Sage Publications.

Bertaux, Daniel, and Martin Kohli. 1984. "The Life Story Approach: A Continental View." *Annual Review of Sociology* 10: 215–37.

Biller, Henry B. 1993. *Fathers and Families: Paternal Factors in Child Development.* Westport, CT: Auburn House.

Billingsley, Andrew. 1992. *Climbing Jacob's Ladder: The Enduring Legacy of African American Families.* New York: Simon and Schuster.

Billson, Janet Mancini. 1996. *Pathways to Manhood: Young Black Males' Struggle for Identity.* New Brunswick, NJ: Transaction.

Blake, Wayne M., and Carol A. Darling. 1994. "The Dilemmas of the African American Male." *Journal of Black Studies* 24 (June): 402–15.

Blauner, Robert. 1989. *Black Lives, White Lives: Three Decades of Race Relations in America.* Berkeley: University of California Press.

Block, Carolyn Rebecca, and Richard Block. 1993. "Street Gang Crime in Chicago." In *Research in Brief.* Washington, DC: National Institute of Justice.

Bluestone, Barry, and Bennett Harrison. 1982. *The Deindustrialization of America.* New York: Basic Books.

Bluestone, Barry, Mary Stevenson, and Christopher Tilly. 1993. "The Deterioration in Labor Market Prospects for Young Men with Limited Schooling: Assessing the Impact of 'Demand Side' Factors." Paper presented at the annual meeting of the Eastern Economic Association, March 14–15, Pittsburgh.

Blumer. Herbert. 1969. *Symbolic Interactionism.* Englewood Cliffs, NJ: Prentice-Hall.

Bobo, Lawrence, James R. Kluegal, and Ryan A. Smith. 1991. "Laissez Faire Racism: The Crystallization of a 'Kinder, Gentler' Anti-Black Ideology." In *Racial Attitudes in the 1990s: Continuity and Change*, ed. by Steven A. Tuch and Jack K. Martin. Westport, CT: Praeger.

Bonilla-Silva, Eduardo. 1997. "Rethinking Racism: Toward a Structural Interpretation." *American Sociological Review* 6.3 (June): 465–80.

Bordua, David J. 1961. "Delinquent Subcultures: Sociological Interpretations of Gang Delinquency." *Annals of the American Academy of Political and Social Sciences* 228: 120–36.

Bourdieu, Pierre. 1962. *The Algerians.* Trans. by Alan C. M. Ross. Boston: Beacon Press.

———. 1977a. *Outline of a Theory of Practice.* Cambridge: Cambridge University Press.

———. 1977b. "Cultural Reproduction and Social Reproduction." In *Power and Ideology in Education*, ed. by Jerome Karabel and A. H. Halsey. New York: Oxford University Press.

———. 1984. *Distinction: A Social Critique of the Judgement of Taste.* Cambridge: Cambridge University Press.

————. 1986. "The Forms of Capital." In *Handbook of Theory and Research for the Sociology of Education*, ed. by John G. Richardson. New York: Greenwood Press.

————. 1988. *Homo Academicus*. Cambridge: Polity Press.

————. 1990. *The Logic of Practice*. Cambridge: Cambridge University Press.

Bourdieu, Pierre, and Loic J. D. Wacquant. 1992. *An Invitation to Reflexive Sociology*. Cambridge: Polity Press.

Bourgois, Philippe. 1995. *In Search of Respect: Selling Crack in El Barrio*. New York: Cambridge University Press.

Bowman, Philip. 1989. "Research Perspectives on Black Men: Role Strain and Adaptation across the Life Cycle." In *Black Adult Development and Aging*, ed. by R. L. Jones. Berkeley, CA: Cobb and Henry.

————. 1992. "Coping with the Provider Role Strain: Adaptive Cultural Resources among Black Husband-Fathers." In A.K.H. Burlew, W. C. Banks, Harriette Pipes McAdoo, and D. Azibo, *African American Psychology: Theory, Research, and Practice*. Newbury Park, CA: Sage.

————. 1993. "The Impact of Economic Marginality on African American Husbands and Fathers." In *Family Ethnicity*, ed. by Harriette Pipes McAdoo. Newbury Park, CA: Sage.

————. 1995. "Marginalization of Black Men and the Underclass Debate." In *The Decline in Marriage Among African Americans*, ed. by M. B. Tucker and C. Mitchell-Kernan. New York: Russell Sage.

Bowman, Philip, and Tyrone Forman. 1997. "Instrumental and Expressive Family Roles Among African American Fathers." In *Family Life in Black America*, ed. by Robert J. Taylor, James S. Jackson, and Linda M. Chatters. Thousand Oaks, CA: Sage.

Boyd-Franklin, Nancy. 1989. *Black Families in Therapy*. New York: Guilford Press.

Brekhaus, Wayne. 1998. "A Sociology of the Unmarked: Redirecting Our Focus." *Sociological Theory* 16:1 (March): 34–51.

Brodt, Bonita, and other reporters of the *Chicago Tribune*. 1988. *Chicago Schools: Worst in America*. Chicago: Contemporary Books.

Bronstein, Phyllis, and Carolyn Pape Cowan. 1988. *Fatherhood Today: Men's Changing Role in the Family*. New York: John Wiley.

Browning, Harley L., and Nestor Rodriguez. 1985. "The Migration of Mexican Indocumentados as a Settlement Process: Implications for Work." In *Hispanics in the U.S. Economy*, ed. by George J. Borjas and Marta Tienda. Madison, WI: Academic Press.

Bruner, Jerome. 1990. *Acts of Meaning*. Cambridge, MA: Harvard University Press.

Calhoun, Craig. 1993. "Habitus, Field, and Capital: The Question of Historical Specificity." In *Bourdieu: Critical Perspectives*, ed. by Craig Calhoun, Edward LiPuma, and Moishe Postone. Cambridge: Polity Press.

Calhoun, Craig, Edward LiPuma, and Moishe Postone (eds.). 1993. *Bourdieu: Critical Perspectives*. Cambridge: Polity Press.

Chicago Fact Book Consortium. 1984. *Local Community Fact Book: Chicago Metropolitan Area*. Chicago: Chicago Review Press.

Chicago Fact Book Consortium. 1995. *Local Community Fact Book: Chicago Metropolitan Area*. Chicago: Chicago Review Press.

Chicago Housing Authority, Office of External Affairs, Department of Research and Development. 1992. "Statistical Profile 1991–1992." Chicago Housing Authority.

Chicago Panel on Public School Policy and Finance. 1986–92. *Chicago Public Schools Data Book*. Chicago.

Cicourel, Aaron. 1974. *Cognitive Sociology*. New York: Free Press.

Clark, Reginald M. 1983. *Family Life and School Achievement: Why Poor Black Children Succeed or Fail*. Chicago: University of Chicago Press.

Cloward, Richard A., and Lloyd E. Ohlin. 1960. *Delinquency and Opportunity: A Theory of Delinquent Gangs*. New York: Free Press.

Cohen, Albert K., and Harold M. Hodges. 1963. "Characteristics of the Lower Blue-Collar Class." *Social Problems* Spring, 10; 4 (Spring): 303–34.

Cohn, R. M. 1978. "The Effects of Employment Status Change on Self-Attitudes." *Social Psychology* 41, 2: 81–93.

Coleman, James S. 1988. "Social Capital in the Creation of Human Capital." *American Journal of Sociology* 94: S95–120.

Collins, Patricia Hill. 1998. *Fighting Words: Black Women and the Search for Justice*. Minneapolis: University of Minnesota Press.

Connell, R. W. 1995. *Masculinities*. Berkeley: University of California Press.

Cosby, Bill. 1986. *Fatherhood*. New York: Dolphin/Doubleday.

Coser, Lewis. 1965. "The Sociology of Poverty" *Social Problems* 13:2 (Fall): 140–48.

Cottingham, Phoebe H., and David T. Ellwood (eds.). 1989. *Welfare Policy for the 1990s*. Cambridge: Harvard University Press.

Crenshaw, Kimberle W. 1997. "Color-Blind Dreams and Racial Nightmares: Reconfiguring Racism in the Post-Civil Rights Era." In *Birth of a Nation'hood*, ed. by Toni Morrison and Claudia Brodsky. Lacour. New York: Pantheon Books.

Danziger, Sheldon, Gary Sandefur, and Daniel Weinberg (eds.). 1994. *Confronting Poverty: Prescriptions for Change*. Cambridge, MA: Harvard University Press and Russell Sage Foundation.

Darity, William A., Samuel L. Myers, Emmet D. Carson, and William Sabol (eds.). 1994. *The Black Underclass: Critical Essays on Race and Unwantedness*. New York: Garland.

Davis, Allison. 1946. "The Motivation of the Underprivileged Worker." In *Industry and Society*, ed. by William F. Whyte. New York: McGraw-Hill.

Davis, Allison, and John Dollard. 1940. *Children of Bondage: The Personality Development of Negro Youth in the Urban South*. Washington, DC: American Council on Education.

Davis, Allison, Burleigh R. Gardner, and Mary R. Gardner. 1941. *Deep South: A Social Anthropological Study of Caste and Class*. Chicago: University of Chicago Press.

Davis, Theodore J. 1994. "The Educational Attainment and Intergenerational Mobility of Black Males: The 1970s and 1980s." *The Urban Review* 26, 2: 137–51.

Denzin, Norman K. 1978. "The Sociological Interview." In *The Research Act*, ed. by Norman K. Denzin. New York: McGraw-Hill.

———. 1997. *Interpretive Ethnography: Ethnographic Practices for the Twenty-First Century*. Thousand Oaks, CA: Sage Publications.

Denzin, Norman K., and Yvonna S. Lincoln (eds.). 1994. *Handbook of Qualitative Research*. Thousand Oaks, CA: Sage Publications.

DiMaggio, Paul. 1979. "Review Essay on Pierre Bourdieu." *American Journal of Sociology* 84, 6 (May): 1460–74.

———. 1982. "Cultural Capital and School Success: The Impact of Status Culture Participation on the Grades of U.S. High School Students." *American Sociological Review* 47, 2 (April): 189–201.

———. 1997. "Culture and Cognition." *Annual Review of Sociology* 23: 263–87.

DiMaggio, Paul, and John Mohr. 1984. "Cultural Capital, Educational Attainment, and Marital Selection." *American Journal of Sociology* 90, 6 (May): 1231–61.

Dollard, John. 1937. *Caste and Class in a Southern Town*. New Haven: Yale University Press.

Douglas, Jack (ed.). 1970. *Understanding Everyday Life: Toward the Reconstruction of Sociological Knowledge*. Chicago: Aldine Publishing.

Doyle, Bertram Wilbur. 1937. *The Etiquette of Race Relations in the South: A Study in Social Control*. Chicago: University of Chicago Press.

Drake, St. Claire, and Horace Cayton. 1993 [1945]. *Black Metropolis*. Chicago: University of Chicago Press.

DuBois, W. E. B. 1996 [1899]. *The Philadelphia Negro: A Social Study*. Philadelphia: University of Pennsylvania Press.

Duncan, Kevin C. 1994. "Racial Disparity in Earnings and Earnings Growth: The Case of Young Men." *The Social Science Journal* 31, 3: 237–50.

Dyson, Michael Eric. 1989. "The Plight of Black Men." *Zeta Magazine*, February, pp. 51–56.

Elliott, Delbert. 1992. "Longitudinal Research in Criminology: Promise and Practice." Paper presented at the NATO Conference on Cross-National Longitudinal Research on Criminal Behavior, July 19–25, Frankfurt, Germany.

Ellwood, David, and Phoebe Cottingham, eds. 1989. *Welfare Policies for the 1990s*. Cambridge, M.A.: Harvard University Press.

Evans, Brenda J., and James R. Whitfield. 1988. "The Status of Black Males in America: A Database Search." *American Psychologist* 43: 401–2.

Farley, Reynolds, and Walter R. Allen. 1987. *The Color Line and the Quality of Life in America*. New York: Russell Sage Foundation.

Feagin, Joe R., and Melvin P. Sikes. 1994. *Living with Racism: The Black Middle Class Perspective*. Boston: Beacon Press.

Fellner, Jamie, and Marc Mauer. 1998. "Losing the Vote: The Impact of Felony Disenfranchisement Laws in the United States." The Sentencing Project and Human Rights Watch, October.

Fernandez, Roberto M., and David Harris. 1992. "Social Isolation and the Underclass." In *Drugs, Crime, and Social Isolation: Barriers to Urban Opportu-*

nity, ed. by Adele V. Harrell and George E. Peterson. Washington, DC: Urban Institute Press.

Fordham, Signithia. 1996. *Blacked Out: Dilemmas of Race, Identity, and Success at Capital High*. Chicago: University of Chicago Press.

Frazier, E. Franklin. 1932. *The Negro Family in Chicago*. Chicago: University of Chicago Press.

———. 1934. "Traditions and Patterns of Negro Family Life in The United States." In *Race and Culture Contacts*, ed. by E. B. Reuter. New York: McGraw-Hill.

Fredrickson, George. 1987. *The Black Image in the White Mind: The Debate on African American Character and Destiny, 1817–1914*. Second edition. Middletown, CT: Wesleyan University Press.

Freeman, Richard B., and Harry T. Holzer (eds.). 1986. *The Black Youth Employment Crisis*. Chicago: University of Chicago Press.

Furstenberg, Frank F. 1988. "Good Dads–Bad Dads: Two Faces of Fatherhood." In *The Changing American Family and Public Policy*, ed. by Andrew J. Cherlin. Washington, DC: Urban Institute Press.

Furstenberg, Frank F., and K. Harris. 1992. "The Disappearing American Father? Divorce and the Waning Significance of Biological Parenthood." In *The Changing American Family: Sociological and Demographic Perspectives*, ed. by S. J. South and S. E. Tolnay. Boulder, CO: Westview.

———. 1993. "When and Why Fathers Matter: Impacts of Father Involvement on the Children of Adolescent Mothers." In *Young Unwed Fathers: Changing Roles and Emerging Policies*, ed. by R. Lerman and T. Ooms. Philadelphia, PA: Temple University Press.

Gamson, William. 1992. *Talking Politics*. New York: Cambridge University Press.

Gans, Herbert. 1962. *Urban Villagers*. New York: Free Press.

———. 1969. "Class in the Study of Poverty: An Approach to Anti-Poverty Research." In *On Understanding Poverty: Perspective from the Social Sciences*, ed. by Daniel P. Moynihan. New York: Basic Books.

———. 1995. *The War against the Poor: The Underclass and Anti-Poverty Policy*. New York: Basic Books.

Gary, Lawrence (ed). 1981. *Black Men*. Beverly Hills, CA: Sage Publications.

Gary, Lawrence, and Bogart R. Leashore. 1982. "High Risk Status of Black Men." *Social Work* 27, 1: 54–58.

Geertz, Clifford. 1973. *The Interpretation of Cultures: Selected Essays*. New York: Basic Books.

Gerson, Kathleen. 1993. *No Man's Land: Men's Changing Commitments to Family and Work*. New York: Basic Books.

Gibbs, Jewelle Taylor. 1988. *Young, Black, and Male in America*. Dover, MA: Auburn House Publishing Company.

Giddens, Anthony. 1973. *The Class Structure of Advanced Society*. London: Hutchinson.

———. 1979. *Central Problems in Social Theory*. London: Macmillan.

———. 1984. *The Constitution of Society: Outline of a Theory of Structuration*. Cambridge: Polity Press.

Glaser, Barney G., and Anselm L. Strauss. 1967. *The Discovery of Grounded Theory: Strategies for Qualitative Research.* New York: Aldine De Gruyter.

Glasgow, Douglas G. 1980. *The Black Underclass: Poverty, Unemployment and Entrapment of Ghetto Youth.* New York: Random House.

Goffman, Erving. 1974. *Frame Analysis: An Essay on the Organization of Experience.* Cambridge, MA: Harvard University Press.

Gordon, Edmund T., Edmund W. Gordon, and Jessica Gordon Nembhard. 1994. "Social Science Literature Concerning African American Men." *Journal of Negro Education* 63, 4: 508–31.

Granovetter, Mark. 1978. "The Strength of Weak Ties." *American Journal of Sociology* 78: 1360–80.

———. 1983. "The Strength of Weak Ties: A Network Theory Revisited." *Sociological Theory* 1: 201–33.

Griswold, Robert. 1993. *Fatherhood in America: A History.* New York: Basic Books.

Griswold, Wendy. 1987. "A Methodological Framework for the Study of Culture." *Sociological Methodology* 17: 1–35.

Grossman, James. 1989. *Land of Hope: Chicago, Black Southerners, and the Great Migration.* Chicago: University of Chicago Press.

Hannerz, Ulf. 1969. *Soulside: Inquiries into Ghetto Culture and Community.* New York: Columbia University Press.

———. 1972. "What Ghetto Males Are Like: Another Look." In *Black Psyche,* ed. by Stanley Guterman. Berkeley: The Glendessay Press.

Harper, Phillip Brian. 1996. *Are We Not Men? Masculine Anxiety and the Problem of African American Identity.* New York: Oxford University Press.

Harrell, Adele V., and George E. Peterson (eds.). 1992. *Drugs, Crime, and Social Isolation: Barriers to Urban Opportunity.* Washington, DC: Urban Institute Press.

Harrington, Michael. 1962. *The Other America: Poverty in the United States.* New York: Macmillan.

Hawkins, Darnell F. (ed.). 1996. *Ethnicity, Race, and Crime: Perspectives across Time and Place.* Albany, NY: State University of New York Press.

Heckler, Margaret. 1985. *Report of the Secretary's Task Force on Black and Minority Health.* Washington, DC: U.S. Department of Health and Human Services.

Hemphill, Essex, and Joseph Beam (eds). 1991. *Brother to Brother: New Writings by Black Gay Men.* Boston: Alyson.

Herbert, Bob. 1994. "Who Will Help the Black Man: A Symposium." *New York Times Sunday Magazine,* November 20.

Hertz, Rosanna (ed.). 1997. *Reflexivity and Voice.* Thousand Oaks, CA: Sage Publications.

Hirsch, Arnold E. 1983. *The Making of the Second Ghetto: Race and Housing and Chicago, 1940–1960.* New York: Cambridge University Press.

Hochschild, Jennifer L. 1995. *Facing Up to the American Dream: Race, Class, and the Soul of the Nation.* Princeton, NJ: Princeton University Press.

Hofstadter, Richard. 1945. *Social Darwinism in American Thought, 1860–1915.* Philadelphia: University of Pennsylvania Press.

Holzer, Harry J. 1986. "Black Youth Non-Employment: Duration and Job Search." In *The Black Youth Employment Crisis*, ed. by Richard B. Freeman and Harry T. Holzer. Chicago: University of Chicago Press.

———. 1996. *What Employers Want: Job Prospects for Less-Educated Workers.* New York: Russell Sage Foundation.

———. 2002. "An Initiative to Raise Employment among Young Minority Men." *Poverty Research News* 1 (January/February): 9–10.

Hood, Jane C. 1986. "The Provider Role: Its Meaning and Measurement." *Journal of Marriage and the Family*, 48: 349–59.

Hunter, Andrea G., and James Earl Davis. 1994. "Hidden Voices of Black Men: The Meaning, Structure, and Complexity of Black Manhood." *Journal of Black Studies* 25 (September): 20–40.

Israilevich, Philip, and Ramamohan Mahidhara. 1990. "Chicago's Economy: Twenty Years of Structural Change." *Economic Perspectives* March/April: 15–23.

Jackman, Mary R. 1994. *The Velvet Glove: Paternalism and Conflict in Gender, Race, and Class.* Berkeley: University of California Press.

Jarrett, Robin L. 1994. "Living Poor: Family Life Among Single-Parent, African American Women." *Social Problems* 41: 30–49.

Jarrett, Robin L. 1995. "Growing Up Poor: The Family Experiences of Socially Mobile Youth in Low-Income African American Neighborhoods." *Journal of Adolescent Research* 10: 11–135.

Jencks, Christopher, and Susan E. Mayer. 1990. "The Social Consequences of Growing Up in a Poor Neighborhood." In *Inner-City Poverty in the United States*, ed. by Laurence E. Lynne, Jr. and Michael G. H. McGeary. Washington, DC: National Academy Press.

Jencks, Christopher, and Paul E. Peterson. 1991. *The Urban Underclass.* Washington, DC: Brookings Institution.

Johnson, Charles S. 1934a. "Negro Personality and Changes in a Southern Community." In *Race and Contacts*, ed. by E. B. Reuter. New York: McGraw-Hill.

———. 1934b. "The Cultural Development of the Negro." In *Race Relations*, ed. by Willis D. Weatherford and Charles S. Johnson. Boston: D.C. Heath and Company.

———. 1934c. "Can There Be a Separate Negro Culture?" In *Race Relations*, ed. by Willis D. Weatherford and Charles S. Johnson. Boston: D.C. Heath and Company.

———. 1934d. *Shadow of the Plantation.* Chicago: University of Chicago Press.

———. 1941. *Growing Up in the Black Belt: Negro Youth in the Rural South.* Washington DC: American Council on Education.

Kasarda, John. 1990a. "Structural Factors Affecting the Location and Timing of Urban Underclass Growth." *Urban Geography* 11: 234–64.

———. 1990b. "Urban Industrial Transition and the Underclass." *Annals of the American Academy of Political and Social Sciences* 501: 26–47.

———. 1990c. "City Jobs and Residents on a Collision Course: The Urban Underclass Dilemma." *Economic Development Quarterly* 4 (November): 313–19.

————. 1995. "Industrial Restructuring and the Changing Location of Jobs." In *State of the Union: America in the 1990s*, vol. 1, ed. by Reynolds Farley. New York: Russell Sage Foundation.

Katz, Michael B. (ed). 1989a. *The Underclass Debate: Views From History*. Princeton, NJ: Princeton University Press.

————. 1989b. *The Undeserving Poor: From the War on Poverty to the War on Welfare*. New York: Pantheon.

Katz, Michael B., and Thomas Segrue (eds.). 1997. *W. E. B. DuBois, Race, and the City: The Philadelphia Negro and Its Legacy*. Philadelphia: University of Pennsylvania Press.

Keil, Charles. 1966. *Urban Blues*. Chicago: University of Chicago Press.

Kelley, Robin. 1997. *Yo Mama's Dysfunktional*. Boston: Beacon Press.

Kimmel, Michael. 1996. *Manhood in America: A Cultural History*. New York: The Free Press.

Kimmel, Michael S., and Michael A. Messner (eds.). 1992. *Men's Lives*. Second ed. New York: Macmillan Publishing Company.

Kirschenmann, Joleen, and Kathryn Neckerman. 1991. " 'We'd Love to Hire Them, But. . .': The Meaning of Race for Employers." In *The Urban Underclass*, ed. by Christopher Jencks and Paul E. Peterson. Washington, DC: Brookings Institution.

Kluegel, James, and E. R. Smith. 1986. *Beliefs about Inequality: Americans' Views of What Is and Ought to Be*. New York: Aldine de Gruyter.

Kornblum, William, and Terry Williams. 1985. *Growing Up Poor*. Lexington, MA: Lexington Books.

Kotlowitz, Jonathan. 1991. *There Ain't No Children Here*. New York: Doubleday.

Kozol, Jonathan. 1991. *Savage Inequalities: Children in America's Schools*. New York: Crown Publishers.

Kvale, Steiner. 1996. *Interviews: An Introduction to Qualitative Research Interviewing*. Thousand Oaks, CA: Sage Publications.

Ladner, Joyce, P. 1971. *Tomorrow's Tomorrow: The Black Woman*. Lincoln: University of Nebraska Press.

Lamb, Michael, and Abraham Sagi (eds.). 1983. *Fatherhood and Family Policy*. Hillsdale, NJ: Lawrence Erlbaum.

Lamont, Michele. 2000. *The Dignity of Working Men: Morality and the Boundaries of Race, Class, and Immigration*. New York City and Cambridge, MA: Russell Sage Foundation and Harvard University Press.

Lamont, Michele, and Annette Lareau. 1988. "Cultural Capital: Allusions, Gaps, and Glissandos in Recent Theoretical Developments." *Sociological Theory* 6: 153–68.

Lareau, Annette. 1989. *Home Advantage: Social Class and Parental Intervention in Elementary Education*. New York: Falmer Press.

————. 1999. "Moments of Social Inclusion and Exclusion: Race, Class, and Cultural Capital in Family-School Relationships." *Sociology of Education* 72 (January): 37–53.

Laseter, Robert L. 1997. "The Labor Force Participation of Young Black Men: A Qualitative Examination." *Social Service Review* 71 (March): 72–88.

Laslett, Barbara. 1991. "Biography as Historical Sociology." *Theory and Society* 20: 511–538.

Lemann, Nicholas. 1986. "The Origins of the Underclass." *Atlantic Monthly*, June (vol. 257), pp. 31–61.

———. 1991. *The Promised Land: The Great Migration and How it Changed America*. New York: Alfred A. Knopf.

LeMelle, Anthony J. 1995. *Black Male Deviance*. Westport, CT: Praeger.

Lerman, Robert I. 1993. "A National Profile of Young Unwed Fathers." In *Young Unwed Fathers: Changing Roles and Emerging Policies*, ed. by Robert I. Lerman and Theodora J. Ooms. Philadelphia, PA: Temple University Press.

Levant, Ronald F., and John Kelly. 1989. *Between Father and Child: How to Become the Kind of Father You Want to Be*. New York: Viking.

Lewis, Charlie, and Margaret O'Brien (eds.). 1987. *Reassessing Fatherhood: New Observations on Fatherhood and the American Family*. London: Sage.

Lewis, David Levering. 1993. *W. E. B. DuBois: Biography of a Race*. New York: Henry Holt and Company.

Lewis, Oscar. 1959. *Five Families: Mexican Case Studies in the Culture of Poverty*. New York: Basic Books.

———. 1961. *The Children of Sanchez*. New York: Random House.

———. 1966. *La Vida: A Puerto Rican Family in the Culture of Poverty, San Juan and New York*. New York: Random House.

Liebow, Elliot. 1967. *Tally's Corner: A Study of Negro Streetcorner Men*. Boston: Little, Brown.

Lin, Nan. 2001. *Social Capital: A Theory of Social Structure and Action*. New York: Cambridge University Press.

Linde, Charlotte. 1993. *Life Stories: The Creation of Coherence*. New York: Oxford University Press.

Lukacs, Georg. [1922] 1971. *History and Class Consciousness*. Cambridge, MA: MIT Press.

Luria, Alexander R. 1976. *Cognitive Development: Its Cultural and Social Foundations*. Cambridge, MA: Harvard University Press.

Lyman, Stanford. 1972. *The Black American in Sociological Thought*. New York: G.P. Putnam and Sons.

MacLeod, Jay. 1995. *Ain't No Making It: Aspirations and Attainment in a Low-Income Neighborhood*. 2nd ed. Boulder, CO: Westview Press.

Madhubuti, Haki. 1990. *Black Men: Obsolete, Single, Dangerous?* Chicago: Third World Press.

Majors, Richard G., and Janet Billson. 1992. *Cool Pose*. New York: Lexington Books.

Majors, Richard G., and Jacob U. Gordon (eds.). 1994. *The American Black Male: His Present Status and Future*. Chicago: Nelson-Hall Publishers.

Marks, Carole. 1989. *Farewell, We're Good and Gone: The Great Black Migration*. Bloomington, IN: Indiana University Press.

Martindale, Don. 1981. *The Nature and Types of Sociological Theory*, Prospect Heights, IL: Waveland Press.

Marx, Frederick, Steve James, and Peter Gilbert. 1995. "Hoop Dreams." Videore-cording. Fine Line Features.

Massey, Douglas, and Nancy Denton. 1993. *American Apartheid: Segregation and the Making of the Underclass.* Cambridge, MA: Harvard University Press.

Mauer, Marc. 1990. *Young Black Men and the Criminal Justice System: A Grow-ing National Problem.* Washington DC: The Sentencing Project, 1990.

———. 1999. *The Race to Incarcerate.* New York: New Press.

Mauer, Marc, and Tracy Huling. 1995. *Young Black Men and the Criminal Justice System: Five Years Later.* Washington DC: The Sentencing Project.

McAdoo, John Lewis. 1981. "Black Fathers and Child Interaction." In *Black Men,* ed. by Lawrence Gary. Beverly Hills, CA: Sage Publications.

McAdoo, John Lewis. 1986. "Black Fathers' Relationships with Their Pre-school Children and the Children's Development of Ethnic Identity." In *Men in Fami-lies,* ed. by Robert A. Lewis and Robert E. Salt. Newbury Park, CA: Sage.

———. 1988a. "The Role of Black Fathers in the Socialization of Black Chil-dren." In *Black Families,* ed. by Harriette Pipes McAdoo. Newbury Park, CA: Sage.

———. 1988b. "Changing Perspectives on the Role of the Black Father." In *Fa-therhood Today: Men's Changing Role in the Family,* ed. by Phyllis Bronstein and Carolyn Pape Cowan. New York: John Wiley.

———. 1993. "The Role of African American Fathers: An Ecological Perspec-tive." *Families in Society* 74: 28–35.

McAdoo, John Lewis, and McAdoo, Julia B. 1994. "The African American Fa-ther's Role within the Family." In *The American Black Male: His Present Status and His Future,* ed. by Richard Majors and Jacob U. Gordon. Chicago: Nelson Hall.

McFate, Katherine, Roger Lawson, and William Julius Wilson (eds.). 1995. *Pov-erty, Inequality, and the Future of Social Policy.* New York: Russell Sage Foun-dation.

McKee, James. 1993. *Sociology and the Race Problem: The Failure of a Perspec-tive.* Champagne, IL: University of Illinois Pres.

Mead, Lawrence. 1986. *Beyond Entitlement.* New York: Free Press.

———. 1992. *The New Politics of Poverty: The Nonworking Poor in America.* New York: Basic Books.

Miles, Matthew B, and A. Michael Huberman. 1994. *Qualitative Data Analysis.* Beverly Hills, CA: Sage Publications.

Miller, Jerome G. 1996. *Search and Destroy: African American Males and the Criminal Justice System.* New York: Cambridge University Press.

Miller, Walter B. 1958. "Lower Class Culture as a Generating Milieu of Gang Delinquency." *Journal of Social Issues* 14, 3: 5–19.

Mills, C. Wright. 1940. "Situated Actions and Vocabularies of Motives." *Ameri-can Sociological Review* 5: 904–13.

———. 1963. *Power, Politics, and People.* New York: Ballantine Books.

Mincy, Ronald B. 1994a. *Nurturing Black Males.* Washington, DC: Urban Insti-tute Press.

———. 1994b. "The Underclass: Concept, Controversy, and Evidence." In *Confronting Poverty: Prescriptions for Change,* ed. by Sheldon H. Danziger,

Gary D. Sandefur, and Daniel H. Weinberg. Cambridge, MA: Harvard University Press.

Monroe, Sylvester. 1995. "America's Most Feared." *Emerge* October: 20–28.

Monroe, Sylvester, and Peter Goldman. 1988. *Brothers: Black and Poor.* New York: William Morrow.

Moskos, Charles, and John Sibley Butler. 1996. *All That We Can Be: Black Leadership and Racial Integration the Army Way.* New York: Basic Book.

Moss, Philip, and Christopher Tilly. 1996. *Why Black Men Are Doing Worse in the Labor Market: A Review of Supply-Side and Demand-Side Explanations.* New York: Social Science Research Council.

———. 2001. *Stories Employers Tell: Race, Skill, and Hiring in America.* New York: Russell Sage Foundation.

Moynihan, Daniel Patrick. 1965. *The Negro Family: The Case for National Action.* Washington, DC: U.S. Department of Labor.

Murphy, Raymond. 1988. *Social Closure: The Theory of Monopolization and Exclusion.* New York: Oxford University Press.

Myers, Lena Wright. 1996. "The Socialization of African American Males: A Broken Silence with Empirical Evidence." *Challenge* 7, 3: 75–84.

Myrdal, Gunnar. 1963. *Challenge to Affluence.* New York: Pantheon Books.

Neckerman, Kathryn, and Joleen Kirschenmann. 1991. "Hiring Strategies, Racial Bias, and Inner-City Workers." *Social Problems* 38: 433–47.

Newman, Katherine S. 1999. *No Shame in My Game: The Working Poor in the Inner City.* New York: Alfred Knopf and the Russell Sage Foundation.

O'Connor Alice. 2001. *Poverty Knowledge: Social Science, Social Policy, and the Poor in Twentieth-Century U.S. History.* Princeton: Princeton University Press.

O'Connor, Alice, Chris Tilly, and Lawrence Bobo. 2000. *Urban Inequality: Evidence from Four Cities.* New York: Russell Sage Foundation.

O'Connor, Carla. 1997. "Dispositions toward (Collective) Struggle and Educational Resilience in the Inner City: A Case Analysis of Six African American High School Students." *American Educational Research Journal* 34 (Winter): 593–629.

O'Connor, Carla, and Alford A. Young, Jr. N.d. "Working Paper on an Expanded Vocabulary for Individual Perceptions of Expectations, Aspirations, and Life Chances." Unpublished paper.

Ogbu, John. 1978. *Minority Education and Caste: The American System in Cross-Cultural Perspective.* New York: Academic Press.

Oliver, William. 1994. *The Violent Social World of Black Men.* New York: Lexington Books.

Omi, Michael, and Howard Winant. 1994. *Racial Formation in the United States: From the 1960 to the 1990s.* 2nd edition. Routledge: New York.

Orbuch, Terri L. 1997. "People's Accounts Count: The Sociology of Accounts." *Annual Review of Sociology* 23: 455–78.

Park, Robert. 1950. *Race and Culture.* Glencoe, NY: Free Press.

Parke, Ross D. 1981. *Fathers.* Cambridge, MA: Harvard University Press.

Parkin, Frank. 1979. *Marxism and Class Theory: A Bourgeios Critique.* New York: Columbia University Press.

Parsons, Talcott, and Neil Smelser. 1956. *Economy and Society.* New York: Free Press.

Pearlin, Leonard I., M. I. Lieberman, Elizabeth G. Menaghan, and Joseph T. Mullan. 1981. "The Stress Process." *Journal of Health and Social Behavior* 22: 337–56.

Persons, Stow. 1987. *Ethnic Studies at Chicago.* Urbana, IL: University of Illinois Press.

Peshkin, Alan. 1991. *The Color of Strangers, The Color of Friends: The Play of Ethnicity in School and Community.* Chicago: The University of Chicago Press.

Peterson, Paul E., and Adele V. Harrell (eds.). 1993. *Drugs, Crime, and Social Isolation: Barriers to Urban Opportunity.* Washington, DC: Urban Institute Press.

Petterson, Stephen M. 1997. "Are Young Black Men Really Less Willing to Work?" *American Sociological Review* 62 (Aug.): 605–13.

Poland, Blake, and Ann Pederson. 1998. "Reading between the Lines: Interpreting Silences in Qualitative Research." *Qualitative Inquiry* 4, 2: 293–312.

Portes, Alejandro. 1998. "Social Capital: Its Origins and Applications in Modern Sociology." *Annual Review of Sociology* 24: 1–24.

Price-Bonham, Sharon and Patsy Skeen. 1979. "A Comparison of Black and White Fathers with Implications for Parent Education." *The Family Coordinator* 28: 53–59.

Psathas, George (ed.). 1973. *Phenomenological Sociology: Issues and Applications.* New York: Wiley.

Rainwater, Lee. 1970. *Behind Ghetto Walls: Black Family Life in a Federal Slum.* Chicago: Aldine.

Rainwater, Lee, and William Yancey. 1967. *The Moynihan Report and the Politics of Controversy.* Cambridge: MIT Press.

Riessman, Catherine Kohler. 1993. *Narrative Analysis.* Newbury Park, CA: Sage Publications.

Riessman, Frank. 1962. *The Culturally Deprived Child.* New York: Harper.

Robbins, Derek. 1991. *The Work of Pierre Bourdieu.* Boulder, CO: Westview Press.

Rodman, Hyman. 1963. "The Lower-Class Value Stretch." *Social Forces* 42: 205–15.

Rolison, Gary L. 1993. "Non-Employment of Black Men in Major Metropolitan Areas." *Sociological Inquiry* 63 (Summer): 318–29.

Sampson, Robert. 1987. "Urban Black Violence: The Effect of Male Joblessness and Family Disruption." *American Journal of Sociology* 93: 348–405.

Sartre, Jean-Paul. 1967. *Search for a Method.* New York: Alfred Knopf.

———. 1976. *Critique of Dialectical Reason.* Atlantic Highlands, NJ: Humanities Press.

Sawhill, Isabel V. 1995. *Welfare Reform: An Analysis of the Issues.* Washington, DC: Urban Institute.

Schultz, David. 1969. *Coming Up Black: Patterns of Ghetto Socialization.* Englewood Cliffs, NJ: Prentice-Hall.

Schuman, Howard, Charlotte Steech, Larry Bobo, and Maria Krysan. 1997. *Racial Attitudes in America: Trends and Interpretations.* Cambridge, MA: Harvard University Press.

Schutz, Alfred. [1932] 1967. *The Phenomenology of the Social World*. Evanston, IL: Northwestern University Press.

——. 1962. *The Collected Papers of Alfred Schutz*. Vol. 1, *The Problem of Social Reality*. Ed. by Maurice Natanson. Boston: Martinus Nijhoff.

——. 1964. *The Collected Papers of Alfred Schutz*. Vol. 2, *Studies in Social Theory*. Ed. by Arvin Brodersen. Boston: Martinus Nijhoff.

——. 1970. *On Phenomenology and Social Relations*. Ed. by Helmut R. Wagner. Chicago: University of Chicago Press.

Schutz, Alfred, and Thomas Luckmann. 1973. *The Structures of the Lifeworld*. Evanston, IL: Northwestern University Press.

Scott, Daryl Michael. 1997. *Contempt and Pity: Social Policy and the Image of the Damaged Black Psyche 1880–1996*. Chapel Hill: University of North Carolina Press.

Scott, Michael B., and Stanford Lyman. 1968. "Accounts." *American Sociological Review* 33: 46–62.

Sears, David, James Sidanius, and Larry Bobo. 2000. *Racialized Politics: The Debate about Racism in America*. Chicago: University of Chicago Press.

Sewell, William H. 1992. "A Theory of Structure: Duality, Agency, and Transformation." *American Journal of Sociology* 98 (July): 1–29.

Sigelman, Lee, and Susan Welch. 1991. *Black Americans' Views of Racial Inequality*. New York: Cambridge University Press.

Simmel, Georg. [1949] 1971. "Sociability." In *Georg Simmel: On Individuality and Social Forms*, ed. by Donald Levine. Chicago: University of Chicago Press.

Smith, Robert C. 1995. *Racism in the Post-Civil Rights Era: Now You See It, Now You Don't*. Albany, NY: State University of New York Press.

Snow, David A., and Robert D. Benford. 1988. "Ideology, Frame Resonance and Participant Mobilization." In *From Structure to Action: Social Movement Participation across Cultures*, ed. by Bert Klandermans, Hanspeter Kriesi, and Sidney Tarrow. Greenwich, CT: JAI Press.

——. 1992. "Master Frames and Cycles of Protest." In *Frontiers of Social Movement Theory*, ed. by Aldon D. Morris and Carol McClurg Mueller. New Haven, CT: Yale University Press.

Snow, David A., E. Burke Rochford, Jr., Steven K. Worden, and Robert D. Benford. 1986. "Frame Alignment Processes, Micromobilization, and Movement Participation." *American Sociological Review* 51: 464–81.

Song, Miri, and David Parker. 1995. "Commonality, Difference, and the Dynamics of Disclosure in In-Depth Interviewing." *Sociology* 29, 2 (May): pp. 241–56.

Stack, Carol. 1974. *All Our Kin: Strategies for Survival in a Black Community*. New York: Harper and Row.

Staples, Robert. 1982. *Black Masculinity: The Black Man's Role in American Society*. San Francisco: The Black Scholars Press.

Steinberg, Stephen. 1995. *Turning Back: The Retreat from Racial Justice in American Thought and Policy*. Boston: Beacon Press.

Stone, Gregory. 1962. "Appearances and the Self." In *Human Behavior and Social Processes*, ed. by Arnold Rose. Boston: Houghton Mifflin.

Sullivan, Mercer L. 1989. *Getting Paid: Youth Crime and Work in the Inner City*. Ithaca, NY: Cornell University Press.

Suttles, Gerald. 1968. *The Social Order of the Slum*. Chicago: University of Chicago Press.

Swartz, David. 1997. *Culture and Power: The Sociology of Pierre Bourdieu*. Chicago: University of Chicago Press.

Swidler, Ann. 1986. "Culture in Action: Symbols and Strategies." *American Sociological Review* 51: 273–86.

Tarrow, Sidney. 1992. "Mentalities, Political Cultures, and Collective Action Frames: Constructing Meaning through Action." In *Frontiers of Social Movement Theory*, ed. by Aldon D. Morris and Carol McClurg Mueller. New Haven, CT: Yale University Press.

Taub, Richard. 1991. "Different Conceptions of Honor and Orientations toward Work and Marriage among Low-Income African-Americans and Mexican-Americans." Paper presented at the Chicago Urban Poverty and Family Life Conference, October 10–12, Chicago.

Taylor, Robert Joseph, Bogart R. Leashare, and Susan Toliver. 1988. "An Assessment of the Provider Role as Perceived by Black Males." *Family Relations* 37 (October): 426–31.

Taylor, Robert T. and Waldo Johnson, Jr.. 1997. "Family Roles and Family Satisfaction among Black Men." In *Family Life in Black America*, ed. by Robert J. Taylor, James S. Jackson, and Linda M. Chatters. Thousand Oaks, CA: Sage.

Tolleson, Jennifer. 1997. "Death and Transformation: The Reparative Power of Violence in the Lives of Young Black Inner-City Gang Members." *Smith College Studies in Social Work* 67, 3: 415–31.

U.S. Bureau of Labor Statistics. 2002. *Vital Statistics, 2002*. Washington, DC.

U.S. National Center for Health Statistics. 1994. *Vital Statistics of the United States, 1994*. Washington, DC.

———. 2000. *Vital Statistics of the United States, 2000*. Washington, DC.

———. 2002. *Vital Statistics of the United States, 2002*. Washington, DC.

Valentine, Charles A. 1968. *Culture and Poverty*. Chicago: University of Chicago Press.

Venkatesh, Sudhir Alladi. 1994. "Getting Ahead: Social Mobility among the Urban Poor." *Sociological Perspectives* 37 (Summer): 157–82.

———. 1997. "The Social Organization of Street Gang Activity in an Urban Ghetto." *American Journal of Sociology* 103 (July): 82–111.

———. 2000. *American Project: The Rise and Fall of a Modern Ghetto*. Cambridge: Harvard University Press.

Wacquant, Loic J. D. 1989. "The Ghetto, the State, and the New Capitalist Economy." *Dissent* Fall: 508–20.

———. 1992. "The Social Logic of Boxing in Black Chicago: Toward a Sociology of Pugilism." *Sociology of Sport Journal* 9, 3: 221–54.

———. 1995. "The Pugilistic Point of View: How Boxers Think and Feel about Their Trade." *Theory and Society* 24, 4: 489–535.

Wacquant, Loic J. D., and William Julius Wilson. 1989. "Poverty, Joblessness, and the Social Transformation of the Inner City." In *Welfare Policy for the*

1990s, ed. by Phoebe H. Cottingham and David T. Ellwood. Cambridge, MA: Harvard University Press.

———. 1990. "The Cost of Racial and Class Exclusion in the Inner City." *Annals of the American Academy of Political and Social Science* 501.

Waller, Maureen R. 2002. *My Baby's Father: Unmarried Parents and Paternal Responsibility*, Ithaca, NY: Cornell University Press.

Warner, W. Lloyd. 1936. "American Caste and Class." *American Journal of Sociology* 42 (September): 234–37.

Warner, W. Lloyd, and Allison Davis. 1939. "A Comparative Study of American Caste." In *Race Relations and the Race Problem*, ed. by Edgar T. Thompson. Durham, NC: Duke University Press.

Wells, Amy Stuart, and Robert L. Crain. 1997. *Stepping over the Color Line: African American Students in White Suburban Schools*. New Haven, CT: Yale University Press.

West, Cornel. 1993. *Race Matters*. Boston: Beacon Press.

Whyte, William Foote. 1943. *Street Corner Society: The Social Structure of an Italian Slum*. Chicago: University of Chicago Press.

Willis, Andre (ed.). 1966. *Faith of Our Fathers: African American Men Reflect on Fatherhood*. New York: Dutton.

Willis, Paul E. 1981. *Learning to Labor: How Working Class Kids Get Working Class Jobs*. New York: Columbia University Press.

Wilson, William Julius. 1987. *The Truly Disadvantaged: The Inner-City, The Underclass, and Public Policy*. Chicago: University of Chicago Press.

———. 1991. "Studying Inner-City Dislocations: The Challenges of Public Agenda Research." *American Sociological Review* 56 (February): 1–14.

———. 1992. "The Plight of the Inner-City Black Male." *Proceedings of the American Philosophical Society* 136, 3: 320–25.

———. (ed.). 1993. *The Ghetto Underclass*. Newbury Park, CA: Sage.

———. 1996. *When Work Disappears*. New York: Alfred Knopf.

Wright, Erik Olin. 1985. *Classes*. New York: Verso.

Wuthnow, Robert. 1987. *Meaning and Moral Order: Explorations in Cultural Analysis*. Berkeley: University of California Press.

Young, Alford A., Jr. 1997. "Rationalizing Race in Thinking about the Future: The Case of Low-Income Black Men." *Smith College Studies in Social Work* 67, 3: 432–55.

———. 1999. "The (Non) Accumulation of Capital: Explicating the Relationship of Structure and Agency in the Lives of Poor Black Men." *Sociological Theory* 17, 2 (July): 201–27.

———. Forthcoming. "American Dreams against the American Dilemma: Upwardly Mobile Black Men and Confrontations with Race."

Zerubavel, Evitar. 1997. *Social Mindscapes: An Invitation to Cognitive Sociology*. Cambridge, MA: Harvard University Press.

Index

PRINCETON STUDIES IN CULTURAL SOCIOLOGY